W9-CZX-563

Cities of Peasants

Explorations in Urban Analysis

Edited by Professor R. E. Pahl, Professor of Sociology, University of Kent and the late Professor H. J. Dyos, Professor of History, University of Leicester

Volume 1

CITIES OF PEASANTS: The Political Economy of Urbanization in the Third World by *Bryan Roberts,* Professor of Sociology, University of Manchester

Volumes in preparation for this series include: John Lambert (Sociology, University College, Cardiff) on "The Inner City"; James Bater (Geography, Environmental Studies, University of Waterloo) on "The Soviet City"; Peter Burke (History, University of Sussex) on "Cities and Social Change"; Gareth Stedman Jones (Fellow, King's College, Cambridge) on "Urbanization and Class Consciousness"; David Eversley (Policy Studies Institute, London) and Helen Meller (History, University of Nottingham) on "Planning for Urban Happiness."

Cities of Peasants

The Political Economy of Urbanization
in the Third World

Bryan Roberts

 SAGE Publications   Beverly Hills / London

CARNEGIE LIBRARY
LIVINGSTONE COLLEGE
SALISBURY, N. C. 28144

Copyright © Bryan Roberts 1978.

First published 1978
by Edward Arnold (Publishers) Ltd
41 Bedford Square London WC1B 3DP

Published in the United States of America 1979
by Sage Publications Inc.
275 South Beverly Drive
Beverly Hills California 90212

Hardcover ISBN 0-8039-1290-0
Paperback ISBN 0-8039-1291-9

Library of Congress Catalog Card No. 79-87589

SECOND PRINTING

All rights reserved. No part of this publication may be reproduced, stored in a retrieval system, or transmitted in any form or by any means, electronic, photocopying, recording or otherwise, without the prior permission of the publishers.

This book is published in two editions. The paperback edition is sold subject to the condition that it shall not, by way of trade or otherwise, be lent, re-sold, hired out, or otherwise circulated without the publishers' prior consent in any form of binding or cover other than that in which it is published and without a similar condition including this condition being imposed upon any subsequent purchaser.

307.76
R643

Contents

1/2019

Preface

This volume was written mainly when I was visiting the Department of Sociology at the University of Texas at Austin. To the Director of the Population Research Center of that university, Dr Harley Browning, I owe an especial debt for his help, intellectual stimulation and friendship. The facilities of the Center and the excellent library of the university, with its Latin American collection, made the awesome task of reviewing a continent's development more pleasant. Though I have discussed the themes of this volume with many colleagues in the Americas and in England, I would especially like to thank Jorge Balan, Elisabeth Jelin and Jorge Dandler for the help they have given me. Not only did they read the manuscript, but they kept patience with someone whose understanding of the historical detail and nature of Latin American development is less than their own. Also, I want to thank Norman Long who co-directed with me a project in the highlands of Peru financed by the British Social Science Research Council. We have worked so closely together over these last years in writing and in talking that it is difficult to acknowledge adequately the ideas and help that I have received from him.

The editors of this series, *Explorations in Urban Analysis*, also deserve thanks. This is the first volume of the series and posed unusual difficulties to editors attempting to reconcile historical and sociological perspectives. They both put a great deal of work into the organization of the volume, and offered help that went beyond what can normally be expected of series editors.

Last but not least is my debt to my family. This volume interfered with many a weekend excursion into the wilds of Texas, severely curtailed a holiday exploration of Mexico and lingered on to cut into family time in Manchester. My wife, Sue, also read the manuscript and helped me by her comments and editing.

Introduction

This volume is intended to be introductory. Although the range and historical depth of the material make the theme complex, I have tried to present the argument as simply and coherently as possible. This has been done by using, as far as possible, readily understandable terms and by following a single line of argument throughout. Such a procedure has, however, certain limitations of which the reader should be warned. My perspective is that of political economy but it is not intended to be as scientifically rigorous in its use of terms and concepts as, for example, are certain lines of marxist enquiry. Secondly, by presenting a single framework of interpretation to cover a great range of data, I run the risk of, at times, obscuring the difference between hypothesis and established fact or underemphasizing alternative explanations. I have tried to avoid this danger by signalling clearly those interpretations of data which are mainly hypothetical and need further research. The bibliographical references in the text are not simply meant to justify a particular argument: they refer to interesting material which the reader can use to develop his own explanations. Lastly, this is a book about a particular issue—the expansion of capitalism in underdeveloped countries. It does not attempt to survey the situation of those underdeveloped countries which are not part of the capitalist system. This omission is a necessary one because of the limitations of space and my own knowledge, but it does imply an important limit on the generality of this analysis.

I will outline briefly the argument of the volume to provide some sense of its overall organization. My aim is to show how the form of economic expansion that occurred in Europe from the sixteenth century onwards has shaped the patterns of growth in underdeveloped areas of the world. My focus is urbanization since it is the increasing concentration of population in urban centres and in non-agricultural employment that is often seen as a necessary condition of economic development. Thus, in the first chapter, I will examine different ways in which we can conceive the link between urban growth and economic development. I will suggest that the most convincing framework for our analysis is that of the economic interdependency of nations and of regions within nations.

Interdependency implies that the economic and social institutions of any one area are shaped by the relationships which this area maintains with others. There is, thus, no single model of economic growth or social change which all countries must emulate if they are to achieve development. The potential of any one area, such as its urban or industrial growth, is formed by that area's position within a wider world economic system. In this system, some areas acquire a predominant place and others a subordinate one. Wealth and poverty, modernity and traditionalism are, in this way, the reverse sides of the same coin of economic growth.

To deepen this argument, I will look at the contrasting cases of Britain and the United States which, in different ways, became the powers that from the nineteenth century onwards most deeply affected the area of the underdeveloped world that is our focus—Latin America. Despite the importance of external factors in limiting economic development, we will see that the major force for change within underdeveloped countries is their internal economic growth. This growth takes on different forms in different countries, bringing new social and political forces into play. These forces affect the development of political institutions and of class organization and, in turn, institutions and class conflict determine the character of economic growth. It is this type of analysis which helps us understand why there is a diversity of responses to the common situation of underdevelopment.

The second and third chapters are organized historically, covering the colonial period, the nineteenth century and the twentieth century until the contemporary period. The aim of these historical chapters is to examine the changes in the pattern of urbanization in underdeveloped countries resulting from the increasingly close economic relationship between underdeveloped countries and the advanced capitalist countries. I will contrast the type of urbanization present in colonial Latin America with that which took shape when the subcontinent was more closely integrated into the European and North American economies in the nineteenth and twentieth centuries, noting the radical effects of industrialization on the agrarian structure and on producing an increasing concentration of economic activities in a few metropolitan centres. By comparing four countries (Argentina, Brazil, Peru and Mexico) with different patterns of economic development, we see how the systems of production dominant in underdeveloped countries shape class organization and the development of the state. Recent political developments such as populism are, however, the result of a convergent economic process, that of industrialization.

It is the dominant pattern of contemporary economic growth,

based on industrialization, and *not* traditionalism or inertia that prevents a more even and rapid agrarian development. The characteristics of present-day urban migration are thus viewed in terms of the economic activism of the rural population as well as in terms of the greater economic opportunities present in the cities. The issue that best helps us understand why cities can continue to attract population is that of urban economic dualism. Economic growth concentrates in the large-scale sector of the urban economy which offers the best profits, salaries and wages. Yet, a small-scale sector of the urban economy continues to thrive, though on low wages and low profits through the interdependence of the two sectors. The large-scale sector makes use of the small-scale sector as a reserve of unskilled and casual labour, as a means of putting-out work and as a means of providing cheaply services, such as transport, commerce and repairs, which facilitate the expansion of the large-scale sector. The small-scale sector absorbs labour, using the income opportunities provided by the large-scale sector. We will see that part of the explanation for the persistence of this dualistic structure is the growing importance of the state in the economy. The state acts to foster rapid economic growth, but at the expense of investment in social infrastructure.

The nature of the dualistic urban economy affects social relationships, housing, local-level politics and even religious practices, producing a situation in which the poor are active but unincorporated members of the urban populations of underdeveloped countries. The poor are, however, fragmented ideologically and by their short-term economic interests. Since no class or class fraction has sufficient strength and appeal to form the basis of stable government, there is a permanent crisis in government which makes it difficult to obtain the consensus needed to resolve the problems of an increasing technological and financial dependence, internal inflation, lack of private investment in production and so on. The increase in authoritarian and often military government in Latin America and other underdeveloped countries is thus seen as a 'solution' to the current bottlenecks of economic growth, resolving temporarily the class conflicts brought about by industrialization and urban development.

1
Urbanization and underdevelopment

The theme of this book is the contemporary urban problems of underdeveloped countries. The discussion will be confined to the capitalist underdeveloped world and most of the examples will be taken from one continent of that world—Latin America. This restriction is necessary if we are even to attempt to come to grips with the complexity of our theme since comparisons have more meaning when examined within a broadly uniform economic context. Also, the analysis that I will use requires a certain historical depth and attempting to provide it for one continent, let alone two or three, is a daunting task.

In the period following the second world war, underdeveloped countries urbanized rapidly so that, between 1940 and 1975, the urban population doubled and in some countries half or more of the population is now living in towns of 20,000 or more. Population is also concentrated in relatively few urban centres which have high rates of growth, often in excess of five per cent a year, and such places as Mexico City and São Paulo in Brazil are likely to attain sizes of 20 million or more before the end of this century. As staggering as the size of such cities is the evident poverty of much of the urban population of the underdeveloped world. Contrasts between wealth and poverty, between 'modernity' and 'traditionalism' are sharp. Modern skyscrapers, sumptuous shopping, office and banking facilities co-exist with unpaved streets, squatter settlements and open sewage. In the central streets of the cities of the underdeveloped world, the elegantly dressed are waylaid by beggars and street vendors; their shoes are shined and their cars are guarded by urchins from an inner-city slum whose earnings are a vital part of the family budget.

It is not surprising that to many observers the problems of urban growth in underdeveloped countries are those of the lack of stable, well paid industrial employment. These cities are frequently viewed as being overpopulated, with high levels of unemployment or underemployment. The concentration of jobs in 'non-productive' activities in government, commerce or personal services is sometimes cited as one of the evils of contemporary 'underdeveloped' urbanization.

In the course of this book, I shall argue that this emphasis on urbanization without industrialization is misleading and claim instead that the pattern of urban life in underdeveloped countries, including the poverty and apparent economic marginality of much of the population, is an integral part of the current economic growth of third-world countries.

Although 1940 is a somewhat arbitrary date to use as the beginning of this 'urban explosion', it is significant in the sense that it marks the definitive shift of underdeveloped economies towards industrial production, following the curtailment of external supplies of manufactures as a result of the war. Many underdeveloped countries, especially in Latin America, had already begun to develop a local industry long before 1940, but it was with the second world war, and especially with the expansion of international trade after it, that underdeveloped countries began to industrialize rapidly. These are also the years in which the pace of urbanization increased dramatically (table 1.1). In later chapters I shall examine how and why this process of industrialization occurred and illustrate its extent by taking the example of Latin America where, in almost every country by 1970, industry contributed a greater share of the gross national product than did agriculture.

I shall examine the contradictions present in an urban situation in which increasing industrial growth and concentration is accompanied by an inadequate urban infrastructure and by the continuing poverty of much of the urban population. One of these contradictions is a process of capital accumulation in the cities of the underdeveloped world which is based on access to cheap and abundant labour, not only to power the factories but to provide complementary services and ancillary manufacturing.

The contradictions of contemporary urban capitalist development are not only, or even mainly, internal to industry, but appear in many facets of urban life. The city must provide the basic facilities that workers and their families need for survival—housing, shops and markets, transport and public services such as health, water and electricity. Indeed, creating and maintaining urban labour power involves more than providing material facilities. Specialized schooling and training facilities are needed to prepare people for the different types of jobs created by a complex production system. Even maintaining order and fostering a sense of civic responsibility and work-discipline are necessary preconditions for industrial production. These processes provide for the reproduction of labour power in the sense of maintaining a supply of labour both physically able to work—in that, for example, workers are healthy and live near to places of work—and prepared, culturally and ideologically, to work under the prevailing conditions of capitalist production. (See Castells, 1977, 145–91, for some of the theoretical issues in-

Table 1.1: Percentage of population of the world and of each world region that is urban (in places of 20,000 or more) (%)

	1920	1930	1940	1950	1960	1970	1975
WORLD TOTAL	14.3	16.3	18.8	21.2	25.4	28.2	29.7
MORE DEVELOPED MAJOR AREAS	29.8	32.8	36.7	39.9	45.6	49.9	52.1
Europe	34.7	37.2	39.5	40.7	44.2	47.1	48.2
Northern America	41.4	46.5	46.2	50.8	58.0	62.6	65.4
Soviet Union	10.3	13.4	24.1	27.8	36.4	42.7	46.4
Oceania	36.5	38.0	40.9	45.7	52.9	57.9	57.1
LESS DEVELOPED MAJOR AREAS	6.9	8.4	10.4	13.2	17.3	20.4	22.2
East Asia	7.2	9.1	11.6	13.8	18.5	21.7	23.7
South Asia	5.7	6.5	8.3	11.1	13.7	16.0	17.4
Latin America	14.4	16.8	19.6	25.1	32.8	37.8	40.5
Africa	4.8	5.9	7.2	9.7	13.4	16.5	18.1
MORE DEVELOPED REGIONS*	29.4	32.6	37.0	40.0	46.0	50.5	52.8
LESS DEVELOPED REGIONS†	5.8	7.0	8.6	11.4	15.4	18.5	20.3

*More developed regions refers to Europe, Northern America, Soviet Union, Japan, temperate South America, Australia and New Zealand.
†Less developed regions refers to East Asia without Japan, South Asia, Latin America without temperate South America, Africa and Oceania without Australia and New Zealand.
Source: Frisbie, 1976, table 4, based on United Nations, *Growth of the world's urban and rural population 1920–2000*, Population Studies no. 44 (New York: UN, 1969), table 31.

volved in the analysis of the reproduction of labour in urban situations.)

Private enterprise is rarely able or willing to provide directly for the reproduction of urban labour power. The nature of the facilities needed are such that they must often be provided collectively and through the agency of the state. Moreover, private enterprise normally puts pressure on the state to provide the infrastructure that contributes directly to its own profitability (good roads, telecommunications and so on) and, increasingly, to take over the less profitable but necessary branches of production. As cities increase in size, the costs of providing an adequate urban system rise considerably and the social pressure to do something about them also increases, if only in order to avoid the dangers of epidemic, traffic chaos and so on. However, investment in the social and physical infrastructure of the city is not directly profitable and private enterprise is reluctant to pay the taxes needed for such an investment. R. C. Hill (1977, 82) put it this way in referring to the urban fiscal crisis in the United States: 'The increasing socialization of costs and the continued private appropriation of profits creates a fiscal crisis—a "structural gap" between state expenditures and state revenues.'

The state is thus faced with contradictory pressures of ensuring the profitability of industry by providing the needed infrastructure and by keeping taxes low and of meeting (or at least appearing to meet) the demand of urban residents for 'non-productive' investments in housing, schools and other social services. This type of analysis has become a relatively familiar one in the literature on contemporary urbanization in Europe, in which the urban system is seen as one of the major arenas for the class struggle (Pickvance, 1976; Castells, 1977). The contradictions in many cities of the underdeveloped world are sharper because capital is relatively scarcer and less easily transferred for investment in the urban infrastructure. Also, though the urban poor are an integral part of the urban capitalist system, few of them are directly employed in it and they do not form an important part of the internal market for consumer goods. Under these conditions, it follows that the urban system in underdeveloped countries is organized to exclude much of the population from its material benefits. We have therefore to examine the extent to which the state comes to rely on coercion as a means of capitalist development rather than on the integration of the urban population through democratic politics or through direct improvement in their standards of life (Mingione, 1977; Sorj, 1976, part 2).

The theme running throughout the discussion in the following chapters and linking the historical analysis of urbanization with that of the contemporary urban structure is one of class and class conflict. Class alliances and conflicts comprise the dialectic process by which change takes place; the emergence of new forms of production creates new class interests and threatens those interests tied to an established and perhaps superseded form of production. The struggle of different classes to expand and defend their interests results in social and political institutions (political parties, trade unions, new forms of legal contract or of regulation of work) that contribute to the form of later economic development.

By focusing on the class struggle it becomes easier to recognize the specificity of each country's and each city's development, enabling us to compare, for example, the problems of manufacturing cities with those of cities that are mainly commercial and administrative centres. Although cities in the underdeveloped world may seem to be facing similar problems and to be seeking similar solutions to those problems, the manner of fostering and coping with economic development is, in fact, quite different from country to country. Some countries have conservative, authoritarian military regimes, while others have reformist and left-wing military regimes; there are also civilian governments with widely differing degrees of popular support. The extent to which the state intervenes in the urban economy and provides urban infrastructure also differs from country to country.

Naturally we must broaden our focus to take in the whole process of urbanization and not simply that of contemporary urban growth. Moreover, as cities are the products of broader socio-economic changes, they cannot be considered in isolation from them. Urbanization in its most formal sense merely constitutes the increase of the urban population as compared with the rural one, but it includes and results from far-reaching economic transformations on the national and international plane.

Urbanization and development

Urbanization, in the modern period, has entailed a profound process of social and economic transformation. Agriculture has become a less direct source of livelihood and a steadily decreasing proportion of the population in both developed and underdeveloped countries is employed on the land. Urbanization has also implied an increasing territorial division of labour. Agricultural areas become specialized in the production of certain crops to provide foodstuffs for urban populations at home and abroad; towns and cities specialize in branches of industrial activity. Urban and rural areas become increasingly interdependent economically and this interdependence leads to an international division of labour as each nation specializes in different branches of production for export. In a survey of forty countries, including both developed and underdeveloped countries, Gibbs and Martin (1962) show fairly close correlations between an index of urbanization (expressed as a percentage of population in metropolitan areas) and the dimensions of the division of labour in terms of industrial diversification, technological development and the territorial dispersion of the sources of consumer goods imported.

Specialization and interdependence are thus the product of industrialization and it is this pattern of urbanization that distinguishes the modern period from earlier ones. As Lampard (1965) indicates, there is a long history of urban civilization in which cities served as residences of elites, craftsmen and traders and as centres for the organization and appropriation of the agricultural surplus; it is only factory-based industrialization which has given rise to an incessant urbanization based on increasing specialization and interdependence.

One of the most common approaches to economic development stresses the necessary contribution which urban industrialization makes to economic development. The approach here is to measure economic development in terms of growth in national productivity and rise in per capita income. From this perspective, the concentration of people in urban-industrial places contributes to economic development by reducing over time the proportion of the population in a nation's economy engaged purely in agricultural subsistence. Thus, Rosenstein-Rodan's (1943) programme for promoting urban industrialization in the depressed areas of eastern and south-eastern Europe, after the war, was echoed later in the declarations of leaders of underdeveloped countries that were seeking to escape dependence on the industrialized countries. Nkrumah in Ghana, and the Economic Commission for Latin America, were some among many who wished to embark upon a pattern of urban industrialization similar to that of the developed world (Brookfield, 1975, 71). It was recognized that increases in the urban population might not at first be absorbed into industrial employment; but it was claimed that the availability of such labour stimulated industrial investment. Other commentators have stressed the advantages of urbanization from a sociological and psychological perspective. Levels of education are thought to improve with urbanization, if only because the urban milieu is supposed to combat illiteracy (Lerner, 1958). Likewise, various patterns of traditional behaviour are thought to be less likely to persist in an urban environment (Sjoberg, 1965). Kinship structures or ritual observances might persist, but it has been held that unless they are compatible with the new forms of economic organization and an urban style of living, their function will merely become ceremonial (Hawley, 1971, 314). These perspectives can all best be regarded as theories of modernization.

It is not my purpose to provide an extensive review of the literature on modernization; nor is it my intention to present the modernization perspective as a homogeneous or simplistic one. The analysis of the ways in which traditional forms can acquire a new and vigorous content during economic development has been an important part of modernization analysis (Feldman and Moore, 1962). Likewise, 'modernizers' such as Wilbert Moore (1964) have emphasized the important differences between the development experience of underdeveloped and developed countries, stressing for example, the importance of state intervention in underdeveloped countries. What modernization perspectives have in common is a view of development as a convergent and evolutionary process in which simpler forms of organization are increasingly absorbed into more centralized and complex ones (Moore, 1977).

Such a focus means that an implicit model of necessary stages in urbanization is often used to evaluate the significance of variations in urbanization throughout the world. Reissman (1964, 155–79) has analysed urbanization in underdeveloped countries as a replication, albeit in a more concentrated and uneven form, of the urbanization experience of the European nations at the time of their urban industrialization. The similarities that he emphasizes are the rural-urban migration process, the rapid growth of cities and the social problems to be found within the cities of nineteenth-century Europe. On the basis of this analysis, Reissman creates a typology of change which represents the stages through which a society must pass in order to achieve a balanced urban–industrial development; the factors that he identifies as complementing each other in this development process are urban growth, industrialization, the presence of middle classes and nationalism. Imbalance between these factors, such as urban growth without industrialization, is conceived as creating social problems and constitutes a hindrance to progress at the next stage. Societies in these phases of development are described as transitional to more complex forms of organization; this viewpoint is similar to Sjoberg's (1965, 220) categorization of cities in underdeveloped countries as transitional to the urban–industrial structure of the developed world.

Concepts such as transition and convergence have, however, a limited usefulness in understanding the experience of urbanization. We shall see later that there are important differences here, even among the advanced capitalist countries. Moreover, to stress convergence is to overlook the interdependent nature of the urbanization process in different parts of the world. Urbanization is essentially the product of capitalist development and expansion. This expansion has not occurred evenly or in the same historical periods throughout the world, but it has affected, to different degrees, most areas of it. The industrial expansion of the first developed countries, such as England, led to rapid urbanization at home, but it also created different patterns of urbanization elsewhere. Ports and trading towns developed in the colonies and in Latin America as a consequence of the growth of trade between industrializing Europe and regions that could supply the primary products needed for industry and to feed the urban population of Europe.

How, then, are we to take account of the factors that explain the persisting differences in the development of cities and regions? One influential approach uses the analysis of market forces as a means of identifying and differentiating patterns of economic development. For example, the formal relationship between spatial patterns of urbanization, economic specialization and interdependence is often analysed in terms of central place theory (Berry, 1967, 35-77). Central place theorizing is concerned with constructing a model of how a region can be organized spatially to maximize both economic specialization and integration. It concentrates on market factors and inter-firm linkages, but is less concerned with how regions or nations have actually acquired their pattern of urbanization. The aim is to provide a model for discriminating among the economic forces that influence the pattern of regional development. It is similar to certain types of regional development theory such as growth pole theory, which stresses that industrial and infrastructural investment, if correctly located, will trigger off a self-sustaining development process (Lasuen, 1972; Hermansen, 1969).

Of perhaps greater relevance for historical analysis of urban development is the use of neoclassical economics to analyse the supply of and demand for the factors of production (land, labour and capital) at different periods of the growth of a country or city. The explanations deriving from this approach are often offered as alternatives to those which take account of political or social factors. (See Habakkuk, 1967, for the use of this perspective in an historical analysis.) Morley and Williamson (1977), for example, compare contemporary Brazil with the United States in the first half of the twentieth century. They argue that income inequality in these two contrasting situations is better explained by factor demand than by exogenous variables such as union strength, industrial concentration, the party in power and so on. They claim that these latter explanations are a form of 'ad hocery' in that they are devoid of any coherent analytic basis.

Since the findings of economists and economic historians are frequently used throughout this book, we need to be clear about the difference in perspective between their accounts and this one. In this volume, political and social forces are attributed as much importance as is the market in shaping the course of economic development. In particular, I find the distinction between exogenous and endogenous factors blurred and of questionable utility when long-term trends in economic development are analysed. Markets do not exist in a vacuum but, as we shall see, are often created by government action and by coercion. The demand for a product does not simply depend on income distribution, but is affected by various exogenous factors such as customary patterns of consumption or the marketing skills of the large modern corporation. The availability of labour and the distribution of work skills depend on factors such as government immigration policy or educational traditions. The analysis of market forces is, of course, a useful means of evaluating policy alternatives or of estimating short-run trends; but a broader perspective is needed if we are to understand how the decisions are made and the resources mobilized that produce a given pattern of factor supply and demand. (See Felix, 1977 for an economist's critique of the limitations of neoclassical economics for the analysis of development issues.)

The importance of broadening our perspective is brought out in John Goldthorpe's (1978) analysis of the factors underlying inflation. He argues that inflation is basically produced by socio-economic trends which make people less willing to tolerate income inequalities, while making governments more sensitive to popular demands. He argues that in the British case government sensitivity to unemployment and 'unrealistic' wage demands by unions are not the result of irrationality, bad economics or the like, but are calculated responses to the realities of the economic situation. This situation is based on a pattern of industrial development and of social mobility which, over time, created a highly solidary working class and undermined the values and hierarchical relationships that had previously restrained wage demands. Goldthorpe points out that, from a sociological perspective, the market destabilizes social relationships, creating expectations and competitive pressures which are inherently inflationary. Achieving a non-inflationary situation depends not only on correct monetary policies, but on a political and social context which, for example, dampens expectations and leads people to accept, as normal, income inequalities. We will find many similar examples of the ways in which the characteristics of the state and the pattern of class relationships shape economic organization. By focusing on class and class conflict, we will thus be able to take account of the diverse ways in which capitalist development has taken place in underdeveloped countries. We must keep in mind, however, that the class relationships of underdeveloped countries are conditioned by the historically created dependency of these countries on the advanced industrial world. In the following section I will explore the significance of this spatial component of inequality. I will also examine more carefully than hitherto the relationship between class conflict and the expansion of capitalist production.

Dependent development

Development is an interdependent process in which some countries and regions acquire a predominant place within the division of labour, using coercion to organize production elsewhere, as in the case of colonialism, or control of capital or advanced technology and markets. The division of labour that results is unequal in terms of the relative advantages that each part derives: the dominant partner reserves for itself the most lucrative activities, using the other as a source of cheap raw materials or foodstuffs and as a market for manufactures. This situation is expressed in two related concepts, that of dependency and that of the core-periphery relationship.

Dependency as analysed, for example, by A. G. Frank (1971) and Samir Amin (1973) who uses the term neo-colonialism, can be seen in terms of the structural relationship by which the advanced capitalist world at once exploited and kept the third world underdeveloped. Underdevelopment can thus be seen as being produced and maintained by the way in which capitalist expansion occurred in Latin America, Africa or Asia. The dominant capitalist powers (first England and then the United States) encouraged the transformation of local political and economic structures, both directly and indirectly, to serve their interests. Colonial territories were organized to produce the commodities needed by the metropolis—first precious metals and some agricultural products (such as sugar) and then, increasingly, the gamut of primary products needed for industrial expansion and to feed the urban populations of the advanced capitalist world. Characteristically, the situation under dependency is one in which the local population does not have sufficient control over its resources to be able to extract better terms of exchange with the dominant powers or to sustain a locally based pattern of balanced economic development (Amin, 1974, 15–20). A colonial power is able to reorganize native society to the economic advantage of the metropolis, thereby creating a kind of vassalage. Thus, Spain reorganized village life in Mexico and Peru to provide labour for the mines from which it extracted its richest treasure.

However, the situation of dependency is not simply produced by colonialism; it is also an internal structure of class relationships which work to the economic advantage of the metropolis and to the progressive underdevelopment of the periphery. At the periphery, there is a disarticulation of the economy, with sectors only marginally engaged in exchange with each other (Amin, 1974, 16). Foreign merchants and financiers provide a market for the primary materials and the locals use the revenues to purchase luxury goods from the advanced capitalist world. This free trade makes it difficult for local industry to develop in the face of competition from foreign imports; but the protection of local industry is rarely to the advantage of local oligarchies committed to the export economy. Even with formal independence, a former colony can, in these ways, remain securely tied to the interests of the colonial power.

From this point of view the chain of exploitative relationships that links the metropolitan country to the major city and dominant classes of the dependent country extends from these classes to traders and producers located in provincial towns, right down to the peasant producer or to the landless rural worker (Stavenhagen, 1965). At each stage of appropriation or expropriation there must always be a class of people who derive advantage from their situation and are prepared to act as agents in channelling the local resources to the metropolis. The surplus that remains in the dependent country does little to stimulate development: the life styles and values of the dominant classes of landowners and merchants entail, it is claimed, that this surplus is consumed in luxury expenditures rather than productive investments.

This analysis of dependency rests on an analysis of the logic of capitalist development. Capitalism is to be seen as becoming a dominant world economic system from the sixteenth century onwards, with the expansion of capitalism as co-terminus with that of colonialism and underdevelopment. The problems of Latin America from the colonial period onwards, for example, are thereby to be understood in terms of the way in which capitalism has penetrated that continent. Even apparently traditional institutions, such as the *hacienda* or Indian community, can be seen to have been shaped by capitalist expansion; it can be argued, therefore, that such institutions are not simply the survival or transplant of non-capitalist forms of organization and production, such as feudalism or primitive communism.

A comprehensive view of this aspect of dependence and interdependence is Brookfield's (1975) survey of the literature dealing with economic development and with the consequences of the creation of an interconnected world economic system. This world system made possible the emergence of complex organizations to sustain it at the national and regional level, but had the additional effect of concentrating control over the allocation of scarce resources and production. Together these had the effect, as Brookfield (205–9) puts it, of alleviating scarcity for some at the cost of increasing the relative impact of scarcity on others. This perspective is similar to the line of analysis developed by Wallerstein (1974a) in his concept of the modern world system. In his view, the world system is based on the specialization of different regions at different stages and under different aspects of the production process. In the early modern period, Wallerstein distinguishes between the core industrial regions, such as England, semi-peripheral regions specializing in commerce and in organizing the production of primary products, such as Spain, and peripheral regions, such as Latin America and Eastern Europe, which were organized to provide primary products for the core countries.

This line of argument provides an alternative perspective to that of growth pole theories of regional development. Friedmann (1972a, 1972b), for example, emphasizes the political dimensions that are important for regional development and stresses the concentration of power that develops in the economically most dynamic regions. He calls these regions core regions and examines the processes whereby such regions organize the production of peripheral regions; this organization has the effect of concentrating resources at the core and creating a progressive economic and political dependence of the periphery on the core. His major point is that the dominance of core regions is a self-reinforcing process since innovations in technology or culture tend to be developed first in core regions. Proximity to centres of decision-making, the presence of a highly developed consumer market and the presence of organizational resources for innovations are among the many factors which can be cited to explain this concentration of innovation. Economic advantages accrue to the earliest innovators and all innovation tends to reinforce and extend the control of the core over the periphery. More traditional competitors at the periphery will be forced out of business and less productive enterprises will be displaced from the core to the periphery.

The dominance of the core tends to produce or reinforce what appears to be inefficiency or traditionalism at the periphery. Indeed, the dynamism of the core depends, in great part, on creating conditions of scarcity at the periphery. Thus Friedmann argues that, in the case of Chile, the predominance of Santiago has deprived provincial city government of any financial resources; in this situation, local government appears inefficient since it does not provide adequate urban services nor foster local economic development. Taxes and local banking deposits channel capital to Santiago, where it promotes the economic growth of the core region. In the face of the dominance of the core, the dominant provincial classes in many countries may espouse regionalism, stressing the traditional virtues or ethnic characteristics of their region as a means of challenging the dominance of the core. These potential conflicts between periphery and core may in the long run limit the expansion of the core, giving rise to counter-elites at the periphery and perhaps to the eventual withdrawal of the periphery from the influence of the core (Friedmann, 1972a, 96–8).

Studies focusing on the structure of dependency or on that of the core-periphery relationship, have, however, tended to overlook those local-level forces making for change in the situation. Dependency 'theory', as Fernando Cardoso (1976) points out, has become reified, in some hands, as a purely mechanical analysis of the ways in which external agents, such as foreign governments or multinational corporations, dominate local politics and economic life. Yet substantial transformations have occurred in the economic and social structures of almost all underdeveloped countries, despite the unevenness of this development, and these transformations must be analysed in terms of the internal processes of change, as much as of the external context. For this reason I use the term development in this book, as well as the apparently more neutral terms growth or change. Provided that we remember that no optimistic view of progress is implied by its use, the term development has the advantage of drawing attention to the increasing specialization and differentiation that is taking place within even the most underdeveloped countries.

We will look, in subsequent chapters, at the systems of production that emerge in dependent countries and regions as a result of capitalist expansion. These systems of production are based on differences in the labour, capital and technological requirements of different commercial crops, raw materials or manufactures. Associated with these systems of production are particular types of class formation and class conflict. This form of analysis stresses that dependency is not a uniform condition, but includes many different situations of dependency. One of the most complete versions of this approach is that given by F. H. Cardoso and E. Faletto (1969), in an essay entitled *Dependency and Development in Latin America*. They argue that within the constraints of the international capitalist system an uneven development had taken place within Latin America. They have succeeded in showing that this development varied economically and politically as a result of the specificity of the class struggle and that this was based on differences in the organization of production.

These perspectives on the relationship between urbanization and economic development are similar, in certain respects, to the staple theory of economic development (Watkins, 1963). This theory, which has been mainly developed and applied in terms of Canadian experience, concentrates on the way national or regional economies are shaped by the specific production or extraction requirements (including income distribution, processing and transport) of the primary products exported to world markets (see Brookfield, 1975, 93–7).

Staple theory is helpful for understanding the diversity of development experiences because it draws attention to the variety of ways export crops shape social, economic and political institutions. The relationship is not a mechanical one. It is mistaken to think, for example, that certain crops are inherently 'democratic' in their effects and that others are 'authoritarian'. The value of staple theory is that it helps analytically to break down capitalist expansion into its different components so that their particular consequences for institutional development can be identified.

Hirschman (1977) has extended his own linkage approach to development to suggest a comprehensive view of the impact of different staples. He is interested in the direct backward and forward linkages generated by both primary and manufacturing production; but he extends the linkage concept to include the consumption patterns generated by the staple and to take account of whether or not the staple stimulates the development of the state's fiscal mechanisms. Certain staples lend themselves more easily to state taxation than others: for example, their ownership and control may be in foreign hands, as in enclave production, and they represent a visible target for government seeking revenue. Other staples, and coffee is often such a case, are owned nationally and by a relatively large number of influential landowners. In this case, the state may find it hard initially to tax production in face of the opposition of the dominant local classes, although, as happened with coffee in Brazil, the need of producers to seek guaranteed prices in face of world market fluctuations became an important factor in stimulating the development of the state's fiscal mechanisms.

Hirschman's suggestions are not meant to be applied mechanically; his major point is that we should pay more attention to the dialectic process that is involved in the expansion of any system of production. This production creates new class interests and the possibility of clashes among them. An expanding system of production entails clashes of interests between those committed to the new production and those whose position is threatened by its growth. For example, labour may be attracted away from older forms of production by higher wages and these older forms may also find that the policies advocated by the new interests, such as tariff reform, are counter to their own. Staples also differ in the extent to which they lend themselves to foreign or to national control of production.

Hirschman stresses the social and political factors in development, even to the point of identifying the advantages of staples which *do not* create opportunities for linkages, as in the case of sophisticated processing plant or equipment. His argument is that, in the early stages of development, such linkages would inevitably be controlled by the foreign investors of capital, relegating the grower of the staple to the agricultural role. In contrast, where the staple requires only a few simple operations (drying and bagging, for instance) and its value per unit of weight justifies the grower himself transporting it to market, then the grower is more likely to extend his interests into commerce and transport. The profits of such a staple would thus contribute to a more widespread local development.

I will extend this approach further in this book by taking into account the types of labour required for different forms of staple and industrial production, the political institutions needed to obtain such labour and the implications these have for the development of the class struggle. Following this line of analysis, I shall stress the ways in which capitalism has expanded *within* underdeveloped countries. My concern is less with the ways in which the advanced capitalist world continues to exploit underdeveloped countries (continuity within change according to Frank), than with the patterns of social, economic and political life that have resulted from the exigencies of capitalist expansion in an unevenly developed economy.

Urbanization in the advanced capitalist countries

I will conclude this chapter with a brief description of the patterns of urbanization following the Industrial Revolution in Britain and in the United States. The first aim of this description is to remind ourselves of the national and international context that shaped the urbanization of the developed world. As we saw above, the experience of Britain and the United States has often been used as a benchmark for subsequent patterns of urbanization. It is still common for observers to take isolated aspects of urban life in underdeveloped countries and compare them with the nineteenth-century experience of the advanced capitalist world, pointing to similarities or differences in migration or in family life in the cities and so on. Such comparisons can be useful provided that the differences in the context of urbanization are kept in mind since we are dealing with an interdepedent development process. In this respect, the British and US patterns or urbanization are interesting because they contrast not only with those of underdeveloped countries but with each other, in the ways in which social and political structures affect economic development.

The experiences of Britain and the United States in the nineteenth and early twentieth centures are also significant since these two countries had a major impact, in this period, on the economies of the underdeveloped world. Britain was clearly the dominant industrial power and was the major source of capital investment for other countries until the early twentieth century (Thomas, 1973). Of the underdeveloped world, Latin America, though not a British colony, was by 1913 the most important focus of British investment in publicly issued securities. It received 20 per cent of the total compared with 10 per cent for India and Ceylon. The United States received 20 per cent, Canada 13.7 per cent, Australia and New Zealand 11.1 per cent and Europe 5.8 per cent (RIIA, 1937, 121).

By 1913, British investment was some 80 per cent of total foreign investment in Latin America. From approximately the 1940s the United States became the dominant trading partner in Latin America, replacing the previously dominant European powers (UN, 1964, table 159). In the 1940s Latin America was the major location for US direct private investment abroad (Bureau of the Census, 1975, 870). Indeed, during the 1950s the direct private investment in Latin America was greater than US direct private investments in Europe and all other countries of the world combined, with the exception of Canada.

I will suggest that the British and United States form of economic imperialism had a very different impact on the underdeveloped world. Economic imperialism can be defined for our purposes as the search for, and creation of, overseas markets for the products and investments of the metropolitan country. (See Brookfield, 1975, 15–18, for a short review of the different perspectives on economic imperialism, contrasting the emphasis on the search for new markets (Luxemburg) with that on the export of capital (Lenin).) The difference between Britain and the United States was due, in part, to the different stage of capitalist development at which each country was dominant. Britain was dominant in the competitive stage when industrial production was relatively small-scale and fragmented and the United States in the monopoly stage when capital was concentrated and centralized through large industrial conglomerates, banking institutions and so on. This international context must be kept in mind when we consider the internal transformations taking place in the underdeveloped countries, since the change in the dominant capitalism has, as its counterpart, a change in the organization and control of production in underdeveloped countries. The following descriptions do not attempt to capture all the complexities of the urbanization experience of Britain and the United States; I will be concerned only with the salient contrasting characteristics of these two experiences as they affect underdeveloped countries.

Great Britain

In Britain, more perhaps than in any continental European country, the urban-industrialization of the nineteenth century was preceded by an almost complete commercialization of agriculture (Landes, 1970, 50). Most agricultural land was owned by large landowners and rented to farmers who, by the eighteenth century, were under increasing commercial pressure to improve their methods and their crops. Wage labour was common in agriculture by this period and there is some evidence, from Lancashire, of an increasing use of casual labour and of labour that lived outside rather than on the farm (Marshall, 1961). England had developed a substantial network of small, but thriving, market centres; some of these were already centres of important manufacturing activity carried out mainly by cottage spinners and weavers. A contemporary observer described the area for forty miles around Manchester as one of the greatest industrial regions of the day, estimating that by 1774 about 30,000 people there were engaged in the cotton industry (Chapman, 1904, 3). Compared, then, with many underdeveloped countries, England was unusual in that agrarian conditions were creating a supply of free labour prior to urban-industrial development.

Even in the English case it was not easy, at first, to recruit labour for the factories. The early textile mills, which were water driven and in rural areas, often had considerable difficulty in obtaining labour. Like the Gregs at Styal, near Manchester, mill-owners often used extra-market mechanisms to recruit labour, such as obtaining apprentices through the Poor Law, or providing tied housing (Boyson, 1970). Some employers continued with the paternalistic organization of the industrial colony, with its company shops, housing, schools and churches, even when labour became more freely available in the nineteenth century. The colony structure, they claimed, brought economic and moral benefits by developing a stable and reliable work force (Marshall, 1968).

By the mid-nineteenth century, factory labour had become abundant and cheap relative to that of the United States (Habakkuk, 1967). The transformation of agriculture and land scarcity meant that, in contrast to the United States, farming and farm work in England were not alternatives to industrial employment: agricultural wages were low and employment possibilities in agriculture were scarcely expanding. Craft industry persisted well into the nineteenth century; but the independence of the artisan had been substantially eroded through the development of the merchant emp-loyer system of hiring outworkers (Fong, 1932, 8–16). In Lancashire there was also a substantial population increase in the eighteenth century which put some pressure on existing employment oppor-tunities (Lawton, 1962). Irish and, to a lesser extent, Scottish migra-tion provided in the nineteenth century an additional supply of labour.

There were other features of English industrialization that made the supply of labour, with the requisite skills, less of a problem than it has been in many subsequent cases of industrialization. Landes (1970, 117–19) points out that the pace of technological change in England was slower than the term, Industrial Revolution, implies. Even in cotton textiles, the first branch of manufacturing to be affected by important technological changes, the dramatic increase in power looms came in the years after 1835 (Fong, 1932, 37). Craft produc-tion persisted well into the nineteenth century even in those branches of manufacture, such as metal and textiles, where factories were established early. In fact, the expansion of factory production revital-ized or even created branches of craft production, such as the clo-thing industry or machine building and maintenance. The vitality of craft production is not surprising since it often complemented fac-tory production, enabling the factory-owner to save capital and increase his flexibility by the putting-out system. Also, the level of technological complexity was not yet such as to give large-scale operations and their economies of scale an overwhelming cost advantage over small-scale ones (Felix, 1977).

This pattern of industrial organization meant that labour would eventually be absorbed by manufacturing industry to a much greater extent than is possible in countries industrializing under the tech-nological conditions of the twentieth century. Moreover, manu-facturing employment in Britain was based on a much wider market than has been available to countries that industrialized subsequently. As early as 1819–21, two thirds of the cotton yarn produced in Britain was exported either directly or as cloth and by 1880–2, this percentage was 84.9 (Landes, 1970, 239). In cotton textiles, for example, employment in the mills rose from 218,000 in 1838 to 340,000 in 1856, despite substantial gains in productivity in the same period (Fong, 1932, 44).

By 1901 almost 40 per cent of the British labour force was emp-loyed in industry and construction. Agriculture in this year provided employment for some 15 per cent of employed males (1901 Census of England and Wales, 82). Moreover, the relatively primitive tech-nology of the nineteenth century created a demand for a mass of unskilled workers in mining, construction and transport. At its high-point, mining absorbed 1,200,000 men or between nine and ten per cent of the economically active male population (Hobsbawm, 1969b).

Since the capital requirements for early factory production were small, they were within the reach of small-scale entrepreneurs with the aid of loans from a few friends. The subsequent growth of the factory was often financed from profits (Landes, 1970, 78). In the Manchester area, those who constructed the new mills came from families which frequently had a long history of local entre-preneurship and landholding, often as outwork manufacturers and traders (Foster, 1974, 11; Boyson, 1970; Chapman, 1904). Thus, most British factories in the nineteenth century were either family firms or partnerships; the efficiency of the money market in provid-ing short-term credit obviated the need, until the end of the century, to raise money publicly through joint-stock companies (Presnell, 1965; Landes, 1970). The structure of manufacturing industry was, for most of the nineteenth century, relatively small-scale. By 1856, for example, there were over 2,000 textile mills in England with an average work force of 166 (Fong, 1932, 32).

These features of British industrialization were not repeated in the experience of later developing European countries, such as Germany and Italy (Gershenkron, 1962, 72–90). In Germany, the predominant pattern of industrialization at the end of the nineteenth century was large-scale units of production in which long-term financing by banks and direct state aid played a much more important role than had been the case in Britain. This industrial organization was one factor in enabling German industry to invest in complex technology and establish a lead in new branches of industry, such as chemicals and electrical engineering.

British urban and industrial development in the nineteenth cen-tury was the result of small-scale, local initiatives and was resistant to state control and planning. City growth was superimposed upon a plethora of archaic administrative jurisdictions. Until 1832, for example, Manchester, with a population of some 160,000 people, was governed by a court leet as a manorial village, with the assistance of a separately constituted body of police commissioners (Redford and Russell, 1940). The movement of municipal reform was a slow one and, despite the example of Birmingham, major cities such as Leeds had not adequately resolved their problems of municipal finance and administration by the end of the nineteenth century (Briggs, 1971, 236). The provision of housing was, likewise, a matter of an uncoordinated and fragmented initiative. Although housing in the industrial towns was sometimes provided by the factory- or mine-owner, this practice became less frequent in the course of the nineteenth century except when the industry was established in a rural area (Marshall, 1968). There is little published research evi-dence, but my own work and that of others suggests that the usual way of providing housing was for local tradesmen or professionals to put up small amounts of capital in collaboration with a local builder. There was an adequate supply of such small-scale capital, partly because capital markets in nineteenth-century Britain were far from perfect and often too specialized for the small investor (Dyos and Reeder, 1973). Although the quantity of housing in the industrial towns was sufficient, by the end of the century, to provide single family dwellings for the working class, the quality was often poor. Local municipal authorities were under pressure from builders, land agents and local tradesmen not to apply standards in order to encourage rapid and cheap development (see Olsen, 1973).

Finding *ad hoc* local solutions to urban development was also the practice in the United States in this period, but it had perhaps more serious consequences in Britain where there was less freedom to manoeuvre in face of the limitations of existing jurisdictions and of lack of space. Robson (1973, 223–8) suggests that British cities lagged behind their German and American counterparts in innovations that depended on the exercise of large-scale control, such as electricity, tramways and the telephone. The backwardness of British town administration in the nineteenth century is a relative matter and much of it was due to the constraints of being the first to install equipment that subsequently became dated. However, with the possible exception of Brimingham, the dominant provincial classes failed to develop a coherent project of local government as a means of sustaining the economic progress of their regions (Briggs, 1971, 234–5). The bickerings of councillors and the rivalries of local committees can be viewed as the inevitable consequence of a fragmented economic structure; but it was a poor basis on which to challenge the power and attraction of London (Mellor, 1977, 24–47).

The role of London in British economic development illustrates many of the features of the core-periphery model outlined earlier. Despite the dramatic growth of industry in the provinces, London in the nineteenth century retained its economic as well as political dominance of the national scene (Dyos, 1971). It was not a factory town but it still contained by far the greatest concentration of industrial employment in the country, with 468,000 workers in manufacturing in 1861 (Hall, 1962, 21). Employment in London benefited from technological innovation and the development of industry in the provinces. London's clothing industry, which employed almost a quarter of all English and Welsh clothing workers, used the sweating system and the sewing-machine to make up the textiles of the north (Hall, 52–66). Since London was the hub of communication and trade, employment in transport and storage activities formed the largest single employment category for males in the 1861 census, with 13.44 per cent and, in 1891, was superseded only by employment in retail and distribution activities (Stedman Jones, 1971, 358–9).

Although a great deal of London's employment was casual or in sweat-shops, even this aspect of the emerging division of labour within Britain was to the advantage of the dominant classes. It meant that the metropolitan working class was more fragmented and less easy to organize than its counterparts in the provinces (Dyos, 1971; Stedman Jones, 1971). The centre of power was, in effect, the locus of the weakest challenge to the existing system of inequality.

London maintained its position of dominance partly because the centralization of English economic and social life had become firmly established before the Industrial Revolution. Dyos and Aldcroft (1969) discuss the way in which the metropolis and its merchants had already shaped the pattern of inland trade before the Industrial Revolution, drawing in supplies from all over the country and using provincial towns as collecting centres for the needs of the city. Early transport innovations, such as the turnpikes, were often financed by London merchants, eager to consolidate their provincial lines of supply. Canals were usually launched by local men, but when they became a commercial success, London capital often took a significant share, as in the case of the Ellesmere Canal (Dyos and Aldcroft, 97). Railways were, of course, to consolidate London's position, bringing even the northern counties within an easy day's travelling of the capital.

London was a magnet throughout the nineteenth century because it remained the largest single market for almost all the commodities that people might wish to buy or sell, from consumer goods, or the arts, to power and social prestige. The provinces attempted to rival the capital with their impressive public buildings, theatres and concert halls, but the attraction of London was usually too great. Provincial industrialists and merchants did, at times, form themselves into counter-elites, seeking to challenge the power of the metropolis over issues such as the corn laws, the abolition of slavery and tariff reform (Williams, 1944, 154–68; Boyson, 1970). Yet is is interesting to see that even someone as forthright as was Henry Ashworth in attacking central government interference and the landed classes should, towards the end of his life, increasingly spend his money on the traditional status pursuits of the English dominant classes—land, hunting and the good life (Boyson, 1970).

British industrialization became associated with a spatial pattern of social inequality which had enduring effects on Britain's economic development. One of the sharpest contrasts with subsequent experiences of industrialization is the early consolidation in the provinces of an industrial working class which, until after the second world war, was largely self-recruiting, socially and geographically. The slowing down in job mobility did not appear at the same time or to the same extent in the different areas. Factory employment spread first in the textile region and then unevenly throughout the country; yet during the nineteenth century, Birmingham contained a vast variety of trades organized in workshop production. Likewise, for much of the nineteenth century there was considerable internal migration—migration from Ireland, Scotland and the continent and, of course, emigration to North America, Australia and New Zealand.

The evidence for increasing immobility is sketchy; but, from the early nineteenth century there are signs that the industrial working class was locally recruited. Edward Thompson (1970, 401–29) stresses the cultural manifestations of this recruitment in the regional customs and dialects that persisted in the factory towns. The predominant pattern of migration was short-distance and probably drawn mainly from villages in which non-agricultural employment predominated (Redford, 1926; Weber, 1899, 225; Anderson, 1971, 34–41). Even in mid-Victorian London about half the migrants came from bordering counties (Lees, 1973). Anderson (1971) shows that in the Lancashire cotton town, Preston, kinship and places of origin continued to be an important basis on which migrants established relationships and coped with the problems of finding work and accommodation.

In the first industrial regions such as the northwest, the population growth of the industrial towns slowed considerably after the mid-nineteenth century. By the beginning of the twentieth century, Manchester and Salford and even 'surburban' Chorlton were beginning to show an absolute decline in population (Lawton, 1962). In my current research on residential mobility in Oldham from 1850 to the present, there is evidence that while families changed houses very frequently in mid-century, the rate of turnover in tenancies declined sharply at the end of the nineteenth and through the first thirty years of the twentieth century. Robson (1973, 96) cites evidence from Leicester that residential turnover there was declining in the early twentieth century.

One topic that merits more research is the extent to which the pattern of industrial growth encouraged residential stabilization. Regions grew on the basis of staple industries—cotton textiles in southeast Lancashire, woollen manufacture in west Yorkshire and Lancashire, iron in the west Midlands, Teesside and south Yorkshire, coal in south Wales and the northeast (Robson, 1973, 94). These regions grew at different periods, but it is unlikely that a growing region attracted a substantial population from other industrial regions. Thus, by 1901, when Lancashire had passed the peak of its economic growth, 89.3 per cent of all those born in Lancashire and still resident in Britain were still resident in Lancashire itself (1901 Census of England and Wales, tables 38 and 39).

In the period up to the first world war the pace of technological change in British industry was uneven and, by and large, once an industry was established there were few changes in the organization or production. (See Landes, 1970, 316–21, for a nuanced account of the British case.) This situation may have encouraged occupational inbreeding and, by particularizing skills, discouraged workers from seeking employment in other industries in times of unemployment. Thus Copeland (1912) labelled cotton-mill operatives in England as an almost hereditary class. The inadequate educational provision for the working class in the nineteenth century was a further barrier to both social and geographical mobility (Landes, 1970, 340–8). In the 1930s, government analyses of the employment situation in the northwest demonstrated a high degree of immobility among the population. This was attributed to the high rate of employment among married females, to house ownership and to the limited horizons of a workforce that had lived in an area dominated by one industry (Manchester, 1936). The strength and character of British trade unions owed much to the development of strong, local work traditions among a stable population. This situation meant that the British working class became very effective in resisting change in work organization that threatened their livelihood.

Britain's lead in the Industrial Revolution meant that it captured overseas markets for industrial products with a relatively simple and inexpensive production technology. There was little association between industrial capital and bank capital (Hobsbawm, 1969a). Banking houses concentrated on what they saw as the greater profits to be derived from overseas trade and from financing infrastructural development, both at home and abroad. One consequence of this capitalist structure was that British capital was not committed by the terms of its own expansion to the internal market; nor was it committed to technological change as a means of deepening that market through introducing more differentiated products. Britain became tied to maintaining and creating an overseas market for basic industrial products and these overseas interests were significant factors in producing the patterns of urbanization in the Americas in the nineteenth century. They meant that British capital was attracted overseas to create the infrastructure that would promote trade exchanges (Thomas, 1973, 244–90). British investment in Argentinian, Brazilian or North American railroads increased, directly and indirectly, demand for British industrial products. These railroads also 'opened up' the interior of the Americas for the production of primary products for export. The slow rate of technological change in British industry meant in the long term, however, that the cycles of investment overseas and renewed investment in Britain did not lead to sustained economic growth at home. This organization of British capitalism generated and sustained a particular pattern of intervention in underdeveloped economies. By 1913, it was estimated that probably over 80 per cent of British overseas investment were placed in countries that were largely dependent on the export of primary products (RIIA, 1937, 122). In many areas of the world, especially when these were not colonies, British economic imperialism remained fundamentally commercial in orientation. The control and organization of local production was left mainly in local hands —though, of course, these 'locals' might be foreign immigrants.

Thus, British investments were concentrated in the development of the economic infrastructure of foreign countries (RIIA, 1937, 148–59). Communications, especially railroads, absorbed the bulk of private investment, followed closely by government securities. Together with public utilities, banks and finance, these functional fields of investment accounted for some 84 per cent of British foreign investment by 1913. The character of these investments differed little between the colonies and dominions and areas, such as Latin America, outside direct British control (Glade, 1969, 219).

The products of British industry were an important part of British trade; but they were not an integral part. The time would come when British traders in Latin America and British banking houses would find it more profitable to trade in US or German products. In contrast to US investors, British traders and investors made little attempt to develop and take control of local manufacturing industry and coordinate it with manufacturing in Britain by, for example, purchasing British capital goods. Nor did British capital make a concerted effort to control primary production and tie it to the needs of British industry (Singer, 1975). One implication of this type of foreign capitalist penetration, as we shall see in the next chapter, was that it encouraged in underdeveloped countries a diversity of regional 'responses' to economic development and divergent patterns of urbanization.

The United States

One of the most striking differences between the urbanization pattern of the United States and that of Britain is the lesser importance of employment in manufacturing and construction. In 1870, 23.5 per cent of the American labour force were employed in construction and manufacturing, with many industries being based on the transformation of the agricultural product; at that date 50.8 per cent were employed in agriculture and 11.5 per cent were employed in distributive services (transport, utilities and trade). By 1920, the transformative sector generated 32.9 per cent of total employment, and by 1960 35.9 per cent were so employed, by which time agriculture employed 7 per cent of the population. The ratio of employment in distributive services to that in the transformative sector remained fairly constant throughout the period 1870 to 1960; by 1900 the ratio of employment in distributive services to that in the transformative sector was 0.60, and in 1960 the ratio was 0.61 (Browning and Singelmann, 1975).

These figures suggest that a different pattern of economic development underlies urbanization in the United States. It was through the development of urban centres that the agricultural regions of the west and mid-west were opened up (Berry, 1967). In contrast to the situation whereby the needs of a scattered farming population give rise to centrally located market centres, urban settlements preceded agricultural development in many parts of the United States.

Wade (1959) describes the way in which the west was developed through towns which acted as bridgeheads for colonization and as service and collection centres for the hinterland. The size of the United States and transport difficulties meant that urban settlement was essential, not only for the transhipment of goods but also for the manufacture of basic items whose transport costs were prohibitive. In this situation, town development was relatively free from the domination of the established eastern centres. Wade emphasizes that the frontier did not necessarily stimulate innovation in urban organization; indeed, the new towns assiduously copied eastern urban patterns. However, located in areas of new settlement, the western towns were not subject to the tangle of archaic jurisdictions that enmeshed their British counterparts. By the end of the nineteenth century, most American western towns had found workable solutions to the problems of finance, public services and government.

Morse (1975) relates this aspect of US urban development to the staple and linkage approaches I discussed earlier. Morse uses a distinction between the plantation and homestead models of economic development to understand why agricultural exports stimulate industrialization under some conditions but not under others. The plantation produces high export earnings, but these earnings do not stimulate widespread local development. Instead, earnings are channelled through one or two major urban centres where they are consumed in sumptuous living, thereby stimulating the import of luxury manufactures and the development of commerce dominated by the major urban centre. In contrast, small-scale, homestead farming requires a local infrastructure of small towns to service it. Scale is important because the needs of large production units, such as the plantation, could be met by shipping produce over a considerable distance, while the dispersion of small producers stimulates the rise of local collection centres. Under these conditions a substantial share of the earnings of the farm product remains locally to stimulate local commerce and industry (Morse, 1975). The low levels of urbanization in the southern parts of the United States in the nineteenth century were due to the predominance of the plantation economy (Rothstein, 1966). As Rothstein (1967) indicates elsewhere, the issue

is not one of the non-capitalist or non-entrepreneurial character of
the planter elite. The southern plantation operated as an economic
enclave in its surrounding territory. Initial shortages of labour led to
extensive plantations worked by slave labour, since the crops needed
to be worked on a large scale to be profitable. The cotton crop was
tended, harvested and ginned by resident labour; it was directly
shipped in bulk to the ports. Thus, the earnings of cotton did little to
stimulate economic development outside the plantation; the plantation did not require the production of foodstuffs, nor did it need
commercial or other services. Indeed, small farmers became dependent on the plantation for ginning and shipping their product, thus
reinforcing the concentration of earnings in the planter elite.

Under these conditions a few port cities developed, mainly as
commercial centres and centres of residence for the elite; their life
styles and consumption patterns were not such as to stimulate local
production. Luxury manufactures were brought in directly from
Europe and the eastern states. Dowd (1956) extends this argument to
the post-bellum period. He points out that even after the abolition of
slavery, institutional patterns kept the south underdeveloped and
relatively unurbanized. Planters used sharecropping arrangements
with poor whites to obtain cotton cheaply. Under these arrangements, and in the factories established to manufacture cloth, poor
white hostility to, and fears of, the blacks was used to keep labour
disorganized and cheap. The profits made were channelled to northern banks and investors. Levels of consumption remained low in the
south and insufficient to extend local commercial and industrial
development.

In contrast, in the west of the United States, despite dependence on
eastern capital, the homestead pattern of settlement provided a market for manufactures while producing, cheaply, the cereals required
for export. The towns of the west thrived as centres of trade and
industry and developed a strong sense of municipal autonomy.

Rothstein (1966) provides a detailed examination of the relationship between the form of agricultural production in the west and
economic and social institutions. He argues that the small-scale
nature and technical requirements of wheat production generated a
variety of middleman activities and demands for agricultural inputs.
Grain was stored in bulk in small towns, stimulating the devlopment
of means to classify and standardize the various small harvests that
made up the bulk. Complicated chains of brokerage developed
around warehouse receipts, leading to innovations in the financial
management and organization of the grain trade, which became
centred increasingly in cities such as Chicago and St Louis. Using
these and many other examples, Rothstein argues that homestead
wheat production helped develop a pattern of urbanization in which
commercial and other service activities could flourish in small

towns, generating profits that were often invested locally. Further-more, the increasing voting power of the western populations com-bined with the interest of eastern finance to secure the development of transport and urban infrastructure.

Since urbanization in the United States was an active agent in developing agriculture as well as industry and services, labour was relatively scarce both in agriculture and in industry, especially in the first half of the nineteenth century. Labour scarcity raised wages to levels higher than those in England in the same period and stimulated technological innovation (Habakkuk, 1967, 12–16).

In contrast, urbanization in Europe concentrated population that could no longer find adequate work in agriculture. Industrialization displaced population from the rural areas of Europe by producing cheap manufactured goods that removed the source of livelihood of rural artisans and that encouraged the rationalization and mechaniza-tion of farming. This process eventually occurred in the United States also; but, even in the period of rapid industrialization from 1870 to 1920, employment opportunities in agriculture *increased* in the United States from 6,430,000 jobs to 11,120,000 (Bureau of the Census, 1975, 138).

International migrations linked the US pattern of urbanization with that of Europe. The rapid development of the US economy was made possible by the immigration of European labour power after the Civil War. This immigration was itself produced by the broader patterns of economic interdependency. While high rates of popula-tion increase and population pressures on scarce land resources were the main factors behind the availability of Europe's agricultural population, European industrialization also contributed to this out-migration. The contribution was less the result of any direct dislocations produced by industrialization than of its indirect conse-quences in flooding the European market with cheap foodstuffs from the Americas and other parts of the world. As first England and then other European powers brought countries into their orbit as markets for manufactured products, so too European capital stimu-lated the specialization of countries as producers of primary pro-ducts. American and Canadian wheat, Argentinian wheat and beef, New Zealand and Australian mutton, sugar and other tropical foods-tuffs entered the European market, driving down food prices and making the situation of the small European farmer more precarious.

The result was a redistribution of population in keeping with a newly emerging territorial division of labour. In Europe, the out-migration relieved, to a certain extent, the pressures on employment in the cities and on the land. Indeed, as some commentators have suggested, it is possible that, without emigration, European cities at the turn of the nineteenth century would have shown more evidence of a marginal population (Graham, 1972; Hobsbawm, 1969b). As it was, the European cities often acted as transit camps for urban and rural migrants to the New World, transferring the surplus population to the cities of the eastern seaboard of the United States. The occupational distributions of European cities might, consequently, have been more akin to cities in the underdeveloped world today, with most employment concentrated in the services. European immigrants not only helped the American economy, but they also helped turn Argentina into a major wheat producer and Brazil into a major coffee producer.

Industrialization in the United States was also facilitated by the investment of substantial amounts of European capital and by the import of capital goods from Europe. Above all, perhaps, United States industrialization was shaped by the rapidly expanding internal market for its product. Labour shortages are likely to have pushed average incomes above those of Britain by the last half of the nineteenth century (Hobsbawm, 1969, 172–7; Habakkuk, 1967, 110–11). The opening up of the west and the urbanization of the east had created, in this period, a mass market for agricultural implements, home utensils, tools and weapons, encouraging the standardization of production and such innovations as interchangeable parts. The scale of operations favoured mergers and the rise of industrial conglomerates, further stimulating the adoption of standards which cut across industries. Unlike the English case, bank capital was involved early in the long-term financing of these operations.

Since industrial production in the United States in the late nineteenth and early twentieth centuries was predominantly for the internal market, the major exports were agricultural commodities and other primary products, especially cotton from the south. The urbanization statistics show that under these conditions even a massive industrialization did not entail a high degree of population concentration. At the period (1896–1900) when US manufacturing production was nearly double that of Great Britain, some 60 per cent of the American population lived in places of less than 2,500 people (Bureau of the Census, 1975). This degree of population dispersal was accompanied by the growth of large cities in certain regions of the United States. Indeed, the pattern of urbanization in the late nineteenth century in the United States diverges widely by region: in 1900, 61 per cent of the population of the northeast region lived in places of 2,500 people or more; in the south the equivalent percentage was 18, in the north central region, 38.6 per cent, and in the west 39.9 per cent (Lampard, 1968, table 2).

The type of large city that emerged in the United States as a result of the interdependency of the Atlantic economy was quite distinct from that of Europe and became the basis for a different pattern of economic development. My concern is not with the issue of whether the large American cities of the first part of this century encouraged a distinctive urban style of life which, over time, would influence the behaviour of all urban inhabitants (Wirth, 1938). The discussion over urbanism as a way of life has made clear the importance and persistence of urban sub-cultures in American cities: in some of these cities, ethnicity and kinship are important means of economic and social solidarity, while for other social and economic groups, urban location may have little significance for behaviour (Gans, 1965; Hawley, 1971, 134–5).

For the international comparisons of this chapter, I will limit myself to general features of the organization of the large American city. First, American cities had more, and cheaper, space available for expansion, partly because land monopoly was not as strongly entrenched in a 'new' country; the use of this space was facilitated by the early introduction of street cars and electricity. Adna Weber (1899) quotes the average densities of cities in the United States, England and Germany at the end of the nineteenth century as being, respectively, 15.2 persons per acre, 38.3 persons per acre, and 25.9 persons per acre. By the end of the nineteenth century Weber (469) was able to document an extensive movement of both industry and residence to suburban locations, showing the greater dispersal of the American urban populations than that of Europe.

International migration, which was mainly directed to the cities, contributed to a low degree of working-class organization and consciousness in American cities. Ethnic differences among urban populations were used by those in power to weaken worker organization, as is shown by the events leading to, and the trial of, the Italian-American radicals, Sacco and Vanzetti (Frankfurter, 1962). This migration became part of the pattern of economic expansion at the end of the nineteenth century. Thomas argues that the American economy became geared to using, profitably, the large numbers of unskilled, and often illiterate, workers that came from Europe (Thomas, 1973, 163–74). Factory production and, especially, assembly-line-type methods of production, were encouraged by the abundance of unskilled labour and the shortage of skilled labour. Since technological innovation often saves skilled labour, it is perhaps not surprising to find labour-saving innovations in American industry at a time when labour was, at last, abundant and cheap (Habakkuk, 1967, 128–31). Also, Habakkuk argues, immigrant labour made it somewhat easier to frustrate the attempts of skilled workers to stop mechanization. Industrial expansion created technical and supervisory job opportunities for workers 'displaced' by the new processes. Jobs in commerce and the services also expanded with mass production and the need to distribute and service the commodities produced. The successive waves of migration from Europe meant that American industry had an almost perpetual pool of unskilled labour to expand production cheaply. The sons of the first generations of unskilled migrants acquired the educational and technical skills to consolidate their hold on the better-class jobs in society (Thomas, 1973, 153).

This economic structure generated the patterns of urban residential succession that became characteristic of American cities. Newly arrived immigrants settled in central city tenements, which were cheap and gave access to various job possibilities; unskilled and unstable work fixed these immigrants in ethnic ghettoes (Ward, 1968). As individuals and ethnic groups acquired skills and education, they obtained better paying and more stable jobs and moved to outlying residential districts of the city. Residential instability, consequent upon economic expansion, affected even supposedly unchanging New England towns, as Thernstrom's restudy of Lloyd Warner's Yankee city shows (Thernstrom, 1964; Warner and Lunt, 1941). Thernstrom (215–16) reports a high degree of population and social mobility for nineteenth-century Newburyport and links these mobilities to the lack of working-class consciousness in American cities.

The social and spatial structure of American cities thus contributed to the pattern of industrial expansion. The segregation of skilled, stable and often unionized jobs from unskilled, unstable work was accomplished through successive waves of immigrants, ethnic ghettoes and residential succession. The effectiveness of this segregation of the labour force—the existence of what has recently been called a dual labour market—promoted American industrial expansion and technological innovation (Gordon, 1972, 67–70).

The investment of American capital in local production in Latin America is a direct consequence of this pattern of economic development. The pace of technological change in the United States and the rapid expansion of its industrial production to meet the demands of the internal market meant that American capital was more interested in controlling production abroad than in the trade of finished products. Control secured the primary resources needed for industrial expansion at home and provided a secure outlet for the export of machines and machine tools. In 1930, direct investments abroad by the United States in industry and commerce constituted about half its total long-term investments abroad, while portfolio investments in government-backed securities made up the other half. In Latin America, the major recipient of US investments, direct investments made up 69 per cent of the total. Of direct investments abroad, 62 per cent was distributed between manufacturing industry (20 per cent), petroleum, mining and agriculture (RIIA, 1937, 185–9). As we shall see later, United States investment in manufacturing industry became more pronounced after the second world war. The control of production enabled American capital to shape the local market rather than simply to respond to its demands.

In subsequent chapters I will examine the extent to which the concentration of the high-income population of Latin America in relatively few urban places created the markets suitable for sophisticated consumer durables. Conversely, access to markets determined the location of industry close to the major urban centres. Within these centres, the organization of space such, for example, as the development of suburban dormitories, encouraged the expansion of the market for the final products (cars, domestic appliances, for instance) of capital-intensive industry. There will be no need to presuppose any concerted conspiracy on the part of American capital; it is simply the case that the pattern of foreign investment and credit and the nature of the world market create advantages for individuals and governments in Latin America that adopt capital-intensive technology—a policy advocated by the Economic Commission of Latin America in the 1950s.

The convergence between the form of the Latin American and North American city should not be overstressed. We will see that twentieth-century patterns of urbanization in Latin America still reveal differences with the experience of the advanced capitalist world and between and within Latin American countries. It is this complexity which makes it necessary for us to concentrate on one underdeveloped region only. The form of analysis that I am using is applicable to other underdeveloped regions of the capitalist world and, throughout the text, examples from these other regions will be used. For these other regions the analysis would, however, have to take into account factors such as the stage and form of their incorporation into the capitalist world economy. Thus, there are sharp differences among both African and Asian countries in the extent to which their economies became organized around the export of primary products. Likewise, the systems of production of the export staples differ from region to region and from country to country. Hopefully, the analysis of the significance of such differences for the Latin American countries will provide some insight into the forces shaping political and economic change in other underdeveloped areas. A satisfactory analysis of these other areas would, however, require a degree of historical and contemporary detail that is beyond the scope of this volume.

Latin America is moreover, in some respects, a special case. It is the first and most deeply underdeveloped area of the capitalist world in terms of the extent to which its political and economic institutions were shaped by the needs of the expanding capitalist system. With the exception of Cuba, Latin America remains one of the most securely capitalist of all underdeveloped regions and it is towards generating an understanding of the contradictions entailed in this position that this volume is aimed.

Conclusion

This chapter has introduced the basic concepts that will guide the analysis in the remainder of the book. The notions of dependent development and of core-periphery will be used to explore both the relationship between Latin American countries and the advanced capitalist countries and that between dynamic regions and less developed ones within the same country. The basic challenge, however, is to take account of the specific development path of each country, while keeping in mind the general forces that determine that development. I have suggested that the analysis of the class struggle, as it develops around the expansion of capitalist production, is the best means to achieve this end. The analysis of the British and US patterns of industrialization and urbanization has served to remind us that there is no single path to economic development. These two cases have also illustrated the ways in which political and social forces shape economic development, creating the context which defines and limits the action of the market. Indeed, the expansion of British and American interests overseas is one of the most important contextual elements to keep in mind when, in the remainder of the book, we concentrate on the internal processes of change in underdeveloped countries.

2
Urbanization and underdevelopment before the modern period

This chapter is an outline of the historical origins of the contemporary patterns of urbanization in Latin America. I shall first examine the role of the colonial city in the development of the Latin American economies. This is a convenient step in the argument because it enables us to explore the early effects of European overseas expansion on underdeveloped countries. Also, we can evaluate the historical significance of the traditional practices and archaic institutions which are often thought to be an obstacle to economic development. I shall look at the kinds of changes that occurred even in the slowly moving colonial economy and estimate the extent to which these changes shaped the pattern of change to come, particularly the fragmentation of the sub-continent into a large number of independent states.

The following section will concentrate on the changes occurring in the nineteenth century when Latin America becomes more closely connected economically to Europe. It is in this period that contemporary patterns of urbanization in Latin America are likely to be shaped as the expansion of primary production for export transforms the agrarian structure. This focus will enable us in the concluding section to examine the divergences in development between regions and sub-regions of the continent which resulted from the characteristics of the dominant classes, of the labour supply and of the system of production.

With the Spanish and Portuguese conquests, Latin America became a peripheral part of a European economy which was becoming predominantly capitalist in terms of its basic ethos and overall organization. The role of Latin America in this economy was to provide commodities, especially precious metals, needed by the core countries and to produce them as cheaply as possible. Its incorporation into the European economy radically changed social and economic structures of the whole sub-continent. To provide the labour needed to extract export commodities and to service clergy, landowners and the colonial administration, people were redeployed and village economies reorganized. This exploitation of the economy was based, in the main, on what might be termed precapitalist forms of production such as forced labour in the mines and workshops, large landholdings worked by tied labour and share-cropping in its various forms.

I will examine the implications of this core–periphery relationship for the patterns of urbanization that developed in the colonial period and lasted until the early twentieth century. The anlysis of urbanization in different periods provides insight into the economic and political contradictions that developed within Latin America and became potential sources of internally generated transformations. These include the conflicts of interest between the Spanish and, to a much lesser extent, the Portuguese state and colonial elites. In the nineteenth century, there were conflicts between traders and manufacturers interested in developing an internal market and those landholders who depended on keeping the native population tied to its customary position as providers of cheap labour and tribute. Class interests and class struggles took on different forms in different regions according to the dominant forms of economic enterprise developed in them, and they varied too according to the possibilities of economic expansion and the problems encountered in obtaining labour. We shall see how these factors produced the fragmentation of Latin America into distinct national and sub-national units. (For more comprehensive accounts, readers can consult William Glade, 1969, or Celso Furtado, 1976, on the Latin American economies, and Fernando Cardoso and Enzo Faletto, 1969, for an analysis of class and class conflict in producing divergent patterns of development.)

The colonial period

Urban development was an integral part of both Spanish and Portuguese colonization and the system of cities that developed had as its main object the control and administration of the new domains. Some cities, such as Salvador in Brazil, La Havana in Cuba, Callao in Peru and Veracruz in Mexico, were established at points which facilitated sea communication with Europe; others, such as Mexico City, Santiago de los Caballeros of Guatemala, Cuzco and Quito, were based on existing urban centres; and in some cases, like Puebla in Mexico and Arequipa in Peru, cities were founded in locations where there were dense indigenous populations. A comprehensive review of the stages of urban settlement, detailing the urban plans and the differences between Spanish and Portuguese settlement, is provided by Jorge Hardoy (1975, 3–56), who stresses the extent to which the location and design of early urban settlements were experimental; by the mid-sixteenth century, however, a uniform pattern was followed throughout Spanish America and this was reinforced by crown legislation.

Morse (1962; 1971a) provides a useful characterization of this urban system, contrasting the centripetalism of the European town, which concentrated and organized the commerce of a region, with the centrifugalism of the Latin American town, which served to control and administer resources based in the countryside. Morse also discusses the modifications to this characterization that a more complex analysis of urbanization in Latin America would require; for example, colonial towns in Latin America were never simply centres of control and administration, but were often developed as part of more comprehensive plans of regional development that included the mining and farming areas (Morse, 1971a, 5–6).

One of the most striking examples of a colonial town that fostered the commercialization of a wide area is Potosi in present day Bolivia. For many years after 1545, the Potosi mines produced more than half of the world's output of silver and with a population estimated at over 100,000 people by the end of the sixteenth century, it was the largest city in South America (Hanke, 1956). Assadourian's (1977) analysis of the town's mining economy suggests that it made extensive use of wage labour and stimulated craft and commercial foodstuff production over a large distance. Apart from the forced labour of Indian villages (the mining *mita*), the city attracted migrants on a more or less permanent basis from all over the viceroyalty of Peru. This type of town development suggests that even in the sixteenth century, integration into the European economy favoured commodity circulation and undermined the self-sufficiency of local agrarian structures in Latin America.

It is clear, however, that the development of the urban system in colonial Latin America gave primacy to the political and fiscal needs of the empire (Glade, 1969, 60–2). The urban hierarchy of city and village, often imposed upon pre-existing native jurisdictions and urban institutions, preserved and enforced status distinctions between categories of the population. The categories of Indian, slave, mestizo (of Spanish and Indian parents), mulatto (of Spanish and black parents), and Spaniard had different sets of rights and obligations in terms of tribute, forced labour, taxes, military service, trading and debt contraction. Glade contrasts this form of colonization with Turner's characterization of the North American frontier as a source of economic and political autonomy and innovation. In Spanish America there was merely a geographical and not an institutional frontier, since the process of settlement or the opening up of new lands did not free the colonial population from centrally imposed legal and economic restraints.

In this situation, towns in Spanish America (even less perhaps than those in Europe at this period) did not serve to generate economic progress in a 'backward' countryside (Merrington, 1975). The town jurisdiction was not restricted to a specific urban area, but included the surrounding countryside up to boundaries of the next urban jurisdiction; towns owned their hinterlands both in the sense of economic proprietorship and in the sense of politico-administrative control (Portes and Walton, 1976, 9). These towns became dominated by the landed classes who resided in them and who used municipal jurisdictions to consolidate and enlarge their estates, often at the expense of native communities (Glade, 1969, 61–2). The *vecinos* (chartered land proprietors), with rights to participate in municipal government, were few in the early period; in 1561, for example, the municipality of Lima was estimated to have 99,000 inhabitants in both city and hinterland but of these no more than 40 had the title of *vecino* (Portes and Walton, 1976, 17–19).

Brazil represents a somewhat different case in this period since the Portuguese did not impose as extensive or rigid a system of state control on their dominions as the Spaniards did. There was no densely settled indigenous population in Brazil, nor at first did Brazil seem to offer good prospects of yielding precious metals or other valued commodities. Sugar production for the European market soon developed in the northeast on the basis of imported black slaves. England and other European powers were given important trading concessions. Colonization in Brazil was entrusted much more to private initiative than was the case in Spanish America; moreover, commerce figured prominently in the early economy. Portuguese settlement concentrated along the littoral and mainly in the north; this settlement was managed through relatively independent colonies which were often promoted as business ventures (Glade, 1969, 155–63).

The relative decentralization of early colonial Brazil meant that the towns did not acquire the degree of political and administrative pre-eminence enjoyed in Spanish America. One consequence of lasting significance was that the large plantation acquired considerable importance in northeastern Brazil as a centre for local administration as well as for economic life. The structuring of the economy and polity of the northeast of Brazil around the plantation contrasted with the more town-based developments that occurred in the central south with the discovery of gold in Minas Gerais in the eighteenth century. Rio de Janeiro became the administrative centre of Brazil in 1763 as the nearest port to the thriving gold region. A system of towns developed in the interior of the central south, stimulating commerce and agricultural production.

The regulation of political and economic life in Latin America by Spain, and to a lesser degree by Portugal, did not mean that the local economies were totally subordinated to the metropolises. Assadourian (1973) shows how misleading it is to characterize the colonial economy in Latin America as consisting simply of the export of primary products and the import of those commodities (textiles, metal implements, luxury goods) demanded by the colonial middle and upper classes, with the mass of the population subsisting on crafts and foodstuffs produced for domestic consumption. There was a substantial amount of trade taking place within colonial Latin America, both short-distance and long-distance and based on a large variety of commodities in which production was relatively specialized and regionalized (wine, wheat and corn, potatoes, hides, coarse textiles). The most intense exchanges occurred within regions such as that of colonial Peru, but trade also moved between Peru, other regions of Spanish America and even Brazil. The relative weakness of the Spanish and Portuguese economies, coupled with administrative regulation, did at least afford some protection to trade and manufacture within the colonies, which was to be lost with the coming of independence: 'Breaking in pieces the colonial mediations and articulations, with cannons, guns and banners of liberty, our poor and heroic national revolutions go forward to receive the fighter's reward, the technically more refined domination of the English' (Assadourian, 1973, 174).

One of the clearest examples of the internal transformation of the colonial economy is the impact of mining on the Mexican Bajío in the eighteenth century (Brading, 1971; Wolf, 1957). The requirements of the mines provided a stimulus to other forms of commercial enterprise. Mining products were transformed and handled by large numbers of animals and men who needed to be fed; *haciendas* developed in the Bajío plain to meet these needs. The *haciendas* used labour tied through debt peonage; these peons purchased clothing and other goods in the *hacienda* stores. The labour power of both the commercial *haciendas* and of the mines provided a market for manufacturers—especially textiles. The population growth of the Bajío urban centres was rapid in this period: by 1803, Querétaro had 50,000 inhabitants and, in the same year, Guanajuato was estimated to have 71,000 inhabitants, making it the second largest city in Latin America after Mexico City (Wolf, 1957, 184; Morse, 1974, tables 1–7).

The Bajío case also illustrates the basic limitations imposed by the colonial system of government on capitalist development. Government officials saw the population of the Bajío towns as a dangerously volatile element in colonial society, for ethnic and status distinctions among them had become blurred as a result of common working conditions (Wolf, 1957). Riots in the mining towns at the end of the eighteenth century led the government to impose restrictive legislation on the free economy of the towns in the interests of public order. This policy should not be seen simply as the reaction of a backward colonial government. As Brading (1971, 47–86) shows, even the dominant classes in the colonial economy—the large merchants and landowners—had little interest in free economic exchange. To obtain labour or to sell goods within a predominantly subsistence economy required non-market mechanisms of compulsion; these mechanisms, by imposing legal and status constraints on the local population, further restricted the impact of market forces on local production. It has been argued, in this respect, that the form of corporate organization of Indian communities in Mexico and Peru was less a legacy of pre-colonial society than a response to the requirements and pressures of the colonial system (Wolf, 1957; Samaniego, 1974). This was the enduring contribution of the colonial period to the development of the post-independence states of Latin America. It produced a situation in which, as many commentators have pointed out, non-capitalist forms of production and 'archaic' social formations were reinforced as a result of the incorporation of Latin America into the capitalist world economy (Wolf, 1957; Frank, 1971; Laclau, 1971).

This is the context in which the relationship between urbanization and underdevelopment was established. The internal dynamic of economic transformation in Latin America became linked to the needs and expansion of the European market. Within this territorial division of labour, the towns and cities of Latin America had only a limited generative role. As points of initial settlement and conquest and subsequently as centres of administration and of the export trade, towns spread rapidly throughout Latin America in the colonial period. By 1630 there were, according to Hardoy (1975, 23), at least 165 'cities' in Spanish America, but the urban population remained relatively small. By the end of the eighteenth century, Mexico City had over 100,000 inhabitants and six cities had over 50,000 inhabitants—Rio and Salvador in Brazil, Puebla and Guanajuato in Mexico, La Havana in Cuba, and Lima in Peru. In general, the concentration of population in urban centres was low; according to the figures assembled by Richard Morse (1974, table 10), Brazil had some five per cent of its population concentrated in its four largest cities in 1803. Aggregating Morse's data for some 30 of the largest cities in Latin America at this time, we find that they contain only about seven per cent of the population of the continent.

Thus, though the conquest and economic colonization of Latin America were accomplished through a network of urban centres, for most of the colonial period these centres were relatively unimportant in terms of population concentration. It is this fact that gives substance to Morse's characterization of the urban system as centrifugal: cities and towns served merely as administrative centres and as bridgeheads to settlement, while the bulk of the population and the main economic activities lay outside them. The colonial city, Brading (1976) argues, was an alien enclave 'with an elite which in dress, culture and ethnic background differed from the rural masses'. The city was the centre of conspicuous consumption by the elite: the dress, style of life and ornate palaces of the wealthy were one of the chief means of consuming the residue of the colonial economic surplus left to it. This type of expenditure extended also to the church and the religious orders—the major landholders in Spanish America by the end of the colonial period. Thus, Brading calculates that most of the *hacienda* agriculture of the rich Oaxaca valley in Mexico was devoted to providing an income to support the secular priests of Oaxaca and, above all, a large convent in which nuns maintained separate suites of rooms, servants and private dining facilities.

This use of revenue from agriculture or mining meant that the urban economy had a large service sector, providing employment for domestic servants, shopkeepers, street vendors, musicians, barbers and so on. Much of this employment was casual, with people moving back and forth from city to countryside. Transport required a large labour force to attend the mule trains, and to cart produce and people; in the Argentinian town of Mendoza this 'floating' transport workforce made up ten per cent of the total (Halperin, 1970, 44). Despite the 'splendour' of the colonial city, contemporaries frequently remarked on the disorderliness, filth and poverty of the majority of the population (Brading, 1976).

There was a certain amount of urban artisan industry, though the importance of this in the urban economy appears to have varied from one place to another. Textiles in Peru were largely produced in the countryside whereas in Mexico they came from towns such as Puebla or Mexico City. Likewise, Brading reports 8,157 artisans and another 1,384 men engaged in textiles and other productive industry for Mexico City, while in Lima at the same date (1790) there were 1,007 artisans and 60 *frabricantes*; in Lima, clergy and the religious orders numbered 1,306 males and females, and in Mexico City, 1,134.

Though the colonial city played only a marginal role in the expansion of a market economy, it was an integral part of the colonial economic system. As Cardoso and Singer have pointed out, the towns were the organizing and control centres that made possible commercial agriculture and mining (Cardoso, 1975; Singer, 1973, 97). Despite the apparent isolation and self-sufficiency of the Brazilian sugar plantation, plantation production also depended on a strong urban system. The existence of communities of escaped slaves and the constant danger of slave revolts made planters dependent on the legal and coercive backing of the government (Singer, 1973, 99). The profits of the colonial economy were distributed by means of these urban centres to government, merchants and the church, and were protected from pirates and smugglers within the more easily defendable and taxable cities. Mines and plantations depended in the long run on a strong central authority prepared to enforce labour services, impose order and quell revolt. In effect the situation that developed in Latin America towards the end of the colonial period was almost that of a city-state system; poor inter-regional communications and a weakly developed or non-existent interregional division of labour meant that the commercial and landed interests of the difficult regions depended on the political and administrative power of their local city. Halperin (1970, 44–7) emphasizes the internal fragmentation of Spanish America produced partly by the difficulties of transport. He cites the high costs of overcoming distance, such as those involved in transporting wine overland from San Jaun to Salta in Argentina, a journey of 40 days. The attempts by the Spanish government to impose a more effective central control, by-passing regional centres and regional elites, threatened to undermine the local basis of power and profit. Like-wise, the economic interests of the elites of the major colonial centres such as Mexico City and Lima were opposed to those of the less important cities, since they had more direct access to crown mono-polies and to the other perks of centralization.

Singer argues that the implication of such a centrifugal city system was the fragmentation of Spanish America into a large number of independent states. These independent states were essentially city states, based upon one of the predominant colonial urban centres. The scope of influence of these urban centres defined the new national units; thus, the antagonism between Buenos Aires and the interior provinces of the old viceroyalty of the Rio de Plata led eventually to the fragmentation of the viceroyalty between Uruguay, Paraguay, Bolivia and Argentina.

The persistence of Brazil into the nineteenth century as a single territorial unit is at first sight surprising, given the size of the country and the existence of regional economic differences. There were important seccessionist movements in the early nineteenth century, but these ultimately collapsed as local elites preferred to pursue their interests independently rather than exhaust themselves in long cam-paigns (Singer, 1973, 104). As late as 1932, the state of Sao Paulo had its own army and fought the federal forces and those of neighbour-ing states in an ill-fated attempt to defend local interests against federal encroachment. The maintenance of union in Brazil in the nine-teenth and early twentieth century was made possible by permitting a considerable degree of autonomy to regional elites. Portugal was a relatively weak colonial power and tended to respect local jurisdic-tions. The central authority was an arbiter between regional elites, and the imperial bureaucracy provided a degree of administrative stability without threatening the control of land and labour by the elites (Halperin, 1970, 71; Cardoso and Faletto, 1969, 68). Since Brazilian society was concentrated near the coast, communication between even the most remote regions was easy enough. Thus, centri-fugal forces were weaker in Brazil than in Spanish America.

The pattern of urbanization is only one factor in the complex events which shaped Latin America in the period of independence. The purpose of placing such emphasis on urbanization is to show the importance of the partial and fragmented nature of economic development in the continent for its subsequent evolution. Singer criticizes commentators like Quijano and Castells, who to his mind place too much emphasis on external factors in explaining the fragmentation of Latin America (Singer, 1973, 64–5; Castells, 1972; Quijano, 1968). While recognizing that external interests like Britain's played an important part in the balkanization of Latin America, Singer makes the point that it is the internal structure—and in particular the local class struggles, based on the requirements of local systems of production—that made external interests so successful. This class struggle against the colonial power united the diverse regional centres of Spanish America; after independence, however, the class struggle became particularized, depending upon the economic configuration of each of the independent states.

Increasing integration into the European economy

In the nineteenth century the patterns of urbanization in Latin America changed as the continent became more closely integrated into the European and later the North American economy. The general factors at work were, first, the new technologies of the Industrial Revolution, which raised the productivity of European industry and enabled it to market widely used goods (non-luxury textiles, tools and so on) far more cheaply than the traditional craftsmen of underdeveloped countries could supply them in their own localities. Secondly, new forms of transport substantially lowered the costs of carrying goods overseas or inland (Dyos and Aldcroft, 1969, 234–47). The time (hence the costs) needed to cross the Atlantic was reduced substantially during the course of the century and regular services could be provided that were not dependent on the vagaries of wind-power. Atlantic grain freights fell from 8s a quarter in 1863 to 1s 3d in 1901, and the Lancashire-Shanghai freight costs fell in approximately the same proportion (Dyos and Aldcroft, 244). British naval control of the seas ensured that merchant ships travelled more or less unmolested—a situation in striking contrast with earlier centuries, when privateers constantly interrupted the galleon trade.

Towards the end of the nineteenth century, railway development in Latin America was cheapening the costs of bulk transport of primary products and manufactured goods. In comparison to mule trains and carting, the railway was capable in certain circumstances of reducing the cost of transporting minerals, for example, to as little as a fifth of the rate of animal transport (Miller, 1976). Finally, the

Industrial Revolution in Europe and its accompanying growth of urban populations created a new and continuously expanding demand for non-precious minerals and foodstuffs that could be produced in both the tropics and temperate zones.

These changes in technology and patterns of consumption were occurring throughout the nineteenth century and help to explain the timing and nature of economic change in the different sub-regions and countries of the continent. It was not until the end of the nineteenth century that even the most economically powerful of the Latin American republics, such as Argentina, had fully developed their export economies. Before analysing these divergences in the next section, we need to identify the general trends in urbanization that accompanied them and affected the whole continent.

The initial consequence of independence in Spanish America appears to have been a decrease in the degree of urbanization. Morse's statistics suggest that during most of the nineteenth century a lower proportion of Latin America's population was living in the major cities than was the case at the end of the eighteenth century (Morse, 1974, table 10; Wibel and de la Cruz, 1971, 94). The conditions created by the struggle for independence explains some of this decline but disturbances of the early independence period were partially offset by the growth of towns offering greater security. Alejandra Moreno shows how Mexico City and other towns grew in this period through immigration from the rural areas (Moreno Toscano, 1972; Moreno Toscano and Aguirre, 1975). A decline in the degree of urbanization in the nineteenth century is also observable in Brazil, which did not experience the turmoil of the independence movements in Spanish America (Morse, 1974).

Changes in the patterns of urbanization in the nineteenth century are most convincingly explained by the economic processes that were affecting the whole of Latin America in this period. The early nineteenth century in Latin America shows a more intensive exploitation of agricultural resources. Though this exploitation still needed the organization and political support of the towns, the urban infrastructure required was in certain respects a simpler one since the bureaucracy of colonialism was no longer necessary. As political control became regionalized few officials were required. More importantly, the opportunities for commercial agriculture were diversifying, stimulating the colonization of new regions and giving rise to increasing production. The colonial period in Latin America had been one in which staple commodities for export had been precious metals and sugar; in the eighteenth and nineteenth centuries cacao, cotton, coffee, leather, tallow, wheat, and non-precious metals were added.

The closer articulation with the European economies may also

have affected urbanization by undermining the basis for local manufacturing production. Glade (1969, 187) cites some political propa-
ganda written about 1818 in Mexico which claimed that the opening
of the port of San Blas in western Mexico had put out of work some
12,000 persons in the regional craft guilds. The regionalization of
Latin America and the diversification of exports changed this situation in two important ways: more people were themselves able to
afford cheap mass-produced foreign goods and exporters of primary
products found themselves at loggerheads with domestic industry
which demanded tariff protection. The landed elites were in effect
recruited into this exchange system both as suppliers of primary
products and as agents of European or North American importing
houses. Substantial profits were derived from the sale of imported
manufactured products to the plantations, mines and towns of their
region. This close identification of local elites and foreign interests
was sealed often enough through intermarriage with foreigners,
especially Europeans. Alejandra Moreno and Enrique Florescano
(1974) provide an account of the effect of these processes on Mexican
regional development in the nineteenth century.

Class interests developed in the port, frontier and commercial
cities based on importing foreign manufactures (such as cotton
cloth) or even staples such as cotton itself. These imports worked
against the industrial interests of regions such as Puebla and Tlaxcala
which specialized in cotton manufacture and in the production of
cotton (Moreno Toscano, 1972, 173). When merchants were unable
to persuade the government to lower tariffs, they achieved their
objective by extensive contraband. Increased competition in the
internal market eventually destroyed much local industry (Moreno
Toscano and Florescano, 1974).

The impact of competition was probably felt most in the larger
cities such as Puebla or Mexico City. There are no adequate data on
the relative rates of small-town growth for most of the nineteenth
century; but it seems likely that the expansion of the export economy
stimulated regional economies and the growth of smaller towns, if
only because the transport of goods by mule train brought business
to them simply through servicing the traffic involved. Offsetting
this diversification of local economies was the tendency for export
production to be based on relatively self-sufficient economies within
plantations, *haciendas* or mines. Halperin (1963) reports the way in
which the early nineteenth-century expansion of livestock farming
in Argentina served to weaken the small town economy in its
vicinity. The livestock *hacienda* became a self-sufficient unit of production in which everything was consumed on the spot; illicit trading in any product was suppressed. Limited investment and innovation in ranches and associated industries (salting and tanning plants)
retarded local commercial or service functions. Thus, depending on

the structure of exports and the means of handling them, local economies might diversify and expand or stagnate.

As we shift our attention to the late nineteenth and early twentieth century, it is easier to identify a number of trends. This was the time when most Latin American countries were strengthening the control of the central government over provincial centres and when the penetration of remote areas by railway brought these within the system of ports and capital cities. The dominant trend in urbanization in Latin America in the nineteenth century is the increasing primacy of the urban system—the situation in which the largest city is many times larger than the second city. (Readers should consult Gilbert, 1974, 92–6, Browning, 1958, 1972a, and Morse, 1974, 425–6, for a general discussion of primacy with reference to Latin America.) Morse views primacy as the outcome of the increasing reliance on a plantation economy in Latin America. The major city acted as a nodal point of the plantation economy and within the city administrative, commercial and other service activities developed. As a place of government, the major city attracted elite groups and became the place of residence of the landowning and merchant class. The purchasing power of these countries also became concentrated in the primate city, stimulating further commercial and service activity, construction and some local industrial production. This growth produced migration from the less prosperous agrarian zones. Once a primate city had emerged, moreover, the process of agglomeration tended to become cumulative since other places were starved of the resources needed to follow suit. For example, Mexico City had been relatively stagnant for much of the nineteenth century in the face of the rise of regional centres profiting from the liberalization of trade (Moreno Toscano, 1972, 173). By the end of the century, and as a result of the centralization produced by the development of a railway network based on the capital, Mexico City recovered its economic predominance. In 1900, it was three times as large as the next biggest city, whereas in 1852 it had been just over twice as large (Boyer, 1972, table 9).

The degree of primacy in the different Latin American countries is also related to the extent of their connection with world economy. McGreevy suggests that there is a correlation between exports per capita and the degree of primacy (McGreevey, 1971b, 125). Cuba, Argentina and Chile had the highest per capita exports in the 1870s and their city-size distributions had shifted from a log-normal distribution to one of primacy far more sharply than those of the other five countries surveyed (Mexico, Columbia, Venezuela, Brazil and Peru). By 1920, most Latin American countries had primate urban systems. Argentina then had the highest primacy of the major countries, whether measured by comparing the size of Buenos Aires with that of the next largest city or with that of the next three largest cities

(Browning, 1972a, table 2). Cuba, Mexico and Chile also had high primacy by this date on both indexes (Morse, 1974, table 10; Browning, 1972a, table 2). Peru and Uruguay were similar to these other countries; by 1900 almost one third of the total Uruguayan population lived in the capital city (Glade, 1969, 413). Although Brazil appears to be an exception to this trend since Rio's predominance had declined by 1920, a bi-primary index (Rio and Sao Paulo compared to the next three largest cities) shows very high primacy (Browning, 1972a, table 3). The two major countries in which primacy was less evident by 1920 are Columbia and Venezuela (Browning, 1972a, table 2; Morse, 1974, table 10).

We can now compare this pattern of primacy in 1920 with that of British and United States investment immediately before this. British investments in Latin America in 1913 were concentrated as follows—37.34 per cent in Argentina, 23.21 per cent in Brazil, 16.21 per cent in Mexico, 6.65 per cent in Chile, 4.81 per cent in Uruguay, 4.46 per cent in Cuba, 2.67 per cent in Peru, 1.04 per cent in Guatemala, and the rest distributed between the other nine independent countries (Glade, 1969, table 7–1). US investments in 1914 were concentrated in Mexico (52.4 per cent), Cuba (17.3 per cent) and Chile (10.6 per cent) (Glade, 1969, table 7–2).

As we noted earlier, foreign investments, especially the British, were deployed in ways likely to increase pimacy by helping to provide the administrative and economic infrastructure for exports; this infrastructure was concentrated in the major city through which exports were channelled. US investments were placed in productive enterprises such as mining in Mexico and Chile or plantations in Cuba, but these actually did little to stimulate provincial economic development. Instead, the product was directly transported out by rail and stimulated in return imports of manufactured products, which were consumed in the major cities. The absence of any pronouned primacy in Venezueia and Columbia in the nineteenth century on the other hand was due to the relatively weak incorporation of these countries into the world economy. This and poor internal transport diminished the primacy effects of the plantation and mining systems in both countries (Galey, 1971; Friedel and Jimenez, 1971). By 1920, however, the absence of primacy in Columbia can be accounted for by a regional pattern of urban development, which I shall discuss later. There can be little doubt that the discovery of oil in Venezuela will bring it rapidly within the world economy under conditions in which the primacy of its urban system will, if anything, become more pronounced.

César Vapñarsky's (1975) analysis of primacy and the distribution of urban places in Argentina provides a useful way of relating this discussion of the determinants of primacy to the overview, in the next section, of the regional divergences in urbanization. Vapñarsky points out that both high and low primacy is compatible with two very different forms of internal urbanization. As we have seen, in a situation in which there is little internal economic integration and the urban centres have only weak economic relationships among themselves, then one urban centre can become dominant and monopolize the external trade of the whole country. However, primacy can still emerge despite increasing internal economic integration and the rise of hierarchically organized urban systems in various regions. In this case, the primate city (for instance, Buenos Aires in the twentieth century) owes its predominance not to the lack of dynamism among potential competitors, but to the continuing advantages of its historic role (as the accumulator of the nation's economic resources). This is to suggest that export-led development of underdeveloped countries tends to produce primacy irrespective of the degree of their internal economic integration or development. Likewise, low primacy can be explained either in terms of a high degree of internal economic integration and a relatively low dependence on exports or in terms of a very low degree of economic integration and a relatively low dependence on exports. This last situation is, in fact, the one that McGreevey suggests as characterizing the colonial situation in Latin America where he finds that urban places exhibit a lognormal distribution (McGreevey, 1971b).

Export dependence does not necessarily imply the absence of strong economic and social organization outside the main city. This economic organization may give rise to class interests distinct from those present in the primate city and these interests may be sufficiently organized to exercise a significant independent effect on the development of the national polity and economy. It is this perspective which is explored in the following section in an attempt to counteract the tendency in some analyses to view economic dependency as a uniform phenomenon.

Divergent trends in national and regional development

The economic forces operating upon Latin America in the nineteenth century made for the creation of export-orientated economies trading in primary products, but the problems of developing these economies were, as Cardoso and Faletto (1969) have pointed out, less economic than political. Basically, these problems were similar to those of the colonial period: sufficient labour had to be secured for the expansion of the plantation system or of mining, and land had to be made available. Both needs required 'political' rather than 'economic' solutions in countries in which, as we have seen, a free market in labour and land had not developed. Coercion at local and national level was necessary to secure labour and to 'open up' new lands for cultivation, usually by appropriating them from existing users. To obtain these ends, the economically dynamic classes (foreigners and nationals linked to the export economy) needed to ally themselves with more traditional interests, such as the military, governmental officials or landowners with unproductive land. The composition of these alliances and these classes differed from country to country and contributed to divergences in their patterns of development. Perhaps more signific-ant still for these divergences were differences in local endowments of labour and land and in the system of export production.

Following this line of analysis, Cardoso and Faletto (1969, 57–65) provide a general picture of the different paths of development taken by Latin American countries in the nineteenth century. Among the most important variables they perceive are (a) the economic dynam-ism of the export staple(s) and its likelihood to encourage economic diversification, giving rise to new social groups and to the begin-nings of an urban–industrial economy; (b) the relative cohesiveness of the dominant class and the capacity of this class to fashion the institutions of the national state to its economic ends; and (c) the strength of foreign interests. They contrast the development paths of Brazil and Argentina, pointing to the relative cohesiveness of the dominant classes in Argentina based on the efficient commercial exploitation of land for the export market (cattle and cereals) and also to the relative fragmentation of those classes in Brazil. The dominant classes in Brazil represented distinctive and powerful regional economic interests in such states as Minas Gerais, São Paulo and Rio Grande do Sul; moreover, the planters of the north-east retained considerable local power. In this situation, the domi-nant classes in Argentina were able to effect a relatively more thorough-going modernization of the economy and society than was possible in Brazil. Cardoso and Faletto also explain how in some countries (mainly in Central America) cohesion of the domi-nant classes is high but local export interests are relatively inert and often subordinate to what might be described as foreign enclave production.

An economic enclave exists when a system of production has no linkages into the economy of the region or nation in which it is located. An example of this is Klaren's (1973) description of the sugar plantations of the north coast of Peru, where the cane was milled on the plantation, the sugar was exported along the company's railway and port, and the workers' subsistence was provided through the company store. Though an enclave rarely exists in pure form (largely because the wages of workers are spent in the surrounding economy and the enclave gives contracts for construction work or the like), it represents a type of production which, while under foreign control, does little to diversify the local economy or contri-bute to capital formation within it. The relative dominance of enclave production in a nation's economy consequently hinders the development of a national bourgeoisie.

We can advance this analysis by examining briefly the concrete relationship between systems of production, the rise of the state, and class conflict in four Latin American countries (Argentina, Brazil, Mexico and Peru) used by Cardoso and Faletto to illustrate differences in nineteenth-century development. Argentina was the most urbanized and modernized of Latin American countries; Brazil, though more unevenly developed with strong regional elites had the economically dominant form of production in local hands; Mexico was an 'intermediate' case where foreign ownership of production was important but where a strong national state developed and national interests remained strong in certain sectors of the economy; Peru was the classic case where foreign interests owned the bulk of export production.

Argentina exhibited considerable internal economic development, including industrialization, by the beginning of the twentieth century, on the basis of its staple exports of wheat and meat. This pattern was reflected in a pattern of urbanization in which a primate city (Buenos Aires) existed within a fairly well integrated regional system of towns. In the material that follows, I want to draw attention to two factors that influenced this pattern of development—the system of production of the staple crops and the constant need to obtain and control labour.

We can look first at the expansion of livestock farming in the beginning of the nineteenth century, which depended on finding ways of recruiting and stabilizing the labour force (Halperin, 1963). The *hacendados* came to dominate local society, acting as magistrates and using legislation against vagabondage to discipline their workers. Control of government in Buenos Aires assured the livestock owners control of their labour; it also enabled them to extend their grazing grounds as new territory was 'rescued' by government action from marauding Indian groups. Livestock investment in one form or another became the basis of the power of post-independence elites in Argentina. These elites were closely allied with foreign merchants—particularly the British—who organized the commercialization and financing of the livestock operation, and also the importation of manufactured products, particularly cloth.

In other regions of Argentina, landholders emerged with a similar interest in the control of labour and in obtaining finance for their operations. Jorge Balán (1976) has analysed the case of the sugar-producing area of Tucumán, in the northwest of Argentina at the end of the nineteenth century: plantations were large and processing was centralized in modern mills which provided the goods and services required by the workers. Small-town commerce and industry were undermined by this economy and wealth became concentrated in the

CARNEGIE LIBRARY
LIVINGSTONE COLLEGE
SALISBURY, N. C. 28144

city of Tucumán. Tucumán was the residence of the planter elite and served as the commercial centre for sugar and as a transport node. The profits of production were not invested in developing local industry and their developmental impact on the region was slight. There was little consciousness of regional interests because of the polarized situation of sugar cane production and the lack of a plurality of regional interests (Balán, 1976, 164). However, Tucumán had an important impact on national developments, and the two presidents of Argentina between 1874 and 1890 (the period in which large-scale international migration began) were from Tucumán. Balán points out that the success of the sugar economy depended on the political power of the sugar elite. In the absence of an abundant cheap labour supply locally, the planters relied on various forms of coercion to obtain labour; they also needed railways to market the sugar. The Tucumán planters thus became active in national politics, both by consolidating their local power and obtaining the railway and by forming alliances with financial groups in Buenos Aires which invested in sugar production.

The international migrations that populated the Pampas and were the basis for the rapid growth of Buenos Aires were also conditioned by the cohesion and political power of these dominant classes. One of the aims expressed in government circles and by the newspapers of Argentina for encouraging immigration was that it would serve to populate the interior in ways similar to the homestead policies of the United States (Scobie, 1964, 116). It is historically doubtful whether the Homestead Act of 1862 had the effect on the settlement of the American west that Argentinian observers supposed, and it is certainly the case that very few of the millions of migrants that came to Argentina at the end of the nineteenth century and the beginning of the twentieth became homestead farmers. Under pressure from large landowners and land speculators, the government did not enact any effective homestead legislation until it was too late to help the immigrant and it gave little support to colonization. Instead, the immigrants were used, directly and indirectly, to open up farming lands and develop large-scale wheat farming for the benefit of large landed and commercial interests. Land appreciated so enormously in value with the extension of the railways and with colonization that landowners could retain their land, renting it on short-term contracts to immigrants. Labour for the harvests was partly provided by seasonal migrations from Italy.

Although Scobie (1964, 86) emphasizes the poverty of the wheat farmer and his economic dependence on the four big wheat-exporting firms in Buenos Aires, the expansion of wheat cultivation undoubtedly stimulated economic development at the local level. Argentinian wheat farming did not produce the extensive economic linkages that occurred in the mid-west of the United States (see first chapter), but the system of wheat production, based on small-scale commercial producers dependent on the market for many commodities, was conducive to regional development. Gallo (1974) shows how the province of Santa Fé expanded on the basis of wheat farming and of foreign immigration. Towns, as well as cities, grew fast, literacy rates improved and the socio-occupational structure diversified. Gallo compares this wheat zone with a wool-producing zone to show that in the wool zone there was a more scattered population and proportionately less industrialization. Elsewhere, as in Mendoza, small-scale commercial farming based on wine began to flourish by the end of the nineteenth century, giving rise to a diversified economic structure and a well integrated network of towns and cities (Balán, 1976).

The cohesion of the dominant classes centralized political and economic control in Buenos Aires. The expansion of the export economy generated the resources that permitted the rapid growth of Buenos Aires in construction, in service employment and, by 1895, in industry. Though the most important industries were linked to agriculture, industrial production increased over eight times between 1895 and 1914 (Cortés Conde and Gallo, 1967, 77–83). In the circumstances it is not surprising to discover that so many immigrants either stayed in Buenos Aires, their port of arrival, or ended up there. The conditions of life on the Pampas were not attractive and the government did little in the early period to encourage people to move out of the city. By 1914, Buenos Aires had 1,576,000 inhabitants, or approximately 20 per cent of the total national population (Lake, 1971, 123). At this date, more than 2,300,000 of the country's population had been born abroad and three out of four adults in Buenos Aires were foreigners (Scobie, 1964, 29). The abundant labour supply encouraged investment in manufacturing and provided the means to build the railways, to man the docks and develop the city. Balán (1973) lays stress on the economic dynamism of Buenos Aires in this period, arguing that its growth was due to the expansion of economic opportunities in the city rather than to the failure of agricultural settlement policies.

My argument here is that the development of a strong, centralized state is partly to be explained by the extent to which the dominant classes needed to control and develop central government to expand their economic interests. Control of labour and the sponsoring of international migration usually need the agency of a strong central government. In the Brazilian case, however, it was the state of São Paulo, and not the federal government, that organized the massive European immigrations needed to power the coffee boom. To achieve this, São Paulo developed a powerful government apparatus by the beginning of the twentieth century. Indeed, so effective was this apparatus that Robert Shirley (1978) argues that this was one of the main reasons for the orderliness of São Paulo's growth when contrasted with that of Manchester, England. For a long time coffee production had been a more attractive proposition than sugar, as indicated by the increasing transfer of the slave population from the northeast to the coffee areas of the central south (Leff, 1972). After the emancipation of the slaves and the opening of the new coffee lands of the São Paulo area, the labour for the new plantations was increasingly provided by migrants from Europe.

At the end of the nineteenth century, the rate of immigration into Brazil, mainly to São Paulo state, sometimes exceeded immigration into Argentina, averaging over 100,000 immigrants a year between 1888 and 1897 (Graham, 1972). The fluctuations in immigration into Brazil were closely related to economic conditions in Italy and in the United States—the alternative destination for immigrants. When coffeee prices fell and production slowed down, many immigrants left Brazil for Italy or Argentina; between 1902 and 1910 more than 330,000 immigrants arrived in the São Paulo port of Santos, but as a consequence of re-embarkation the total gain for the period was only 16,667 (Dean, 1969, 7).

Conditions of work on the coffee plantations were bad and pay low; consequently, there was a substantial turnover in labour as migrants returned to Italy, sought opportunities elsewhere in the rural areas or went to the city (Hall, 1974). The profits of the coffee economy and the attractiveness of investment in coffee were to a considerable extent due to the presence of this abundant, cheap labour force (Lopes, 1977). The system of production of coffee, however, does not seem to have stimulated a rapid urban or industrial development of São Paulo state. After 50 years' expansion of the coffee frontier in São Paulo, the non-agricultural labour force in the state was only 37 per cent of the whole in 1920; only four per cent of the state's population lived in the capital in 1890, and 11 per cent in 1900 (Katzman, 1977, 1978). Likewise, the early growth of the city of São Paulo was, in comparison with the federal capital, Rio de Janeiro, predominantly based on service rather than industrial employment. In 1893, approximately 63 per cent of the labour force of São Paulo was employed in transport, commerce and domestic service, and scarcely seven per cent in manufacturing industry (Fausto, 1976, 30).

Over time, the growth of the coffee economy did become the basis for a rapid urban and industrial growth. The coffee plantations remained in national hands, even though the financing and exporting of coffee were controlled by foreign companies. The planters were resident in the state and pushed for the development of the necessary infrastructure—roads, railways, power plants (Dean, 1969). The availability of a literate and abundant labour force in the city and towns, as well as on the plantations, encouraged investment in the production of goods that could compete relatively easily with imports (construction materials, drinks, textiles, shoes).

The cities of the central south, Rio de Janeiro and São Paulo, grew more rapidly than those of the northeast. By 1900, the combined population of Rio and São Paulo was almost three times greater than that of Salvador and Recife, whereas in 1819 the latter had larger combined populations (Conniff, Hendrix and Nohlgren, 1971). São Paulo's growth between 1872 and 1900 was 8.3 per cent a year, compared with Rio's annual rate of 3.7 per cent in the same period. In 1890, 22 per cent of the city of São Paulo's population was foreign-born, while in the state of São Paulo, 5.4 per cent was foreign-born (Fernandes, 1969, 11). By 1920, 36 per cent of São Paulo's population of 579,033 people was foreign-born and 18 per cent of the state's population was born abroad (Graham, 1972, table 8).

Although occurring at a slower pace than in Argentina, the diversification of the economy in Brazil was also based on an export crop. What was to differentiate the Brazilian experience, however, was the persistence of powerful and distinct regional interests alongside the dominant interest (São Paulo coffee exports were responsible for something like 65 per cent of the value of the country's exports). The regionalism of the dominant classes in Brazil was based, until the 1930s, on the relative self-sufficiency of the regional systems of political and economic organization. The three most economically dynamic states—São Paulo, Minas Gerais and Rio Grande do Sul—maintained a high degree of internal elite cohesion and counterbalanced each other in the federal system (Love, 1975; Wirth, 1975).

The coffee boom reinforced the underdevelopment of the northeast. Commercial enterprises and labour were tied to the northeast in a situation in which the rates of return on their dominant activities were declining. The relatively low rates of outmigration were partly due to transport costs. The supply of labour was generally assured and 'fixed' in the northeast by paternalistic relationships between planter and dependent peasantry, but the supply also depended on political power. The landed elites of the northeast maintained control of regional administration well into the twentieth century, and even during the Vargas regime of the 1930s they sought to retain their influence in national politics to avoid labour legislation hostile to their interests (Lopes, 1976).

Low rates of outmigration meant that there was little stimulus to rationalize production, to convert to new crops or to consolidate holdings (Leff, 1972). The disadvantages of the northeast in these respects were increased by membership of the same political unit as the central south. The northeast was unable to adjust exchange rates to protect its sugar and rice and, since these rates were based on the saleability of coffee, Brazilian sugar was priced out of many markets.

Thus, the emergence of more dynamic economic activities in other parts of Brazil did not produce structural change in the depressed areas of the northeast. Instead, involution occurred and the dominant system of production was maintained, but with an increase in subsistence and labour-intensive activities.

Diverse and often conflicting interests among regions meant that the dominant economic groups (the Paulista coffee interests) could not pursue as coherent a project of economic modernization at the national level as could their Argentinian counterparts. Alliances and counter-alliances were to characterize Brazilian federal politics and to lead, as we shall see in the next chapter, to a somewhat different approach to industrialization than was to be the case in Argentina (Cardoso and Faletto, 1969).

We can now look at two cases—Mexico and Peru—in which the dominance of foreign interests in production was more pronounced than in the case of Argentina and Brazil, with economic enclaves such as mines, sugar plantations and cattle ranches directly linked by rail and ship to the foreign metropolis. The pattern of urbanization associated with enclave production is usually seen as one in which the primate city grows as a service centre to the export economy, in which there is little industrialization and in which regional urban centres decline or stagnate. In both cases the situation was more complex and mercurial than this model suggests. The class conflicts arising from the expansion of export production became significant factors in shaping national development in both countries. Each had substantial indigenous populations so their capacity for providing labour to power the export industries was quite different from that of Argentina and Brazil. However, the supply of labour in Mexico differed from that in Peru, which meant the development of relatively strong and weak central governments, respectively.

Mexico's pattern of economic development and urbanization in the nineteenth century (Moreno Toscano, 1972) showed marked regional differentiation. The by-passing of the Mexico City–Vera-cruz trade axis after independence created opportunities for both legitimate and illicit trade among the small ports and regional centres. Guadalajara, situated to the northwest of Mexico City and beyond the capital's sphere of influence, was well placed to take advantage of commerce on the Pacific coast and to organize the trade of the diversified agriculture of its region. In Guadalajara, the urban growth of the nineteenth and early twentieth centuries was based on small and medium-sized enterprises and a dispersed structure of ownership. Although the region of Guadalajara did contain large landholdings, it was also an important area of small and medium-sized farms, of commerce and of craft production. Guadalajara was also the fastest growing Mexican city in the last half of the nineteenth century, far exceeding Mexico City though remaining by 1900 about a third of the capital's size of 345,000 (Boyer, 1972, table 2).

Other nineteenth-century examples of regional urban development in Mexico were the rise of the northern industrial centre of Monterrey and the growth of Mérida in the Yucatan. The stimulus for both these regional centres was the American Civil War. In Monterrey's case the Civil War led to a substantial rise in commerce through Texas to the Mexican Gulf ports and this stimulated cotton production in the nearby states. In the Yucatan, cotton production also began on a large scale with the Civil War. Both centres developed independently of Mexico City and their growth continued in the late nineteenth century on the basis of new forms of production—sisal in the Yucatan and mining and manufacturing in the Monterrey area. Mérida's growth in the late nineteenth century was second only to that of Guadalajara while Monterrey's growth in the early twentieth century was equally fast (Boyer, 1972).

The development of the Mexican railway system reinforced certain features of this regional pattern of urbanization (Moreno Toscano, 1972). The railways favoured export crops and indirectly undermined local systems of small-scale foodstuffs production (Moreno Toscano, 1972, 180). Thus, the ending of mule transport and the carriage trade deprived many small urban centres of their means of livelihood. The railways made possible, however, the rise of other centres based on export production: the cattle and cotton producing areas of the north of Mexico were centralized through a contiguous group of cities—Torreón, Lerdo and Gómez Palacio. This urban group was not part of Monterrey's zone of influence and both zones became closely and independently integrated into the US market by means of the Mexico–United States railways network. Rail links to the sea and to the hinterland contributed to Merida's dominance in Yucatan. Also, new cities began to emerge to service areas producing tropical export crops: Uruapan, Ciudad Guzman and Cordoba are examples that Alejandra Moreno (1972, 186–7) has used to illustrate the changes in Mexico's pattern of urbanization.

Friedrich Katz (1974) has traced the social and political implications of this regional differentiation and attributed them to factors such as the abundance or scarcity of local labour, the type of production and the quality of the land. He surveys the forced labour practices of the sisal and other export crop *haciendas* in the south of Mexico where, in the absence of local labour, outside labour was tied through debt and physical coercion. He has contrasted this situation with that of the sugar *haciendas* of the centre of Mexico in which such practices were unnecessary owing to the abundance of seasonal labour produced by dispossessing villages of their lands. In the north of Mexico, the mines, cattle ranches and export crop *haciendas* had to offer the workers relatively favourable wages and in other cases sharecropping facilities in order to offset the competitive labour market which extended to the southern United States.

In the centre and south of Mexico, the significance of state power for the expansion of export production is well brought out by Wallace Thompson's account of the situation in 1921: 'So valuable did this labour become that bribery and government coercion, special detectives and policemen had to be called in to capture and return the peons who ran away from their contracts and judges and mayors of towns were induced to arrest the runaways' (Katz, 1974, 21). In the north, landed and mining interests had less reliance on state coercion and, to a greater extent than the landowners of the south and centre, the northern elites joined in the revolutionary uprisings against the Porfirian regime (Katz, 1974, 45–7). However, with the success of the revolution the newly dominant classes inherited and strengthened central government and used it to industrialize.

In Peru, the dominant export enterprises (sugar, cotton, mining) developed in areas away from the major concentrations of population; although dispossession of land did occur, its impact was less than it was, for example, in creating the sugar *haciendas* of the Morelos region of Mexico. Moreover, the supply of labour for the export enterprises came mainly from free peasant communities. These communities had reached a point at which their increasing numbers on limited land had forced the peasants to seek work further afield to supplement their local craft and agricultural activities (Long and Roberts, 1978). Although the *enganche* (a form of debt labour) was used to recruit labour for the mines and plantations, there is little evidence that such enterprises had any need to invoke the law or the government to enforce these contracts (Scott, 1976). Instead, the process of recruitment was handled by intermediaries who were usually the richer farmers or traders from the villages. In this context there was less pressure from the dominant foreign or national interests to strengthen central government: the mines and plantations provided most of their own infrastructure, and local development (roads and irrigation) was left, for the most part, to the initiative of local communities.

The expansion of sugar exports did lead, however, to new forms of class conflict in one of the most important of the sugar areas of the north coast—the Chicama valley (Klaren, 1973, 50–64). This valley was dotted with small but flourishing towns which had developed on the basis of Indian communities whose communal landholdings had been partly redistributed with the liberal reforms of independence. In the same valley there were over 50 small and medium-sized sugar *haciendas* and *fundos*. The towns prospered on commerce and on independent farming of crops such as corn, wheat, rice and other staples. By 1920, travellers commented upon the extent to which these towns had decayed and attributed their decline to the expansion of sugar cultivation (Klaren, 1973, 52). Sugar cultivation had, in this period, become concentrated into large combines; over 50 sugar holdings had been concentrated by 1927 into three largely foreign-owned companies. The concentration of holdings was accompanied by increasing production for export; whereas the old *haciendas* often left a substantial part of their land uncultivated, the new companies brought all land under cultivation. To do this, they secured control of water resources for irrigation, thus depriving the independent towns of an adequate supply. This concentration of landholding ended by undercutting the fortunes of the provincial capital, Trujillo. In the first stage of the expansion of the sugar industry, Trujillo and other urban centres had prospered, supplying food to the workforce of the plantations and distributing imported manufactures; but in due course the large plantations became self-sufficient. The largest of these, Casa Grande, operated its own port facilities through which goods were directly imported. Soon the competition from the plantation's stores was arousing bitter hostility from Trujillo merchants (Klaren, 1973, 74–83).

These events created a significant regional dimension in Peruvian politics. The large corporations that controlled the plantations needed government approval to consolidate their operations; for example, Casa Grande's port operation was a government concession. Representatives of the companies were active in Peruvian national politics to keep government from interfering with new economic interests. At the same time, the activities of the companies aroused hostility from other regional groups ; local merchants and professionals were opposed to the foreign-owned monopolies and were joined in opposition by railway workers whose jobs were threatened by the plantation's own railway operations and by the workers in the sugar mills and cane fields. These workers had become increasingly conscious of their class position through claims for better working conditions and wages (Klaren, 1973). Klaren attributes the origins of the powerful populist political party, APRA, to this conjuncture of class interests on the north coast of Peru. However, even in Peru the expansion of export production often stimulated a region's urban growth. In other areas where enclave production was strong, as in the mining towns of the central region of Peru, miners' incomes and revenues from contracts for food supplies, transport and construction for the mining company substantially raised regional income levels. This flow of cash made possible the diversification of village economies and the expansion of crafts; many of these activities were essentially new ones, such as repair workshops for cars and trucks.

I have stressed this expansion of opportunities created by the export economy since it would be difficult otherwise to understand why the dominant agro-mining classes in Latin America who were opposed to tariff protection for industry should receive such sub-stantial popular political support. In Argentina, even those classes not directly linked to the agro-exporting economy still supported a policy of free trade, on the grounds that it helped agriculture and promoted a 'healthy' competition for local manufactures. This explains why labour unions in Argentina at the end of the nineteenth century were against tariff protection for industry just as most of the urban middle classes were (Cortés Conde and Gallo, 1967).

Conclusion

I have argued that it is the particular way in which capitalism has expanded overseas that produced economic and social backwardness among the local population in terms of the persistence of archaic institutions and an uneven pattern of development in which vast cities exist alongside stagnant provincial economies. We have also found, however, that economic growth has important transforma-tive effects even when it is based on the export of primary products and confined to forms of production which do not develop strong linkages into the local economy. We must, then, pay particular attention to the way in which capitalism expands within underde-veloped countries and not simply focus on the mechanisms through which the dominant world economies have extracted a surplus from underdeveloped countries.

For this reason, the emphasis in this chapter has been on the various patterns of development that are possible when countries occupy a similar, subordinate position within the world economy. Latin American countries in the nineteenth century were underde-veloped in terms of their low levels of productivity in agriculture and in industry, and in terms of the poverty of the mass of their inhabit-ants. It is important, however, to recognize that economic growth did take place throughout the continent. This growth created new opportunities for national and foreign entrepreneurs; but in order to make use of these opportunities, the entrepreneurs had to bring new social and political forces into play. Labour had to be recruited and used as cheaply as possible. Political institutions had to be shaped to serve the needs of the new production. Rival elites had to be concili-ated or defeated. These processes constitute the dynamic of the situation of dependency in Latin America. The forces that are brought into being by the drive to expand production are not passive participants in the next stage of the development struggle; and it is to this participation and its impact on industrialization that we now turn.

3
Urbanization and industrialization

In this chapter the analysis departs from the historically based discussion of the uneven pattern of capitalist development in Latin America to a consideration of contemporary patterns of urban life. This transition will be made through surveying the stages in Latin America's industrial development in this century. Urban-based industrialization has become the dominant economic force in Latin America, gradually displacing in importance the rurally based agro-mining sector. The growing importance of industry raises two crucial issues for the development of my argument. First, we need to examine the way in which industrialization created new situations of dependency by altering the role of underdeveloped countries from one of suppliers of raw materials and foodstuffs to one of consumers of imported technology. Consequently, much of the analysis in this chapter is aimed at uncovering the internal and external factors that have shaped industrialization in such a way that it is not a force making for greater independence from the advanced capitalist countries. Secondly, we need to examine the new political and social forces brought into play by industrial development since these forces here helped to mould contemporary developments by introducing new forms of class conflict alliance and by influencing state policy.

In the twentieth century, the export sector retains its importance in underdeveloped countries as a source of foreign earnings and of finance for industrial development; but developing the internal market for manufactured products becomes an increasingly significant economic strategy for national governments and for national and foreign entrepreneurs. This situation has social and political implications which we will begin to explore in this chapter; they entail, over time, a convergence in the pattern of social and political organization as a result of a similar capital-intensive pattern of industrialization. There is a contrast with the divergent patterns of economic and political development that we noted in nineteenth-century Latin America. This convergence is not, however, identical in all respects of political and economic life and we will need to explore those variations in the organization of the state and of the social classes that continue to differentiate the development experience of Latin American countries.

We will be examining a crucial stage in dependent development which, to different degrees, is affecting the rest of the underdeveloped world in the contemporary period. In making any comparisons it will, of course, be necessary to keep in mind the sharp differences in the level of industrialization *within* the third world. While there is no African country (excepting South Africa and Rhodesia) which has a higher proportion of its gross domestic product produced by manufacturing industry than by agriculture, many Latin American countries generate more of their gross domestic product in manufacturing (UN, 1975, 60–97). The industrialization of underdeveloped countries means that new social and economic forces are brought into play—an industrial working class, an industrial bourgeoisie committed to the expansion of an internal market, an expanded commercial and administrative middle class, improved internal communications; 'traditional' groups may, however, still be numerically important and retain their political and economic power. In the twentieth century, industrialization and the conflicts that it entails have become a crucial issue for the dominant political and economic elites. In place of the transient populations of mining camps and plantations, many of which preserved links with village economies, governments and elites face the 'problem' of a masssive, permanent urban population whose presence is necessary to the expansion of the economy. Not only does this permanently resident population raise for the elites the spectre of working-class organization and of overt class conflict: it also involves cost in social and material infrastructure (housing, welfare, sanitation) that both governments and the dominant elites are loath to pay.

The general context of industrialization in the twentieth century

In their first analyses the Economic Commission for Latin America (ECLA, 1957, 41) drew attention to two associated structural changes in Latin America–industrialization and urbanization. The ECLA report estimated that the rate of urbanization in the decade 1945–55 was probably more rapid than in previous decades and attributed this very largely to the role of industrial expansion in economic growth from 1945–55. An analysis by Schnore (1961) also suggested a close association between urbanization and industrialization in Latin America and other underdeveloped countries. Industrialization did not come as rapidly, or as early, in some countries as it did in others; but the tendency for the centre of economic gravity to shift from agriculture towards manufacturing is unmistakable.

From the 1940s onwards, the trend in all Latin American countries is similar: in each decade agriculture contributes a lower percentage of the gross domestic product while manufacturing, with some fluctuations, contributes a higher percentage. In some countries, the predominance of manufacturing was observable by 1940: Chile had a higher percentage of its net domestic product at factor cost generated by manufacturing in that year than was generated by agriculture (un, 1948, 44). By 1945 Argentina, which had been a wheat and animal products exporting economy, had almost as much of its gross domestic product generated by manufacture as by agriculture (un, 1948, 24). The estimates given by the United Nations of the industrial origin of the gross domestic product of Latin American countries show how this trend has affected even the less developed countries: the share of agriculture in the gross domestic product of Bolivia drops from 32 per cent in 1958 to 14 per cent in 1972 and, in this latter year, manufacturing also contributes 14 per cent of the domestic product. In Brazil, the agricultural share declines from 28 per cent in 1948 to 12 per cent in 1973, while manufacturing increases its share in these years to 19 per cent. In Peru, agriculture contributed 35 per cent of the gross domestic product in 1950 and 16 per cent in 1972; whereas, manufacturing contributed 15 and 21 per cent in those years respectively (un, 1975; 1967). By 1960, there is not one Latin American country listed by the United Nations in which agriculture contributes as large a share of the gross domestic product as it does in India (47 per cent). In Asia and Africa, agriculture represents a higher share of the gross domestic product, and manufacturing a lower one, than in Latin America; but in all three continents the manufacturing product is growing more rapidly than that of agriculture (un, 1975, 112–21).

The un estimates should be taken only as rough guides to changes in the economic structure of Latin America; in all countries, it is the service sector of the economy (trade, transport and communication, government, real estate and finance) which contributes the highest percentage to the gross domestic product. What these statistics indicate is a change in the dynamic of underdeveloped economies: increasingly both foreign and local investment is channelled into manufacturing industry rather than into agricultural enterprises. Agriculture does not necessarily decline in this period and, indeed, both the ECLA statistics and those of the United Nations indicate that the agricultural product continues to increase throughout the underdeveloped world, though at rates barely above those of the increase in population (ECLA, 1957, 28; un, 1975, 112). However, agriculture begins to contribute less to the creation of new jobs and to income opportunities than do those sectors of the economy linked to urban-industrial expansion. ECLA (1965, table 4) estimated that between 1925 and 1950, the agricultural sector in Latin America absorbed 40.3 per cent of the net increase in the economically active population, whereas between 1950 and 1960 agriculture absorbed only 26.7 per cent of the increase.

In many Latin American countries industrialization had begun before the end of the nineteenth century. We saw in the last chapter how a strong export economy led to economic diversification and industrialization in Argentina but to a lesser extent in Brazil. Even in Peru, where the export economy was weaker than in these other countries, there was a significant spurt in industrialization at the turn of the century (Thorp and Bertram, 1976). In the 1920s the Antioquia region of Columbia was to industrialize rapidly with Medellin as its base. Economic development in Antioquia was based on coffee produced by small-scale farmers who required local arrangements to finance, commercialize and store the crop. This situation had produced, by the early twentieth century, a thriving urban system with the city of Medellin at its head. A market was created for textile and other mass consumption goods and capital was accumulated locally and invested in local enterprise (Friedel and Jimenez, 1971). Medellin became an important industrial centre, producing textiles, beverages and processing food. Monterrrey in Mexico also industrialized rapidly in this same period, helped by its location close to the us–Mexican border and the investment of us capital (Balán, Browning and Jelin, 1973; Walton, 1977). These well known cases of early industrialization emphasize the fact that in most Latin American countries industrialization had begun before the ending of the boom period in the export of primary products.

Some of the reasons for the increase in industrial growth in the twentieth century were outlined in the first chapter: foreign investment began to concentrate in manufacturing. Between 1912 and 1929, 32 us companies opened branches in Brazil. Unlike British investments, these companies were mainly industrial and aimed at exploiting the internal market. Some of the engineering companies were linked to the export of products from the United States to Brazil (Singer, 1975; Graham, R., 1973). External events, such as the Great Depression and two world wars, stimulated the local production of needed industrial goods.

Also, in the first half of the twentieth century the dangers of relying on the export of primary products became increasingly apparent. There was, in this period, a substantial growth in export competition for Latin American products, especially from those underdeveloped areas which were more directly under the control of the colonial powers (Glade, 1969, 364–75). British planters first experimented with rubber in Brazil and then transplanted it to Malaya, where it could be grown under colonial protection (Singer, 1975, 361).

Rubber from southeast Asia destroyed the Brazilian rubber boom and growing supplies of sugar from the European beet industry, as well as from the Carribean and from Asia, severely depressed world sugar prices. Copper, cacao and coffee were produced in Africa and competed increasingly with Latin American products.

We can also note that the development of chemical industries in the advanced countries began to replace the demand for natural fibres and nitrates. The increase in these different forms of competition combined with climatic variability to make exports of primary products an unstable and risky basis for national prosperity. The benefits of free trade and of the 'natural' exchange of primary for manufactured products were increasingly questioned as the European powers and the United States adopted more restrictive commercial policies (Glade, 1969, 368). Tariff and quota systems closed markets to Latin American products. Under these conditions it is not surprising that even those Latin American economic interests based on the export of primary products began to seek means of diversifying the internal economy. The social forces produced by the development of the export economy in the nineteenth centruy added a strong impetus to industrialization. Plantations and mines had increasingly militant workforces and, in times of recession, their interests combined with those of the urban working and middle classes to attack the stranglehold of foreign interests on national economies. Foreign-owned railways and telegraphs, foreign managers and technicians were evident restrictions on the possibilities of native enterprise and limited the chances of social mobility.

In all the countries that were strongly articulated with the world economy by the beginning of the twentieth century, nationalism became a strong force for promoting industrialization and diminishing dependence on the external market. Peron came to power in Argentina in the 1940s with a policy of nationalizing key foreign enterprises and promoting industrialization. In the 1930s, Vargas in Brazil also pursued a nationalist, pro-industrial policy and this was the case with Cardenas in Mexico in the 1940s. Although Peru had not industrialized to the extent of these other countries, the APRA political party, based on the sugar economy of the north coast, became a powerful force towards nationalizing foreign-owned enterprises and creating local industry. I shall examine these political movements in greater depth in a later section; for the moment it is enough to note that the conjunction of economic and political forces in the early twentieth century created the basis for industrialization.

The industries established in the first part of the century produced simple consumer goods, construction materials and tools; ECLA (1975) listed the following industries as comprising this early stage of development—textiles and leather, food and beverages, simpler chemical preparations, basic pottery, china and glassware and wood processing. These industries had already begun to develop in some countries at the end of the nineteenth century and by the 1940s this stage of industrialization was well advanced in many Latin American countries. Some countries, notably Argentina, Brazil and Mexico, began to move into what ECLA labels the third phase of industrialization, with the development of the rubber industry, the steel industry, the cement industry and petroleum refining. The chief characteristic of the early stages of industrialization was that industry, even factory industry, was small-scale and used simple processes, permitting local capital to promote industrialization. Also, the form of production was relatively labour-intensive, enabling the manufacturing sector to absorb manpower on a fairly intensive scale from 1925 to 1950.

Though factory production tended to displace domestic industry in some lines of production (such as textiles), this was offset by the expansion of small-scale artisan production in urban centres, often in competition with factory production (ECLA, 1957, 37). Since even simple manufactured goods had previously been imported, there were in effect opportunities for import substitution for both factory and artisan production. From 1925 to 1950, both factory and artisan production absorbed part of the increase of the economically active population.

The different responses to industrialization

Although the conditions favouring industrialization were present in most Latin American countries in the first part of the twentieth century, significant differences appeared both in the extent of industrialization and the role of the state in industrialization.

Cardoso and Faletto (1969) make three general distinctions between Latin American countries in their analyis of these divergent responses to industrialization. First, they examine the case of Argentina as an example of industrialization undertaken primarily by a national bourgeoisie and without economic intervention by the state to any significant degree. This response they call 'liberal' industrialization and it is based almost entirely upon private enterprise. The preconditions for this type of industrialization are the existence of an internal market and of a vigorous, dominant, agro-exporting class. This class is linked through the financial system to the industrial bourgeoisie and to the internal market. Under the conditions of the 1920s and 1930s these classes sponsored industrialization based on Buenos Aires that was sufficient to absorb most of the available labour force as an industrial working class.

The second type of industrialization to be identified is 'national-populist'. This is the Brazilian case and occurred when there was no hegemonic class. The economically dominant classes (the coffee and industrial interests of São Paulo) have never been strong enough to neutralize altogether the power of the traditional agrarian interests. Nor have they been able to provide sufficient industrial employment to absorb the increase in numbers of the urban and rural population produced by the expansion of the export economy (for example, through the international migrations and the rapid turnover of labour on the plantations). Under these conditions, the state, from 1930 onwards, has assumed an important role in constituting the industrial system. The state has provided not only the infrastructure and institutional regulation required by the system, but has set up public enterprises itself. This state intervention was 'imperative for a country that was urbanizing, whose previous agrarian economy had deteriorated and which did not have a capitalist sector which had accumulated sufficiently to respond rapidly to massive employment needs' (Cardoso and Faletto, 1969, 119). In Brazil, the industrial working class has thus remained numerically less important than in Argentina down to the middle of the present century. Also, Brazil's industrialization has taken place in a context in which the mass of the population were rural workers and peasants, or the urban poor employed in the services and in artisan industry.

The third type of industrialization is that brought about by what Cardoso and Faletto call the developmentalist state. This type occurs in those countries in which the dominance of the enclave economy prevented the rise of a strong national bourgeoisie. However, the expansion of the export economy had stimulated the growth of administrative and other services, to varying degrees, and had created in the urban centres both a middle and a working class. With the crisis in the export economy, it was therefore the state that took control in promoting industrialization, both because the groups that controlled the state needed a means of rapid capital accumulation and because this policy expanded employment opportunities for the middle and working classes.

The role of the state in industrialization depends, in part, on the existence of strong central government; it also depends on the strength of the class interests supporting or opposing its policies. Thus, both Mexico and Chile had strong central governments by the 1920s and in both cases the state sponsored the beginnings of industrialization when faced with the crisis in the enclave economy. In Mexico, however, as Cardoso and Faletto suggest, the absence of strongly organized rural or urban working-class support for nationalistic policies meant that the government was susceptible to pressures from foreign interests. They contrast this with the situation in Chile, where both working and middle classes were strongly organized prior to industrialization and where politics has been characterized by overt class conflict over control of the state and its economic policies. We can contrast both Mexico and Chile with the case of Peru, in which the enclave economy was also dominant. In Peru, central government was relatively weak until the 1960s and the urban middle and working classes were neither numerous nor strongly organized. In this situation, the favourable opportunities for industrialization in the early twentieth century were neglected (Thorp and Bertram, 1976). This last analysis would apply also to situations such as those of the Central American Republics and Ecuador.

My aim here is not to provide a comprehensive account of the variations in the recent economic history of Latin American countries but rather to illustrate the type of analysis and the type of variables that can be used to understand why countries faced by a powerful force for convergence—that of urban industrialization—may still diverge in their pattern of political and economic development. This 'mixed' situation of divergence within an overall trend to convergence is represented by the political phenomenon of populism.

Populism, in Di Tella's (1965) definition, represents an alliance of classes in which, under predominantly middle class and elite leadership, important segments of the working class are given access to political power. These are usually organized in unions and represent workers in the dominant sector of the industrial economy. Di Tella uses the term populism to characterize most of the recent civilian regimes in Latin America up to the 1960s, including, for example, Peron in Argentina (1943–5; 1974–6), Vargas, Kubitschek and Goulart in Brazil (1930–64), the APRA-Prado coalition in Peru (1955–60) and the PRI ruling party of Mexico. For our purposes, the significance of populism is that it represents the 'solution' at the political level of the contradictions emerging with the stage in urban industrialization that began more or less in the 1920s (Weffort, 1973; Germani, 1966; Di Tella, 1965). My analysis differs, however, from that of Gino Germani and of Torcuato di Tella. In their analysis, populism is a political movement which results from the imbalances in economic development present in urbanization in underdeveloped countries. The rapid growth of cities based on the influx of rural migrants creates an urban working class with little political experience and which traditional political institutions are unable to accommodate. This working class is responsive to the appeal of populist politicians who offer social welfare and jobs and stress patriotic themes such as the nationalization of foreign enterprises.

In contrast, I stress that the low-income groups incorporated by populist regimes are not economically marginal populations, but those which are most necessary to the growth of industrial capitalism. Industrial capital supports, directly or indirectly, populist regimes because such regimes solve the problems confronting capital at a particular stage of its development. This stage occurs at a time when industrial interests are becoming predominant in the economy, but when their power is not sufficiently consolidated to enable them either to incorporate other groups through economic benefits or to coerce them through control of the state apparatus. One of these other groups is likely to be the landowners producing for the export economy. This class loses some of its authority as a consequence of the crisis in the export sector in the early part of the century; but it remains a major source of finance for industrialization. The other group is the working class created by the industrialization process.

Lopes (1961) provides a case study of the dilemmas that the increasing concentration of industry has entailed for industrialists in Brazil. In the early industries in the Minais Gerais and São Paulo regions, industrialists used paternalistic techniques to control work-, ers and keep wage demands to an acceptable level. Workers were housed on company property which at times composed a textile colony made up of ex-workers from the owner's plantation. Owners and administrators provided welfare benefits and acted as god-parents to their workers. However, as more industries were developed and concentrated in the towns, competition between industrialists led them to seek to save on labour costs as far as possible, ending many paternalistic favours. Also, the workers came into contact with each other and could move from factory to factory in search of better conditions. This process led both to an increasing organization of the working class and to an increasing recognition on the part of the employers that they needed to combine and seek government help to resolve their labour problems. By the 1930s São Paulo industry was beginning to export to other states of the federation and was restricted by inter-state customs duties; on this count, too, industrialists became more conscious of the need to strengthen federal power (Love, 1975, 67).

The increasing concentration of working-class populations occurred in situations in which there already existed traditions of radical working-class political movements. In both Argentina and Brazil, immigration from Europe had, to an extent, entailed the importation of European socialist and radical traditions (Hall, 1974; Germani, 1966). However, even in countries such as Peru, without such immigration, there was an upsurge of working-class radical political movements in the early years of the twentieth century; indeed, the origins of APRA, though responding mainly to local conditions, were partly based on European revolutionary socialism (Yepes, 1974; Klaren, 1973, 108–11).

The early working-class political movements in the cities of Latin America were weak, however, even in those cities where there was a sizable industrial working class. Anarcho-syndicalists in São Paulo failed, in the 1920s, to organize the immigrant working class, despite bad working conditions and in face of severe police repression (Fausto, 1976). Likewise, there was in Argentina no successful organization of the rapidly growing industrial proletariat of the 1930s and

1940s into independent, single-class parties (Germani, 1966). A crucial factor in these failures was the geographical mobility of labour; both in Argentina and Brazil, mass migrations provided a readily exploitable force. Hall (1974) points out that this mobility took place on a scale comparable to that of the United States and, citing Thernstrom and Knight (1970), argues that it had a similarly devastating effect on working-class consciousness.

Other factors, such as an industrial workforce which, in the early stages, had high proportions of women and children need also to be considered; above all perhaps was the strength of state repression. Labour militants in early nineteenth-century England battled with a relatively ineffective police force and an army whose resources were tightly stretched (Foster, 1974). Those of Latin American cities were faced, even in the early twentieth century, with a large-scale, relatively professionalized repressive apparatus. Robert Shirley (1978) contrasts Manchester and São Paulo in this respect, showing that although both cities had approximately the same population (600,000), Manchester had in 1898 1,037 police and São Paulo in 1920 had 8,814.

Since working-class militancy was identified by industrialists and other sectors of the urban middle class as a potential threat to their well-being, they supported the development of a repressive apparatus of this size. Also, the emerging commercial-industrial elites needed direct economic assistance from central and local governments; to develop industry they needed a favourable tariff policy and assistance in providing the roads, energy sources and other infrastructure. This assistance from government implied the gradual taking away of resources from the landed elites, either through taxation or tariff policies. To obtain support for such policies the commercial-industrial elites were prepared to sponsor non-militant, working-class organization.

The populist alliance emerged under such conditions. Populist regimes collaborated in industrializing their countries; Peron's early period of power was one of rapid, government-assisted industrialization based on national entrepreneurship. Vargas in Brazil also sponsored the industrialization of São Paulo and its region. The working classes were incorporated directly, through unions and political parties affiliated to the regime; working-class interests were protected through labour legislation on minimum wages, social welfare and job security. Although the traditional landed classes were increasingly marginal to the alliance between organized labour and industrial-commercial interests, they too received some consideration under populist regimes. Labour legislation was not vigorously applied to the rural areas or not applied at all, enabling the commercial agricultural interests to continue their use of cheap, seasonal labour or labour tied to farms by sharecropping and other interests (Lopes, 1976; Weffort, 1973).

The success of populism rested to a great extent on the capacity of industrialization to create employment in the cities. In the 1930s and 1940s there is evidence that urban growth in both Argentina and Brazil was accompaned by a substantial increase in employment in the transformative sector of the economy (Balán, 1973; Faria, 1976; Germani, 1966). In this situation, most of the urban classes derived advantages from urban-industrialization. The middle classes received profits and high salaries from the increase in industrial productivity and the increasing demand for commercial and other services which it entailed. The working class, many of whom were of rural or of immigrant origin, could also feel themselves to be in a better situation.

Thus, Weffort (1973, 144–51) emphasizes the importance of the individual social mobility which accompanies this stage of urban growth, as opportunities in manufacturing and in allied sectors of the economy expand as fast as does the urban population, with urban wages higher than those in the rural areas. Industry is heterogeneous in terms of levels of technology and size of enterprise, creating a variety of working-class situations and many opportunities for social mobility within the urban economy. Workers with some years of urban experience are able to find relatively well paid employment in the more advanced sectors of industry; these workers are 'replaced' in their previous, low-paid jobs by recent migrants from the countryside.

The contrast with the European working class in its formative stage is thus twofold: in Latin America there is a greater heterogeneity of working situations within industry and, linked to this, the working class in Latin America is confronted by an industrial bourgeoisie that is only in the process of establishing itself. The middle classes have only a weakly developed, independent productive base. Most of them are dependent on the services or, directly, on state employment, and the agrarian-based export sector still provides the finance to expand these employment opportunities. Following this line of argument, Weffort (1973, 45) characterizes populism as follows: 'The peculiarity of populism, when compared with other types of popular movement, is that none of its component groups appears as representative of the general interests of the classes to which they belong.'

These common traits in the nature and origins of populism must not obscure the differences between populist regimes in Latin America. In Argentina, the industrial working class was strongly developed by the time of Peron and populism provided effective channels of participation for that working class. The strength of labour unions and their capacity to force some redistribution of national income are continuing factors in limiting the freedom of economic action of either populist or military regimes. In contrast, neither the Brazilian industrial working class nor the industrial bourgeoisie were as strongly developed and, in Brazil, populism was used to further capitalist accumulation directly. Populist regimes provided the mechanisms to control labour through union discipline and stable collective bargaining. There is some evidence that, in Brazil, the minimum wage legislation actually contributed to cheapening labour by reducing wage differentials and weakening the bargaining power of the workers in a situation in which there was a relative shortage of skilled labour (Lopes, 1976). In any event, Brazilian populism provided the means to incorporate, gradually, the mass of workers without giving them effective access to power (Cardoso and Faletto, 1969, 120–1).

In other countries of Latin America, populism was not to be as powerful a political force as in Argentina and Brazil. In some countries, the low levels of industrialization meant that the political contradictions to which populism is a response were not as sharp. Thus, in Peru the traditional agro-mining exporting elites maintained themselves in power until the 1960s and the Peruvian populist party (APRA) never achieved office. Indeed, its access to power in the period 1956–60 was possible only through an alliance with its hitherto inveterate enemy—the Peruvian oligarchy.

Likewise, in those countries where the state has taken an early and preponderant role in fostering industrialization, populism has a distinctive character. In Mexico, for example, strong labour unions were created under Cardenas, partly to offset foreign pressure against attempts to extract better returns from foreign enterprises in Mexico. Entrepreneurial, middle-class and peasant organizations were similarly created and brought within the organization of the ruling party—the PRI. Thus Mexican 'populism' is not so much a response to the existing contradictions of industrialization, but a vehicle through which the state has organized the politics of economic development, granting access to groups when their collaboration becomes crucial to that development.

The transition to the second stage of industrialization

It was in the context of populist regimes seeking to industrialize that ECLA's early assessments of what needed to be done to promote further development were made. The Commission was not entirely homogeneous in its viewpoints and prescriptions for action, but it sought an alternative mode of economic development to that of dependency on the export of primary products. The role of Latin American countries as exporters of minerals and agricultural products and as importers of manufactured products was identified by ECLA as a prime cause of the slow rates of economic development in the continent. Part of the argument was that the unfavourable terms of trade of primary products with respect to manufactured products inhibited capital formation in underdeveloped countries.

However, the social structural implications of reliance on the primary sector were also identified as harmful to development. Primary sector exports were seen to be based, in part, on a structure of land tenure which inhibited agrarian development. Thus *latifundia*, in order to produce for export, maintained a dependent group of labourers and peasants and limited the land available for local foodstuffs production. ECLA (1957, 17) pointed out that the poverty of the Latin American countryside inhibited the development of small and medium-sized towns. Productivity was shown to be low and to be associated with widespread underemployment of males (table 3.1).

Table 3.1: Latin America: gross product per employed person and percentage distribution of total gross product by sectors, *c*. 1950

Sector	Percentage distribution of the gross product*	Percentage distribution of the labour force	Indices of productivity of labour by sectors (average productivity of all sectors = 100)
Agriculture	24.5	53.0	46
Mining	4.3	1.1	410
Manufacture	18.2	14.5	126
Construction	4.6	3.7	122
Other activities	44.4	27.7	175

*Percentages do not add up to 100, because the contribution of housing rents, representing four per cent of the total gross product, is not included. Source: ECLA, table 16.

Industrialization was favoured by ECLA as a way of retaining a greater part of the profits of the export sector. Industries created job opportunities and stimulated a rural-urban migration which could reduce pressure on land and permit higher productivity in agriculture. Employment in industry was also regarded as absorbing 'unproductive' employment in the existing commercial and service sector of the urban economy. Indeed, by 1956 ECLA was already signalling some of the dangers of the expansion of the service sector of the Latin American economies, though viewing this as a transitional problem. Basing its comparisons on the situation in the advanced capitalist world, ECLA pointed out that in a 'properly' balanced development, such as that in western Europe, the service to manufacturing employment ratio was close to 1; only in those countries with exceptionally high productivity, such as the United States, did the service to manufacturing employment ratio reach 1.5. Thus Latin America's ratio of 1.39 in 1950 was seen to be excessive.

Some of the city-ward migration was viewed as being absorbed in marginal activities which served to depress productivity; such service employment was characterized by ECLA (1957, 40) as 'overburdening' the urban population and as being 'excessive'. A similarly disapproving note entered into its characterization of small-scale industry, which was seen as diminishing productivity in its sector—'a vast mushroom growth of small, inefficient workshops, which can operate at a profit owing to the ample supply of cheap labour, provided by the steady immigration of rural population to towns and by the already existing stock of marginal population' (37). This early characterization of certain types of employment as marginal to and harmful to the development of the modern economy contrasts, as we shall see in later chapters, with the perspective of the marginality theorists. ECLA blames this employment situation on the underdeveloped nature of the agricultural sector and on the slow progress of industrialization.

ECLA looked approvingly, in this period, at those countries which had industrialized early and had achieved fairly high levels of productivity in agriculture. Argentina was characterized as reflecting a high degree of economy maturity and as being the most advanced country in Latin America. By the 1960s, however, a noticeable change had taken place in ECLA's analysis; there was by then some disappointment with the poor performance of industry in increasing employment opportunities. Such 'advanced' Latin American countries as Argentina, Chile and Uruguay were singled out for their slow rates of economic growth and for the 'exorbitant' expansion of service employment. In the 1966 report, industrialization involving technologically sophisticated plant which required relatively little labour and the high-income concentration and mass poverty in Latin American countries were seen to inhibit the expansion of the market for labour-absorbing industry. The analysis of the possibilities of expanding employment opportunities also changed radically from 1956; in 1966, the best chances to expand productive employment were seen to rest with agriculture and construction. Even small-scale industry received a grudging acceptance (ECLA, 1965, 184–5).

The analyses and policy recommendations of ECLA reflect the general tenor of critical thinking about the problem of underdevelopment in the immediate postwar period. The emphasis on the nationalist solution to underdevelopment was stressed, in this same period, in Africa and Asia. Among intellectuals and policy-makers, nationalism and the institutions of the nation-state were seen to provide a possible basis for internal unity and for an economic restructuring which would reduce dependence on the advanced capitalist world. Difficulties facing such a restructuring were recognized, but in general these were viewed as obstacles to change which could be overcome with concerted effort from government and an aware citizenry. This ideology was indeed an integral part of the populist political philosophy. Also, many of the obstacles were identified with reformable aspects of the internal structure of the new nations, such as traditional practices in agriculture, backward elites or low levels of education. One of ECLA's major recommendations, for example, was for an agrarian reform which would make possible the development of small-scale commercial agriculture (Faria, 1976, 44–6).

External dependence and capital-intensive industrialization

A major reason for disillusion, even within ECLA itself, with the policy of import-substitution industrialization, was the evidence that it did not promote an independent economic development. In many countries, industrialization increased the amount of foreign control and participation in the economy. High rates of urbanization did little to increase agricultural productivity, while the employment structure of the cities appeared to become even more weighted to the 'unproductive' tertiary sector. Moreover, the economic development that did occur, as measured by rate of growth in the national and per capita product, produced increasing inequalities in income distribution (Foxley, 1976). An explanation for these trends is provided by examining, as do Cardoso and Faletto and Anibal Quijano (1973; 1974), the internal implications of the economic dependence of underdeveloped countries on the advanced capitalist world.

First, the economies of the advanced capitalist nations are in a constant process of change. Consequently, the nature of their articulation with underdeveloped countries changes significantly over time. We noted in the first chapter that the dynamic of the first phase of economic imperialism to affect Latin America (Britain's) is different from that of American economic imperialism. Such changes in articulation set the conditions of exchange which promote or limit development within underdeveloped countries.

In the twentieth century, American investments have concentrated increasingly in industrial production; their location has shifted over time from extractive industry to manufacturing and, within manufacturing, have become concentrated in technologically sophisticated products such as durable consumer goods. From this perspective, the urban industrialization of underdeveloped countries does not reduce dependence, but is a process closely tied to the economic development of the advanced capitalist world.

Quijano (175, 124) expresses the paradox of expecting underdeveloped countries to develop independently while remaining part of the capitalist system: 'Dependence is . . . a nexus of relationships which are established by virtue of the close correspondence between the basic structural orders of the dependent society and the one that has come to dominate it because of circumstances in their past history. . . . More specifically, this means that, in its basic traits and outward features, the structure of power and conflict in a dependent society is weaker than that of the dominant society and is also basically derived from, and part of, the dependent society's relations with the dominant society in the past.'

Quijano analyses the changes in the advanced capitalist economies which fostered the pattern of industrial urbanization in Latin America and other underdeveloped countries. After the second world war, and partly as a consequence of technological developments produced by that war, the most advanced capitalist economies accelerated their rate of technological innovation. This meant in part that the market for the sophisticated products of these economies was concentrated in the advanced capitalist countries themselves; underdeveloped countries provided only a limited market and then only where there was a sufficiently concentrated high income population.

This changing emphasis of the advanced capitalist economies meant that it became more advantageous for certain sectors of capital to transfer their production activities to underdeveloped countries. With high costs of labour in the developed world, products destined for the general market in underdeveloped countries could often be produced more profitably in those countries. Local production did not compete with the sophisticated technology of advanced capitalism and, in fact, provided a market for machinery and new production processes. Interlocking production activities became possible, as when the simpler parts of an electrical appliance are manufactured locally and the more complicated ones made in the developed countries. Thus, a complex pattern of economic interdependence has emerged in which the advanced capitalist countries retain the most productive economic activities such as those associated with the latest technological innovation (like electronics), but delegate more routine production to poorer countries where costs may be lower.

Fernando Cardoso, in an article entitled 'Dependency Revisited' (1973), argues that a new pattern of economic dependence is constituted by the tripartite alliance between state companies, multinational corporations and the local companies associated with both. The multi-national corporation is the organizational means whereby advanced capitalism overcomes the limitations of its territorial bases. It becomes possible to make use of cheaper costs of production in certain countries or to establish subsidiaries as the only way of getting at local markets, while retaining substantial control over the production process. The technology on which production is based remains directly under the control of the parent company and complementary parts of the production are carried out in another country.

In this situation there are few disadvantages to investment in industrial expansion in underdeveloped countries, provided that there is an internal market. Such investment does not compete with the home products of the foreign company within the international division of labour produced by the activities of the multi-national corporation. Indeed, certain underdeveloped countries may export the industrial products of the 'multinationals' elsewhere; thus, the Brazilian car industry exports to the rest of Latin America. Such exports are often more profitable for the parent company than direct export from the home country, where costs of production and transport are higher.

The emergence of the 'multinational' and the changing characteristics of the advanced capitalist economies are part of the explanation for the increasing predominance of foreign corporations in industrial production in Latin America and elsewhere in the third world. Brazil, which had at first espoused an explicitly nationalistic policy of industrialization, has become increasingly dominated by multinational corporations which control most industrial sectors, often in association with the state (Souza and Affonso, 1975). In Argentina by 1959, of the one hundred enterprises with the highest sales receipts, 55 were multinational corporations and of the top ten corporations, eight were multinational (Arias, 1971). In Peru, the relatively rapid industrialization by the 1950s and 1960s was one in which foreign controlled companies became increasingly predominant (Thorp and Bertram, 1978). By 1969, foreign subsidiaries in Peru formed 54 per cent of 39 of Peru's largest industrial companies (Wils, 1975, 56–7).

This industrialization is capital-intensive and is directed to the final production of consumer goods whose major market is middle- and upper-income groups. Brazil's economic boom of the 1960s was in great part based on the expansion of the automobile industry and on the manufacture of other durable consumer goods (Oliveira, 1972). Traditional industrial production also became more capital-intensive, with both textiles and the food processing industries installing technologically sophisticated machinery which, while increasing output, reduced the labour requirements of a plant. Oliveira (1972, 62–3) argues that the profitability of the new durable consumer goods industries is based on producing a differentiated product for a limited but high-income market; the concentration of this population in a few urban centres further increases the accessibility and profitability of the market. In contrast, more traditional products such as textiles have a less dynamic market and, in Brazil, have needed subsidization to export part of their product.

We need to examine why this trend to capital-intensive industrialization, with its consequent dependence on foreign technology, should have proved so acceptable to third-world governments and to other sections of their populations. We noted how Cardoso characterized the new dependence as an alliance between government, local groups and foreign capital; at first sight, this alliance might appear a strange one given the nationalism of many third-world regimes and the supposition of early Marxist commentators that national bourgeoisies would be the first to reject colonialism and neo-colonialism (Barratt-Brown, 1974, 269–76). Thus, Argentina began this century as a country with a modernizing national bourgeoisie and will in all probability end it with foreign corporations in control of the most productive sectors of the economy.

Technologically based production creates complementarities of interest between local elites and foreign ones because the former can derive their profits from direct production, while the latter can derive theirs from the use of their technologies in production (Alavi, 1972). In a similar fashion, Paul Singer indicates that it is to the advantage of multinational corporations to allow firms not directly controlled by them to use their innovations in production because this enables the multinationals to extend the scale of their operations (Singer, 1973, 85–7). For this reason, branches of production highly dependent on technological advance can be taken over by the public sector or 'let out' to national entrepreneurs without opposition from the foreign monopolies. In return for providing the know-how, the monopolies derive royalties, rights to market the product or concessions in other branches of production.

The constraints on an 'independent' industrial development can be more clearly understood if one considers the implications of the existing internal structure of these countries. Previous stages of economic dependency have given rise to a social structure in which the mass of the population are often peasant farmers with a low consuming power. Our historical overview shows how income has become heavily concentrated among urban elites whose consumption patterns are modelled on those of the more advanced nations. In this context, governments are faced with a serious dilemma: to develop independently, they need to generate capital to diversify and expand the industrial structure of the country. Although they can seek to raise this capital abroad, it is unlikely that they will obtain it either in sufficient quantity or on terms that will permit an independent development (Hayter, 1971). To raise this capital internally, as Fitzgerald shows in the case of Peru, governments must either rely on taxing, directly or indirectly, the profits on industrial production or they must force capital accumulation by seeking to appropriate an important part of the agricultural surplus (Fitzgerald, 1976).

In the existing situation of most underdeveloped countries, the easiest way to achieve these ends is to encourage the 'efficient' use of available capital in forms of production that have a high profitability. It was for this reason that ECLA stated early on that, faced with a situation of capital scarcity, the only effective path to industrialization was through the use of advanced technology (Faria, 1976, 35).

According to ECLA to disperse capital through encouraging labour-intensive industrialization would only slow down the process of accumulation because of the lower rates of return on capital.

The 'efficiency' of this use of capital is one that is dependent on an existing class-based pattern of consumption. The products of advanced technology sell well in underdeveloped countries because of the high concentration of income and because of consumption patterns modelled on those of advanced capitalist countries. It is not easy for governments to adopt alternative industrialization policies in this situation, since most social groups are accustomed to purchasing the products which advanced technology makes more generally available. Transistor radios or factory-produced textiles have become part of the consumption patterns of even the most pervasively peasant population. It is not simply the self-interest of the dominant classes and of governments in Latin America and other underdeveloped countries that perpetuates economic dependence; the type of social structure present in underdeveloped countries makes capital-intensive industrialization, orientated to sophisticated consumer goods, the easiest path to follow.

In Columbia in the 1960s, the government encouraged a move to capital intensification through maintaining an 'overvalued' currency (which cheapened the cost of machine imports) and through direct tax subsidies to those importing such machinery. One group of economists calculated that in certain branches of production the profitability of capital-intensive techniques, in comparison with more labour-intensive ones, was mainly an artifact of these subsidies (Nelson, Schultz and Slighton, 1971). Moreover, the subsidies encouraged entrepreneurs to develop luxury consumer goods industries for the middle- and upper middle-class urban populations. Such cases may appear extreme, but they demonstrate the difficulties of economic planning when the 'normal' or 'most efficient' path to economic development is itself based on an extremely uneven or 'abnormal' pattern of income distribution and social stratification.

In the early part of this century, Russia also experienced difficulties in effecting a radical change from an existing situation of dependent capitalist industrialization. Writing in the 1920s, the Soviet economist and politician, Preobrazhensky (1965), analysed the dynamic of what he saw as the new capitalist imperialism—that of the United States—which imposed economic and political dependency by the export of capital and technology. He pointed to the difficulties faced by the Soviet Union in this context, since capital was needed for development but the mass of the Russian population was peasant and lay outside the socialist production system. Any reliance on the profitability of Soviet industry would fail, argued Preobrazhensky, since that industry was in a relatively primitive stage of development and could not compete with advanced capitalist industry in providing consumer goods for the population. Though Soviet industry could be given a monopoly of the internal market, the sale of such goods was not likely to stimulate peasants and other small commodity producers to exchange their surpluses.

Peasants faced with expensive, crude, local industrial production might simply withdraw their surpluses from the market. Since Russia needed to export a range of primary products to pay, on the capitalist market, for the machinery needed for industrialization, it was crucial that an increasing surplus be extraced from the agrarian sector. The eventual solution in Russia was to force accumulation by withdrawing both the peasant and the urban population from the system of free market exchange; peasant collectivization and restrictions on private consumption ensured that industrial production could be planned for the developmental needs of both industry and agriculture. The dilemma over industrialization was increased, moreover, by the political inexpediency of forcing peasant accumulation when the newly established Soviet regime depended on a worker–peasant class alliance (Preobrazhensky, 1965, introduction). This problem is even more acute in contemporary underdeveloped countries. Few regimes have the political will and class basis of support to compel substantial sections of their population either to reduce or to change their consumption patterns.

The reform policies of the Peruvian military regime since 1968 are examples of this difficulty. Agrarian reform in Peru was used as a device to transfer part of the agricultural surplus to industrial investment; also, the regime took over substantial sections of industry, instituted a limited amount of worker participation in other industrial sectors and attempted to regulate the growth of consumer goods industries (Lowenthal, 1975). These policies have had only limited success in the face of non-cooperation from peasant groups who have sought greater local benefits from agrarian reform (Roberts, 1975); and there has been opposition from the urban middle classes to the poor quality and scarcity of consumer goods.

Private capitalists have been unwilling to invest in industrial production whose profitability they see as being increasingly reduced. The industrial working class is numerically weakly developed in Peru and this class has also been suspicious of the military regime's restrictions on its bargaining power. The military have consequently little organized support outside their own ranks and in recent years have proceeded more and more cautiously with their reforms in the face of demonstrations and riots. Despite an early period of nationalization of important enterprises, as in petroleum, sugar and copper, the regime has sought foreign participation and encouraged foreign and local capital to invest in durable consumer goods and other capital-intensive industries (Sorj, 1976; Ferner, 1977).

It is at this point that we can appreciate the forces making for convergence in the patterns of urbanization in the underdeveloped world. To the extent that the economic dynamic of underdeveloped economies depends on emulating the consumption patterns of the advanced capitalist world, then the spatial representation of those patterns is likely to dominate. The concentration of middle- and high-income populations in a few urban centres makes investments in capital-intensive consumer goods industries attractive. These industries are located in, or close to, the centres of population and contribute to the attraction of the large cities for rural migrants. Improvements in urban infrastructures such as roads, lighting, sanitation and housing are part of the dynamic of this industrialization, extending the market for consumer durables such as automobiles and domestic appliances.

The increasing complexity of the urban environment in the large cities of Latin America is an important reason for technological dependence on the advanced capitalist nations. New and more sophisticated systems of communication and the means of keeping order increase reliance on foreign technicians and on advanced technology. The contrast between the large cities with their skyscrapers, sophisticated highway systems and ultra-modern facilities and the small towns and villages of Latin America is a striking testimony to the urban basis of technological dependence.

Regional development and industrialization

Capital-intensive industrialization reinforces an uneven pattern of development, as can be seen in the problems of regional development. Although the picture is at first sight a pessimistic one, this is partly because I have made somewhat rigid assumptions about the nature of capital-intensive industrialization, seeing it as necessarily resulting from the types of goods produced under the demand structure of societies in which income is highly skewed. However, Kirsch (1975) points out that the same product is often produced under widely differentiated technological conditions in Latin America and that certain basic industries such as food, beverages, tobacco and even textiles are at times more capital-intensive than consumer durable or capital goods industries in the same country. There is also the point that I shall take up in chapter 5: it is by no means certain that the structure of consumption would be significantly altered by a policy of income distribution (Kirsch, 1975, 80; Wells, 1976). These caveats imply that provincial economies may expand even when subordinated to the industrialization of core regions. Also, deliberate policies aimed at fostering more labour-intensive production or at redistributing income may both increase employment and provide the basis for industrial growth and diversification.

I discussed in the second chapter the regional inequalities that develop during earlier stages of underdevelopment. In the analysis of internal colonialism, the provinces are seen to be exploited by means of their own urban centres, to the benefit of the dominant commercial and landed classes residing in the largest cities (Stavenhagen, 1965; Gonzalez Casanova, 1965). In these Mexican studies, the treatment of the mass of the local population as an ethnic group (Indian) with characteristics and rights distinct from those of the dominant groups was shown to facilitate exploitation. Such practices have continued into the contemporary period and are one of the means whereby capitalist enterprises secure relatively cheap labour power.

The period of capital-intensive industrialization has, however, changed the nature of the articulation between the capital city and other large cities and provincial places (Morse, 1971b, 50–3). Rapid urbanization and the development of capitalist production in agriculture have increased the importance of the internal market for both agricultural and industrial production. Improvements in communciations and the penetration of government, commerce and the mass media to even the remotest areas of a country are other factors increasing economic and political integration.

In such a situation, internal colonialism is an inadequate concept to explain contemporary provincial underdevelopment. In the postwar period regional inequalities in income distribution and in social welfare appear to have grown in most Latin American countries (Griffin, 1969; Foxley, 1976). These inequalities are not, however, the result of segregating provincial populations from the 'benefits' of economic development by maintaining their relative isolation and by enforcing local commercial or political monopolies; rather, these persisting and increasing inequalities are the results of the types of economic integration generated by capital-intensive industrialization.

This concern with the ways in which economic development generates regional inequalities is an old one and to some economists such inequalities represent the first stages of economic development, as a dynamic metropolitan centre begins to generate growth for the whole country (Wingo, 1969; Friedmann, 1969).

I noted in the first chapter that in the United States regional inequalities grew in the first stages of economic development and were subsequently evened out. In underdeveloped countries, this issue is an immediate one in that regional inequalities in economic growth contribute to population concentration in a few urban centres.

Even commentators like Wingo, who stress the advantages of spatially concentrating economic development, urge governments to take concerted steps to promote a more balanced regional economic development. The persistence of regional inequalities has led John Friedmann, for example, to modify his optimism about the generative effects of planned large city growth. In his later works, as we saw in the first chapter, Friedmann (1972a, b) has stressed the ways in which economic development projects can perpetuate the economic dependence of peripheral regions on central ones.

In exploring the impact of capital-intensive industrialization on provincial development, it is important to remember that this impact will vary, depending on the strength of the articulation between the region and the economic centre. In Lopes's (1977) analysis of regional agrarian development in Brazil, the patterns of change differed markedly, for example, as between the São Paulo region and the northeastern region. In the São Paulo area, agriculture is becoming transformed in a capitalist direction, with a rural proletariat that provides occasional labour power for the capitalist farms. In contrast, in the northeast and on the frontier, peasant farming is expanding, providing a low-cost agricultural product (rice and beans) for the low-income populations of the cities; but food for high income tastes in the northeast is often imported from the capitalist farms of the central south. The limited high-income market of the northeastern cities is in turn a result of the peripheral role of these cities with respect to São Paulo and the cities of the central south of Brazil. As Faria (1976) shows, the northeastern cities have a greater proportion of 'marginal' economic activities as a direct consequence of their increasing integration into the national economic system.

Such regional inequalities are reinforced by the implantation of capital-intensive production in peripheral regions. Singer points out that such implantations are most likely to benefit the central regions. Factors such as congestion and high land prices may make it profitable for a São Paulo enterprise to locate in a less developed area. This location policy will not, however, diminish the dependency of the northeast on the central south, but change that dependency from a commercial to a financial one (Singer, 1973, 75). Thus, the major part of the profits of the enterprise will be appropriated by the banking institutions of São Paulo. The location of the enterprise in an industrial park means that construction materials, machinery and so on are likely to be imported from the central south. The work may require skills that are not available locally and skilled labour will be brought from other regions; the consumption needs of this labour power are unlikely to be satisfied locally and products will be imported from the more developed regions. Such products may even be sold in branches of São Paulo shops and supermarkets. Kirsch (1973) reports similar difficulties in Venezuela with a petrochemical complex designed to increase employment in a provincial region.

This form of 'enclave' production is thus unlikely to generate much local development; the technology involved will be too sophisticated to permit complementary industries to be developed locally. Furthermore, the dependence of the firm on decisions made in São Paulo subordinates an important element of a region's economy to external interests. Such developments can harm a region's development in the long run; the setting up of capital intensive industry raises local prices of commodities, land and housing. These increases may make it more difficult for the subsistence or near-subsistence producer to survive locally, especially when the industry does not provide economic opportunities for such producers. Out-migration may increase, reinforcing the enclave effects of the implanted industry. The results may be that while the São Paulo interests derive considerable profits from their ventures, the possibilities of local accumulation may actually decrease.

These dilemmas are spelled out in David Barkin's (1975) account of regional development in Mexico. He argues that despite considerable investments in regional production and infrastructure by the Mexican government, the result has been to increase regional underdevelopment. He admits that government projects increase local productivity and improve the infrastructure in ways that benefit local inhabitants through the provision of better communications, health facilities and schools. However, the major beneficiaries of the development programmes are the large-scale capitalist farms. These farms were in a position to take advantage of the improved possibilities of production and could most easily shift production when the market changed. The large farms had better access to credit than the small peasant (*ejidal*) farmers. Government agencies were reluctant to extend credit to the small farmer, since such credits provide a low return on capital.

In contrast, Barkin shows that most government investment went to the richer, industrialized regions of Mexico and into large-scale irrigation projects which benefited the large farms most. He outlines some of the local consequences of these development programmes in the Tepalcatepec River basin project in the states of Michoacán and Jalisco to the west of Mexico City: population in the zone grew slightly less than the rate of natural increase between 1950 and 1970, but the employment structure of the population changed appreciably. The population became increasingly based on agricultural wage labour or urban employment, often in the service sector of the economy. The small farmer found it increasingly necessary to rent his land and to work as a day labourer to sustain his family; temporary migrant labour from other regions of the country came to work on the harvests of the large farms. The region's towns grew rapidly on the basis of the commerce linked to large-scale agricultural production; the towns became centres for the sale of agricultural machinery, seeds and fertilizer and provided a range of services

Barkin comments that this pattern of development increased the economic dependence of the area on Mexico City, through the centralization of financial control and of policy-making in the capital. Many of
the large commercial firms were foreign-owned and almost all were
centred in Mexico City, increasing the outflow of capital.

In analysing these outcomes, Barkin stresses the difficulties attending a balanced regional development in a capitalist economy. There
are no internal restrictions on the movement of capital and so it is to
be expected that capitalist enterprises will take advantage of the
profit-making opportunities created by government investment. In
this context, people in poor regions are at a disadvantage, since they
neither have the resources to make use of economic opportunities
competitively, nor can they defend themselves by controlling the
entry of capital or of industrial products. Thus development projects
serve to integrate and increase the direct economic dependence of a
region on the most advanced sectors of a nation's economy.

The tendency of the state to contribute to regional dependence and
inequality by the pattern of its investment appears to be a general one
in Latin America. Glaucio Dillon Soares (1976) points out that the
bulk of state investment in Latin America is directly economic in
nature. In contrast to state investments in Europe and the United
States at the equivalent period of their development, Latin American
governments invest a relatively small proportion of their funds in
social services and infrastructure.

Essentially similar conclusions are reached by Webb (1975) in
analysing public policy and regional incomes in Peru. The Peruvian
case is interesting because both the present military regime and the
previous civilian, Belaunde regime, espoused an explicit policy of
correcting regional imbalances and of redistributing income to the
lowest-income sectors. Priorities given to industrialization by both
regimes had, however, the effect of concentrating technology and
high productivity; less encouragement was given to agricultural
development and the development policy of these regimes favoured
the urban concentration of industry. Also, Webb demonstrates the
difficulties in attempting to correct imbalances without major social
investments. The few social investments made in education and
health, for example, redounded to the advantage of the urban populations and of those employed in the modern sector of the economy.
Webb's conclusion is that regional inequalities in income and welfare
have increased from 1960 to 1971. He points out that these inequalities are not the result of a policy of internal colonialism in which
income is extracted from poorer regions by fiscal devices, but that
growing inequalities result from the 'natural' tendency of governments to favour capital-intensive industrialization policies.

In this context, it is unlikely that urbanization contributes to a
more balanced regional development. The growth of provincial

urban centres may lead to a more balanced urban hierarchy, but productive investment is likely to continue to concentrate in the largest cities. Gilbert (1975) provides for Columbia a detailed account of the forces which led to such concentration. Capital-intensive industrialization concentrates in centres with ample consumer markets, a skilled labour force and a developed infrastructure; the structure of government employment and the increasing expenditures of local government also reinforce the advantages of the existing large urban centres. Gilbert (1975, 245) suggests that, despite Columbia's past history as a country with a relatively balanced urban system, Bogota may in the future become a primate city because of its increasing dominance.

Capital-intensive industrialization leads to the concentration of employment in manufacturing and construction in the largest cities of an underdeveloped country. In contrast, the growth of provincial urban centres is more likely to be based on the expansion of employment in commerce and in other service sectors. Jobs in these sectors are likely to be in smaller enterprises or to be in self-employment. This was Faria's conclusion for Brazil and it fits much of the existing Latin American data. Thus, the city of Huancayo in Peru has an employment structure which is highly concentrated in smaller enterprises and in the service sector when compared with Lima. Huancayo has a large proportion of government employment and is the place of residence of government employees, such as teachers, who work in the villages of the region as well as in the city. The relatively high incomes of government employees are one of the mainstays of the city's economy; government employees have the highest average income of any occupational groups in the city. Many employees do not permanently reside in the city and the highest officials maintain a residence in Lima and make minimal investments in Huancayo (Roberts, 1976a). Thus, despite the contribution of government to the regional economy, the gains to the region are offset by the relative lack of local commitment on the part of these elite groups. They are not a source of capital accumulation and development for the region. Indeed, a concrete expression of Huancayo's contemporary dependency on Lima is the fact that many of its most prominent citizens (including its mayor) have been migrants who, in the course of their careers, will pass on to the national capital (Roberts, 1976a).

It would be unwise, however, to assume that provincial regions are stagnant economically and unimportant elements in national decision-making. The truth of the matter is that we often do not know enough about political and economic processes at the provincial level; the focus of studies of underdevelopment has been excessively on metropolitan areas, their economies and politics. This focus will be one that will dominate the rest of this volume, as we examine the way in which population has concentrated in large urban centres. Consequently, we must keep in mind not only national differences in the situation of underdevelopment, but also those that are produced by the territorial division of labour within countries. Small towns, provincial centres and national metropolises differ from each other in their occupational and income distributions, in their polities and in their urban culture. Had we the time and space, it would be possible to show that many of these differences are understandable in terms of the structure of interdependence produced by the uneven industrial development of the contemporary period.

Conclusion

Latin America's historical role as an exporter of raw materials and of foodstuffs stimulated in the course of this century an extensive industrialization which has concentrated economic opportunities in the major cities of the region. Variations between countries in the degree of industrialization can, to a certain extent, be explained by the characteristics of the dominant classes and by the presence or absence of a strong, centralized state. Industrialization has, in turn, brought new forces into play, such as an organized working class and an industrial bourgeoisie. The political strength of these forces was limited by an uneven pattern of development in which agriculture remained controlled by traditional landowners and which, in the cities, resulted in a large service sector, often dependent on government. The inability of any one class to establish a clearly dominant position in this situation meant the emergence of the populist 'solution' to economic modernization by which, through limited concessions, the industrial working class was incorporated into the structure of government.

Industrialization has brought important changes in the economic relationships with developed countries. In a continent scarce of capital and with consumer preferences similar to those of the developed world, industrialization followed the capital-intensive pattern of more advanced countries. The dependence of underdeveloped countries has become technological. Foreign companies set up operations within the underdeveloped country producing basic consumer goods and importing their technology. These companies profit from the cheaper production costs of underdeveloped countries to export their manufactures to both the developed and underdeveloped world. The effects of this situation of technological dependence on economy, politics and life styles will be further explored in the following chapters; but one of its most evident consequences is the stagnation of provincial regions in face of the concentration of economic growth in a few large cities.

4
Migration and the agrarian structure

The importance of industrialization in shaping economy and society in underdeveloped countries must be set within a context in which a large proportion of the population still works in agriculture and lives in small towns and rural villages. In the next three chapters, I will focus on contemporary urban life in underdeveloped countries; but before making this shift in perspective, we need to consider the processes by which agricultural pursuits have become increasingly replaced by urban ones. I have argued that it is economic expansion, not stagnation or traditionalism, that is the basis of the contemporary problems of underdeveloped countries. This argument can now be extended to the agrarian structures of underdeveloped countries which have long been affected and partially transformed by market forces. The agrarian structures of Latin America have, perhaps, been more affected by external political and economic forces than have those of most underdeveloped areas, with the result that village-level society has been fragmented, social and economic relationships individualized and a labour supply made available for capitalist expansion (Jannry and Garramon, 1977).

I have touched on some of these themes in previous chapters and in the present one I will limit myself to a brief analysis of the economic diversity of rural Latin America and of the economic activities of its rural population. These activities are, I will claim, part of the flux of both urban and rural life, contributing to a geographical and occupational mobility which is an important factor in blurring class boundaries and limiting class organization. To understand urban economic activity and social stratification requires us, then, to develop an idea of the total field of action, rural as well as urban, within which urban populations move and survive. (See Long, 1977, for a full analysis of the dynamics of change in the agrarian structure.)

However, we must remember that the importance of agricultural employment varies from country to country, so that in Latin America Argentina, for example, had by 1970 only 15.2 per cent of its employed population in agriculture, while Brazil, Columbia, Peru and Mexico had between 40 and 50 per cent of their population so employed.

The significance of the agrarian structure for urban growth

One feature of rural social changes is the nature of migration movements to the cities. Though the contribution of these movements to the current rates of growth of cities has been overstressed, migrants and the children they have in the city are a significant element in cultural, political and economic change. The sheer volume of movement makes urban migration one of the most evident of the 'problems' of underdeveloped countries; it has been estimated, for example, that almost 600,000 people head for greater São Paulo each year from cities, towns and villages throughout Brazil (Wilheim, 1977). The impact of these migration movements on urban development depends in part on the characteristics of the provincial areas from which the city draws its population. For example, the manner in which migrants cope with urban life is affected by the resources that they bring to the cities—the educational skills, the financial and material capital or access to a network of friends and kin who provide lodgings and information about jobs. In turn, these resources vary from one area to another, depending on the level and type of their economic development and their social and cultural structure. Thus the nature of the hinterland from which a city draws its population is one source of variation in the social structures of cities in underdeveloped countries.

Industrialization entails a certain convergence in the patterns of migration throughout the underdeveloped world; for example, migration movements become a preponderantly rural–urban movement of a relatively permanent kind (Balán, 1973). This migration pattern contrasts with those reviewed in the last two chapters, which included substantial international migrations, seasonal and other temporary labour migration, rural-to-rural migration, and city-ward migration. Although these other patterns of migration are present in the contemporary period, as in the colonization of the agricultural frontier in Brazil, they are quantitatively less important than urban migrations. One of the major reasons for the preponderance of urban migration is that industrialization begins to unify the internal market for underdeveloped countries, bringing even the more remote and less developed regions into direct economic dependence on the major urban centres. The improvement of internal communications is part of this process, so that regional identities and economic commitments are increasingly eroded by these centralizating forces. In the past, as we have seen, regionalism was often reinforced by the weakness of the economic and political links with the national capital and by direct economic links between a region of a country and foreign economies.

Despite this convergence, the present changes in the agrarian structure of underdeveloped countries are complex and vary in their scope and nature from one country to another and from one region of a country to another. This complexity is a direct result of the uneven pattern of economic development. Non-capitalist forms of agricultural production (mainly peasant) not only survive in the present period, but increase in number, providing food for the large urban centres and a subsistence base for those working seasonally in commercial agriculture or, even, in urban employment. The opportunities provided by the growing urban market for foodstuffs also stimulate the expansion of capitalist agriculture, especially around the major urban centres. This agriculture can take the form of small farms worked mainly by the family, with the aid of high levels of mechanization and of seasonal labour, or of large-scale agro-businesses which may export part or all of their product.

This situation is not, however, a dualistic one in which modern agricultural enterprises stand in stark opposition to the backward farming of peasant cultivators. It is likely that the expansion of modern enterprises has given new life to apparently archaic forms of agricultural production and, indeed, has helped to create new modes of peasant farming such as smallholdings managed and worked by females. Thus, members of a peasant household work under different relations of production, so that the wage labour of the male household head is complemented by his wife's work on the family smallholding and by a son's sharecropping on a nearby large landholding. As Goodman and Redclift (1977) argue for Brazil, 'non-capitalist' relations of production are often strengthened by closer integration with capitalist markets, foreign and domestic. As market opportunities expand, some modern farms increase their requirements for a cheap, temporary labour force, while other landowners use extra-economic coercion to extract surplus from tenants and sharecroppers. (See Dandler, Havens, Samaniego and Sorj, 1976, for an analysis of the links between capitalist expansion and the heterogeneity of relations of production in the agrarian structure of Latin America. Cliffe, 1977, and Meillassoux, 1977, provide comparable material for Africa.)

The predominance of one form of agricultural production or another is an important source of variation in rural–urban relationships and in the characteristics of migration. Areas of capitalist farming, for example, 'expel' more people than do areas of peasant farming. Areas of peasant production may present, however, a more complex set of urban–rural relationships in which family enterprises span rural and urban locations, with town migrants retaining rights to land and aiming to return eventually. Though the theme is beyond the scope of this volume, such differences in agrarian structure affect the actions and institutional development of the state, making agrarian reform expedient in one country and a less important issue in another (Long and Roberts, 1978; Lehman, D., 1974).

A final consideration to bear in mind is the demographic situation. Population growth in underdeveloped areas is high. In Latin America, Africa and the Middle East, where the rates of growth were fastest, population was increasing at approximately 2.7 per cent annually in the 1970s. In contrast, population increase in England and Wales in the period of the Industrial Revolution—say 1801–51—was approximately 1.5 per cent a year. The high rates of population increase in underdeveloped countries result from the reduction in mortality consequent on improvements in health, sanitation and medical facilities, while there has been little sign of countervailing trends reducing the birth-rate. Whereas in developed countries birth-rates have declined as a result of the social and economic changes accompanying urbanization and industrialization, this decline is not detectable in underdeveloped countries (Hawley, 1973, 110–14; Caldwell, 1976).

In Latin America and in other underdeveloped regions, there is little difference in the rates of natural increase between urban and rural populations; cities have a higher proportion of young adults than the countryside—a fact that increases crude birth-rates and decreases crude death-rates—and public health is generally better in cities (Davis, 1972, vol. II, 310). Another factor offsetting the tendency of the urban milieu to depress birth-rates is, as Faria (1976) points out, the informal economic organization of cities in underdeveloped countries. This informal organization makes it possible to use child labour at an early age, but entails economic insecurity in old age, thus making children an economic and social asset.

In this situation, migration from rural areas is the main factor in the increasing urbanization of underdeveloped areas. If we compare the growth of the urban and rural populations in six of the largest Latin American countries, we see that the urban population is growing at a faster rate than is the total population (table 4.1). Even highly urbanized countries such as Argentina, Chile, Venezuela and Mexico continue to increase the proportion of their urban populations. The table also shows, however, that urbanization is not depopulating rural areas, though in Argentina and Chile the rural population remained stable. Indeed, between 1960 and 1970 only two Latin American countries (Argentina and Venezuela) did not have an increase in agricultural employment (Kirsch, 1973).

Too much should not be made of this often mentioned 'peculiarity' of contemporary urbanization in underdeveloped countries. In nineteenth-century Europe also rural depopulation was not significant in the early stages of urbanization. In England, agricultural employment and production probably continued to increase during the first half of the nineteenth century (Saville, 1957, 7). In Germany, the small amount of rural depopulation at the end of the nineteenth century is accounted for by the 'promotion' of rural villages to urban status and thus their inclusion by the census-takers under urban population (Weber, 1899, 47–91). What is significant about the Latin American data is that in many countries rapid urbanization is accompanied by an increasing population pressure on a rural structure in which land is unevenly distributed and which, for most of the population, is insufficient to meet even subsistence needs.

This situation can be seen in data from Mexico and Peru; most other Latin American countries would have similar inequalities in land distribution. Despite the effects of the Mexican Revolution in redistributing land, there is still evidence of a high degree of land concentration: in 1960, agricultural units of less than five hectares made up 77.3 per cent of the total of over 1,000,000 private landholdings, but controlled only 10.8 per cent of the total cultivated land. Units of over 400 hectares were 0.2 per cent of the total number of units and 35.5 per cent of the over 13,000,000 hectares cultivated (CIDA, 1970, 97). Even when *ejidal* land (redistributed as communal property with agrarian reform) is included, 2,000 landholdings of over 400 hectares still make up 20.4 per cent of the area cultivated; in contrast, over 2,500,000 landholdings have less than 10 hectares (CIDA, 1970, 99). In Peru, in 1972, there were over 1,000,000 agricultural units of less than five hectares, holding 6.6 per cent of the land, whereas nearly 4,000 units of more than 500 hectares held 66.3 per cent of the total land (II *Censo Nacional Agropecuario*, 1975). Agrarian reform in Peru has from 1968 onwards meant that the largest units are now farmed as government controlled cooperatives.

Changes in the agrarian structure

The persistence of a large and growing rural population in the face of inadequate land resources and the substantial economic and social changes accompanying urbanization and industrialization is the problem posed by Paulo Singer (1973, 78) when he remarks that the basic issue of internal migration is *not* why so many people leave the land but why more people do not do so. In some areas of Latin America, the increasing commercialization of agriculture is transforming relations of production, creating a rural proletariat which works on nearby farms for a wage or migrates from place to place in search of seasonal agricultural work (D'Incao e Mello, 1976). Such rural workers will often live in the towns. These trends have been analysed for Brazil by Lopes (1976), for Mexico by Bartra (1974) and for Peru by Greaves (1970). This transformation of the agrarian structure is the classic case of capitalist development as described for England by Marx; it occurred even in those counties such as Lancashire where domestic industry (handloom weaving) predominated (Marshall, 1964; Roberts, 1978b). This trend meant that when the rural population eventually migrated to urban areas there were few economic ties binding urban populations to their rural origins.

In this section we will examine those factors that keep people on the land, despite the increasing integration of rural areas into an industrial economy. My aim is to explain the presence of two apparently conflicting trends in the agrarian structure—one towards an increasing 'peasantization' of the rural economy and the other towards an increasing proletarianization.

We can begin the analysis by reminding ourselves of the impact of the export economy on the rural areas of Latin America. Subsistence farming, whether in independent village communities or on land rented or sharecropped from *haciendas*, increasingly changed its nature as a consequence of the articulation with capitalist forms of production. From at least the time of the Spanish conquest, subsistence farming in Latin America was not a natural economy based on the self-sufficiency of agricultural and craft production at the village level. Very few subsistence farmers could hope to survive entirely from the product of their land or from domestic industry; increasingly in all parts of Latin America, wage migration became a permanent part of the village economy. Likewise, village households increasingly diversified their economic activities. Women and children might engage in small-scale trading or artisan activities to complement the family budget, men might permanently engage in seasonal migration to plantations or urban centres. Trading and artisan activities became tied into regional and even national networks of exchange.

The processes through which this diversification occurred are not difficult to identify. In part, they result from increasing demographic pressure on existing land. The best lands were occupied by the large enterprises and, with division of inheritance, each generation had less land resources available. Demographic pressure is only part of the explanation, however, because we need to know why so many stayed on the land despite the increasing difficulty of making a living.

Expedients such as temporary migration were an integral part of the survival of the household economy. A husband's or wife's wage labour was generally sufficient to complement small-scale farming or craft activities, but given the low wages of the plantations or mines it was not enough to provide an attractive basis for the permanent migration of the whole family. The defection of one member to seek work permanently outside was likely to have serious consequences for the viability of the household unit. In this situation, the costs of more permanent or long-distance migration were greater since these included the loss that the village-based household enterprise would suffer as a consequence of outmigration. One of the reasons why even the younger members of poor households in the Mantaro valley of Peru did not migrate at the turn of the

Table 4.1: Urban* and rural population distribution trends, 1960–70, and projected to 1980 (in millions)

Country	Urban Total population			Urban Population			Urban %			Rural Population			Rural %		
	1960	1970	1980	1960	1970	1980	1960	1970	1980	1960	1970	1980	1960	1970	1980
Argentina	20.0	23.4	27.0	12.1	15.5	19.1	60	66	71	7.9	7.9	7.9	40	34	29
Brazil	70.0	93.2	121.5	21.9	37.7	57.2	31	40	47	48.1	55.5	64.3	69	60	53
Chile	7.4	8.8	10.6	3.7	5.3	6.9	50	60	65	3.7	3.6	3.7	50	40	35
Mexico	34.9	48.4	68.1	18.2	27.7	42.5	52	57	62	16.7	20.7	25.6	48	43	38
Peru	9.9	13.6	16.8	3.1	5.8	8.0	31	43	48	6.8	7.8	8.8	69	57	52
Venezuela	7.3	10.3	14.3	3.9	6.4	9.9	53	69	69	3.4	4.0	4.4	47	39	31

*Urban population totals were calculated through this procedure: taking 1970 as the base year, cities in each country with more than 20,000 inhabitants that year were considered. For 1960 and 1980 the population of those same cities, enumerated and projected, was tallied. This discounts entirely cities that will have increased from fewer to more than 20,000 inhabitants in the 1970–80 interval. Source: Fox, 1975, table 3.

century was their responsibility for older kin; unless younger members worked as sharecroppers or as *peones*, there would be no one to take responsibility for their older kin.

Wages earned in the mines or plantations, money made from trade and so on became one of the main bases for the diversification of village economies. It provided capital on a small scale for investments in trade, craft production, fertilizer and seed and by so doing made possible the intensification of subsistence exploitation. Larger numbers of people survived on a fairly constant set of resources, not only by increasing their labour input but also by making such a labour input feasible through an increased use of cash to underpin the new ventures.

In certain respects, this process is akin to that described by Geertz when he discussed what he terms the agricultural involution of the village economy in Indonesia (Geertz, 1963a). There, too, the plantation economy uses the labour of the villages and the village economy intensifies its input of available labour to raise food production marginally. Geertz's point is that the process of involution—increasing attention to detail through a high labour input for only a small increase in production—destroys the dynamic of capital accumulation at the village level; productivity is not raised per capita and thus there are few opportunities for local entrepreneurs to accumulate and begin to set in train a rationalization of local production leading to the predominance of capitalist agricultural production. In this context, the increasing commercialization of agricultural production does not necessarily dispossess the peasant farmer of his land or displace agricultural labour; instead, village land becomes one part of a household economy that includes migration as an integral feature of its own survival.

Household-based enterprises persist in the rural areas because access to land provides a secure basis for utilizing all available labour to obtain a certain standard of subsistence; these enterprises produce goods at competitive prices by the working of long hours, using unpaid household labour and accepting low standards of subsistence. It is this kind of farming enterprise that I include under the term 'peasant'. It is the peasant sector of the rural economy which is expanding most rapidly, numerically, in many underdeveloped countries. Even in those countries where capitalist farming is expanding rapidly, such as Brazil, peasant farms are increasing through the colonization of new lands and the renting of land from *latifundia*. Many *latifundia* in the northeast of Brazil, producing crops that compete with the more efficient capitalist production of the central south zone, have substantially reduced the number of their *colonos* (tied labourers) and of the area of land under cultivation. In this situation, the peasant farmer survives because he provides a low-cost product, such as beans and rice, or because he opens up land that the capitalist enterprise may subsequently take over (Lopes, 1976; 1977).

Also, industrialization is often accompanied by an increasing diversification and commercial vitality of the rural, household-based economy. Kemper and Foster (1975) demonstrate the increasing diversification of the village economy in their well documented study of developments over 40 years in the village of Tzintzuntzan in Mexico. Outmigration from the village was relatively rare prior to 1945, but subsequently increased to reach a peak in the 1960–9 period. Tzintzuntzan became linked by good roads to the urban centres. This integration into the national economy was accompanied by increasing sales of urban products in the village and an increasing commercialization of agriculture. During this period, the population of the village increased despite outmigration from 1,003 in 1930 to 2,169 in 1970; moreover, the period of most rapid population increase in the village (3.2 per cent per annum between 1950 and 1960) was also a period when the village economy was closely articulated to the national urban economy. The local economy became increasingly diversified as the number of full-time farmers decreased and the number of craftsmen and small traders increased.

A similar process occurred in the village of Muquiyauyo, in the Mantaro valley of central Peru, despite severe land shortage. In the period from about 1940 to 1960 the local economy increasingly diversified as it became more closely integrated, through migration, into the national economy; the numbers of local stores, craftsmen and farmers making a surplus increased substantially (Adams, 1959; Grondin, 1975). Muquiyauyo's population grew from just over 1,000 at the turn of the century to 3,500 in 1960.

The dynamic of small-scale production is akin to that of competitive capitalism. Small-scale enterprises survive in the face of modern capitalist expansion by a high degree of exploitation of labour and a readiness to undertake the riskier and less profitable branches of production and services (Roberts, 1975; Singer, 1973, 83). Bartra (1974) terms a similar process in Mexico permanent primitive accumulation. The logic of this form of agrarian transformation is that of the small trader, transporter or industrialist, seeking to sell or obtain products in geographical areas and among sectors of the population which are relatively isolated from modern capitalist enterprise. The presence of this process is one of the most crucial variables affecting the pattern of internal migration.

The most successful rural entrepreneurs are those most likely to leave, especially in the early stages, since their activities (or those of their parents) will have generated the capital and skills to make migration feasible. Moreover, their commercial activities will have brought them into contact with the urban centres and provided knowledge of urban job opportunities. The greater economic opportunities offered by the large cities are sufficient reason why such groups should wish to transfer their enterprise or acquired skills (such as educational attainment). The more successful or the better educated represent those groups who are most 'free' to undertake the movement. Their local labour is less necessary to the survival of the household unit or can be more easily replaced by hiring others. Other areas of a country become involved in city-ward migrations as they become internally transformed by economic diversification. Those that leave these more remote or 'backward' areas are likely to be those with superior skills or resources in comparison with the population of origin.

Poor farmers are incorporated into local enterprises to provide occasional labour in the fields, and to aid with local crafts or trading ventures. In certain cases, farmers are attracted from poorer agricultural regions to work in more prosperous regions, cultivating on a sharecropping or rental basis the fields of those who have migrated to live in the city (Roberts, 1976b). In this way, the agrarian structure retains an increasing population while making such a population increasingly mobile.

This description is complicated by the likelihood that in certain regions members of the poorer, more subsistence-based strata of the agrarian population will at times be forced by the development of capitalist production in agriculture to undertake long-distance migration; also poorer families may move by stages to work in other villages, small towns or provincial centres. The permanent long-distance migration of the poorest is, however, less likely to take place than that of the more skilled and prosperous since they will not have the contacts or resources to survive easily in the competitive job market of the big cities.

A further complication is that some of the areas that provided the earliest city migrants may subsequently prove attractive areas to which migrants return. These areas are economically diversified and may have been completely transformed in the direction of petty commodity production; as such, they provide a range of small-scale economic opportunities that city migrants may eventually consider as offering more secure or profitable opportunities than their existing abode. For this pattern to occur, however, it is necessary that such areas do not become completely transformed by modern capitalist production. Lopes's (1979) description of the increasing capitalization of agriculture in the area of São Paulo demonstrates that there are decreasing economic opportunities in this area other than those of wage labour.

Seeing internal migration as a product of local enterprise rather than of local stagnation helps to differentiate the stages of internal migration and the characteristics of those migrating. When the agrarian structure is transformed through the agency of small-scale enterprise, internal migration is a manifestation of the progressive and cumulative incorporation of provincial areas into the dominant national urban economy. This incorporation is one that is organized by the economic activities of provincials; it is not a disorganized response to external pressures. The recognition that internal, city-ward migrations are, under certain conditions, socially and econom-ically organized movements is one key to understanding the nature of contemporary urban organization in underdeveloped countries.

The characteristics of migrants and of migration movements

Studies of the individual characteristics of migrants and the nature of their movements are numerous; but their findings are complex and often contradictory, warning us, as Morse (1971a,b) and Gilbert (1974, 100–16) have pointed out, of the dangers of generalizing without discriminating carefully between migrants of different socio-economic backgrounds and between different urban and rural contexts. With this caveat in mind, I will examine the extent to which the processes of rural economic diversification described in the last section explain the characteristics of migrants and the pattern of their movements. I will qualify this perspective by introducing a time perspective. Migration is influenced by the particular stage and intensity of the industrial development through which a country is passing. Also, migration necessarily changes the social structure of both rural and urban areas in terms of age and sex distribution, educational and occupation qualifications, creating a new situation for future migrations.

The change from temporary labour migration to mines and plan-tations to a more permanent rural–urban migration was a slow and often a partial one. Even in those cases in which the plantation or mine economy was in relative decline and economic expansion was occurring in the urban industrial sector, it often took time for inter-nal migrations to reflect these changes. Douglas Graham (1970) contrasts the patterns of internal migrations in Brazil in the period 1940–50 with the period 1950–60. In the earlier period, despite the poverty of the northeastern region, fewer migrants left this region than left Minas Gerais which, although poorer than the southern area to which its migrants went in search of work, was wealthier than the northeast. It is only in the period 1950–60 that outmigration from the northeast became greater in volume than outmigration from Minas Gerais, and Graham estimates that a substantial pro-portion of northeastern migration was long distance migration to the economically developing areas of the central south. He explains the change in migration patterns between the earlier and the later period by the greater rate of economic growth in the second period, with industrialization proceeding faster than the expansion of agricultural production both in aggregate and on a per worker basis. He also emphasizes the improvements in road networks and in transport that facilitated long-distance migration.

Graham's analysis suggests that in the first stages of urban–industrial expansion it is not necessarily the poorest areas in a nation which have the most substantial outmigration rates but those areas close to the expanding economic centres. The costs of transport and the risks of seeking work far from home counter the attraction of substantially higher incomes. Studies in Chile, Colombia and Mexico show that most migrants come from the areas close to the expanding centres (Herrick, 1965; Simmons and Cardona, 1972; Balán, Browning and Jelin, 1973). This migration pattern is similar to that of England during her industrialization where, also, there was little long-distance migration of poor farmers from the south to the north of England.

Census data on immigration to Lima in Peru since 1940 show some of the social and economic factors underlying and modifying this short-distance migration (*Censo Nacional,* 1940; Cuadro 145). In 1940, the departments (administrative regions) that contributed most migrants to Lima were the neighbouring departments of Ancash, Junín and Ica, the northern department of La Libertad (centre of the sugar industry) and the southern department of Arequipa. All these departments had been substantially affected by the expansion of capitalist enterprises linked to the export economy and were, with the exception of Ancash, among the departments with the highest literacy rates and the highest proportion of people living in urban places. More densely populated and poorer departments, such as Puno in the southern highlands, sent very few migrants to Lima. In the censuses since 1940 other departments have come increasingly to contribute to Lima's growth and these departments are among the remotest and poorest in the country, such as Ayacucho, Huancavelica and Puno. A similar trend is found in the contribution of various regions of Mexico to the growth of the capital city; it is only in recent years that migrants from poorer and more isolated regions such as the state of Hidalgo appear in substantial numbers in Mexico City.

The gradual inclusion of more remote and poorer regions in migration to the major urban centres suggests that contemporary rural–urban migrations are selective processes (Gilbert, 1974, 111–14). Browning argues that migrant selectivity is a general feature of the first stages of urbanization and summarizes data from a variety of Latin American countries and from Africa to show that in the early stages of migration outmigrants are disproportionately concentrated in the young adult age groups, are more likely to be single than the populations of origin, are better educated, and are more likely to have non-agricultural occupations than the populations of origin (Browning, 1971). Migrants to the metropolitan centres in many Latin American countries are drawn disproportionately from urban as opposed to rural places (Elizaga, 1971, 142; Herrick, 1965, 52–3).

The major contrast that Browning finds between Latin American and African migration is that city-ward migration in Latin America is often predominantly female, whereas in Africa it appears to be predominantly male (Caldwell, 1969). Female migration to cities in Latin America is encouraged by the multitude of jobs available for women in domestic and other service activities (Herrick, 1965). Browning (1971) uses data from a detailed survey of the migration and occupational histories of males in Monterrey, Mexico, to demonstrate that over time the selectivity of migrants decreases; the more recent migrants are more like the populations of origin in terms of marital status, education, work experience and so on. The argument is that early outmigration disproportionately reduces the available 'pool' of those with exceptional qualifications, so that subsequent migrants must necessarily be drawn from those whose characteristics are more like the population of origin.

In the Mantaro valley in the central highlands of Peru, we found that a member of a richer household was relatively free to migrate because he could secure the labour of others to tend the farm while he was away; but poor villagers remained to provide that labour or to sharecrop the lands of the rich migrant. The situation changed as migration became a more generalized phenomena in the central highlands. Wage labour in mines and plantations, work on construction projects and industrial work in Lima or in the provincial capital of Huancayo meant that more and more villagers became involved in the migration process. This, in itself, reduced the risks attending migration; friends of family members who had already migrated to work centres acted as bridgeheads, facilitating the entry of those remaining in the village. The migration networks established soon encompassed the entire village populations.

Furthermore, remittances from migrants and increasing numbers of returned migrants contributed towards a change in the village economy, generalizing the marketing of agricultural products and a money economy. Educational facilities at the village level also improved considerably in the period from about 1940, so that most young adults after that period were literate and had finished primary school. In the contemporary period there was no association between the economic and social status of a village family and the likelihood of its members either being migrants or having migrated (Laite, 1977; Roberts, 1976b). It was still the case, however, that those from the richer village families tended to obtain the better urban jobs; indeed, many of the sons of these families were educated to university level.

This emphasis on socio-structural factors in migration is not intended to be a substitute for an analysis of the spatial and economic variables that also determine migration. For example, the distance that a migrant must travel, the nature of his educational and occupational credentials and the relative importance of the economic centre to which he travels are variables whose interaction explains much of the variation between cities in the nature of the migrant 'pool' on which they draw. Such an analysis is, however, insufficient to provide an understanding of migration under the rural conditions of most underdeveloped countries, as can be appreciated by examining the issue of stage migration and its importance in contemporary migration movements. Taebur and his collaborators have described the stage migration process in the United States as follows: 'The aggregate shift from farm to large cities or suburbs is accomplished not by direct moves but by a series of less drastic moves—from farm to village, from village to town, from town to city . . . Many persons participate in these successive displacements, but the typical individual manages only one or two stages in his lifetime' (Taebur, Chiazze and Haenzel, 1968, 95). Stage migration, with its implication that internal migration is predominantly short-distance migration, was the pattern identified by Ravenstein (1885) and Redford (1926) in the British Isles in the nineteenth century. In Brazil, Chile and Columbia stage migration has been seen as the typical pattern of city-ward migration (Singer, 1973, 53; Herrick, 1965, 50–3; Morse, 1971b).

Browning (1971, 280) makes the point that stage migration is most likely to predominate where there is a well developed urban-size hierarchy. This is the urban distribution to which we referred in the first chapter, where a hierarchical series of central places organize geographical space and are functionally interrelated by a set of relationships from the farming areas to local supply and service centres and to more specialized industrial and distributive centres. In this situation, potential migrants will be most familiar with the possibilities in the higher order centre next to them; the travel and social costs of movements to that centre are lower than for alternative centres.

This urban distribution is uncommon in Latin America as we have seen in the second chapter. The size of a country and extended communications produce approximations to this spatial organization and Brazil and Chile are good examples of this situation. Even in the case of Rio de Janeiro in Brazil, Perlman (1976,70) reports that most migrants among her sample of low-income families came directly to the city. In general, however, the development of primacy has meant that regional urban systems are often weakly developed and direct commercial, social and political relationships have arisen between even remote rural areas and the primate city. Thus, in a study of Guatemala City I found that 60 per cent of migrants to the city came directly from a very large variety of small and intermediate size villages (Roberts, 1973a, 69–70). Similarly, in the Mantaro valley of Peru villages which were within several miles of each other differed considerably in the destinations of their migrants; some went predominantly to the provincial capital, other villages sent their migrants predominantly to Lima and others to mining centres (Roberts, 1976b). The observed differences were best accounted for by the commercial and social relationships already established between a particular village and a work centre. Browning (1971) also notes the predominance of direct migration in Mexico.

The understanding of both stage and direct migration in underdeveloped countries requires, then, a detailed analysis of the marketing and institutional organization of rural areas. Very few rural centres acquire sufficient strategic importance to become the focus of migration for an extended hinterland; instead, local marketing tends to increase dependence on, and linkages with, the major cities. This pattern is described by Johnson (1970) as a dendritic model of urbanization in which one or two urban places predominate and other centres are organized in vertical relationship with them.

Arthur Conning (1972) documents some of the institutional reasons for differential outmigration from rural villages in a study of seven villages in a poor region of the coastal plain of central Chile, equidistant from the major urban centres and metropolitan areas of Chile. He found that in the villages which were most dependent on agriculture (and most exposed to the crop blight which had impoverished the region), there was proportionately less migration to urban centres than in those villages which were more closely integrated into the national political and economic system. These latter villages he considered as more differentiated, having better communications and more commercial, educational and government facilities. However, in the most rural villages, the rate of rural to rural migration was higher than in the more differentiated villages. Thus, in the poorest villages, people seek local work opportunities, while in those villages with better contacts with national centres, migrants are more likely to seek the better-paid jobs in urban centres.

The processes we have been examining result in one major uniformity in city-ward migrations in Latin America: migrants, whatever their origins, arrive in the largest urban centres as a result of some prior contact or information. Many migrants have jobs or lodging assured them before arrival in the city. Married men will arrive before the rest of their families if job or accommodation is uncertain and exploratory visits to the city are common before final settlement (Roberts, 1973a, 47–96). The fact that most migration is relatively short-distance migration makes these prior contacts feasible. Most large city migrants have family or friendship contacts on arrival and these are often instrumental in obtaining work for the immigrant (Cornelius, 1975, 22; Perlman, 1976, 69–79; Browning, 1971). The importance of these contacts is illustrated by Whiteford's (1975) study of seasonal workers in sugar cane production in Argentina; these often seek work in large urban centres, such as Beunos Aires, but are unlikely to remain there. These seasonal workers, many of them Bolivian, have few contacts or relationships in Argentinian cities and without such relationships many prefer to settle in Salta, the provincial capital of the cane region where they do have contacts, despite the scarcity of employment opportunities in that centre.

The pattern of migration to Latin American cities has similarities with migration into the English industrial town of Preston in the nineteenth century. Anderson (1971, 37–67) stressed the importance that kinship assumed in helping migrants adjust to the urban-industrial situation; migration to Preston, as to other industrial towns in England, was predominantly short-distance. The one qualification to the predominance of short-distance migration in city-ward migration in both Latin America and in nineteenth-century Europe is that the larger the city the more likely it is that its migrants come from greater distances (Morse, 1971a; Weber, 1899, 283).

The contribution of migration to urban growth

The danger in the analysis of both direct and stage migration is that it sometimes leads to excessive emphasis on the city as the inevitable and final destination for migrants, ignoring the possibility that city-ward migration is one among several lifetime strategies that people adopt in underdeveloped countries to cope with the difficulties of pursuing stable careers in *either* rural or urban areas (Roberts, 1976b). In the last section, we noted that urban populations are often floating populations, seeking job opportunities at a particular stage in their lives, but with the possibility of moving back to the village or on to another place if opportunities offered. To provide an idea of the characteristics of these circular migration movements, I will use data drawn from a survey that I conducted in the central highlands town of Huancayo in Peru, whose population is currently 125,000.

In Huancayo over half the adult male population born in the town had migrated elsewhere to work or study for periods of more than a year; the adult male population is predominantly immigrant and some 60 per cent of that population was born outside the city. Of these immigrants about a quarter originated in Lima and in the coastal provinces near to Lima; the majority of these adult males estimated that they would return eventually to their place of origin. These migrants from Lima and the coast were mainly employed in government administration, in the professions or in the larger trading establishments; some of them had arrived in Huancayo as part of an administrative or business career and would shortly move on. Others had come to take advantage of the active commercial life of the city and, when they had built up a little capital, they would leave for the coast.

A similar range of commitments is found among those who had migrated to Huancayo from the nearby villages of the central highlands of Peru. A higher percentage of such migrants expected to spend the rest of their lives in Huancayo than did migrants from Lima; however, a substantial percentage of these immigrants planned either to return to their home villages, investing any money saved in the city in building up their farms or in establishing a small rural business, or to move on to other work centres such as Lima. Lima was not a permanent destination even for these migrants. Our surveys in the small villages of the area indicated a high percentage of migrants who had returned from Lima, often in a late stage of their life-cycle. Of Huancayo's present population, approximately 30 per cent of the adult males (excluding those born in Lima) have spent one or more years in Lima, indicating that migration to even a capital city should not necessarily be regarded as a definitive commitment.

Other studies such as that of Chi and Bogan (1975) in four communities of the Chancay valley of Peru, also demonstrate that return migration is a frequent phenomenon and not simply confined to those who failed to find adequate work in the city. The village retains its attraction in face of the city, especially when it continues to offer some basic security, such as access to land, housing or opportunities to trade. Such security acquires particular significance at certain periods of the life-cycle such as old age or early child rearing, when the uncertainties of life in the large cities become more acute.

Also, the importance of migration in urbanization must not obscure the equally important fact that the population of even a fast-growing city is often mostly born in that city. Davis (1932, 310) has calculated the proportion of urban growth attributable to the natural increase of urban populations and found that in the less developed countries, 43.2 per cent of urban growth in 1960–70 was the result of natural increase, which accounted for 38.4 per cent of the growth of their *city* populations.

In many Latin American countries migration has played a less important part in urban growth in recent years than has the natural increase of the urban population. George Martine (1972) provides a case study of the growth of Rio de Janeiro since 1920, showing the decreasing importance of migration in that city's growth over time.

In the period 1920 to 1940, internal migration accounted for at least 60 per cent of Rio's growth to 1,764,100; international migration accounted for another 15 per cent and natural increase for the remainder (Martine, 1972). By 1950, the city's population was 2,377,450; 69.1 per cent of the increase was accounted for by internal migration and 4.1 per cent by immigration. In 1960, a population of 3,281,910 had increased 45.6 per cent through migration and 45.2 per cent by natural increase. By 1970, natural increase accounted for 57 per cent of population growth.

In Guatemala City, approximately 40 per cent of the city's growth between 1950 and 1964 was due to immigration (Roberts, 1973a, 28). About one third of Mexico's urban population growth from 1960 to 1970 was the result of migration and, in contrast to previous decades, between 1950 and 1970 natural increase was more important than migration in the growth of urban population (Cornelius, 1975, 16; Unikel, 1975, 395–400). The annual rate increase of Mexico's total population in 1960 to 1970 was 3.37 per cent and the rate of growth of the urban population was 5.37 per cent (Unikel, table 2).

The absolute number of rural outmigrants in Mexico is now greater than in previous decades when migration was the predominant factor in urban growth; since Mexico's urban population is now larger than its rural population, even a relatively small percentage contribution to urban growth from migration means a large outflow from the rural areas. As a country urbanizes, natural increase within the city becomes an increasingly dominant contributor to urban growth simply because of the sheer size of the urban population relative to the rural population (Davis, 1972, 310).

The preponderance of migration in urban growth thus occurs mainly in the first stages of rapid urbanization. Not all Latin American countries began to urbanize at the same period and consequently in those countries which were already in a late stage of urbanization migration may appear to have been less of a 'problem' than in those countries, such as the Central American countries, which have only just begun their urbanization. Even within highly urbanized countries, the importance of migration to urban growth will vary according to how recently established the urban centre is or, to differences between cities in their rate of growth. Intermediate sized cities are now often growing much faster than the very large cities. Thus, in Brazil, cities such as Brasilia, Curitiba and Fortaleza have grown much more rapidly and more as a consequence of internal migration than the larger cities of São Paulo, Rio de Janeiro or Recife (Fox, 1975, table 4).

The contribution of migration to urban growth is, however, a cumulative one; children of migrants born in towns or cities are counted as part of the natural increase of urban places. Consequently, even in those countries in which net migration contributes a minor fraction of urban population growth, the migration experience may still be an important one in the urban social structure. Stella Lowder (1976) has calculated, for example, that in Lima, Peru, the chances of a child who was born in the city having both parents who were also born there is less than one in ten. Furthermore, since migrants are disproportionately drawn from those age groups who are economically active (14–60), the adult and working population of a city may be predominantly migrants even when the majority of the population has been born in the city, since a large part of this majority is likely to be made up of children under 14.

Internal migration is also more significant to urban growth than it might appear from the statistics. As we noted above, the urban populations of Latin America are, in some respects, floating populations. A city grows not only through the addition of the newly born or the migrant to an existing stable population, but also through the increasing flows of people who pass through the city and who are recorded as the resident population at the census points. Even those born in a city may not have resided there for their whole lives; many will have left to work elsewhere, often in other urban areas, before returning to their native city.

Despite these variations in migration patterns, the overall trend in city-ward migration is increasingly to concentrate populations in the large cities of Latin America. Robert Fox (1975, table 5) shows that in the six major Latin American countries of his survey, the large cities (250,000 and more) increasingly concentrate the urban population; in 1960, they contained 63.5 per cent of the total urban population and by 1980 he estimates that they are likely to contain 69.6 per cent. The shift from economies orientated to the export of primary products to those which are internally focused and based on urban industrialization has thus intensified population concentration in Latin America.

Browning (1972a) shows that up until the 1960s, there was an increasing trend towards urban primacy in all but one of the eight major Latin American countries. The exception to the trend is Brazil, but in this case the exception is produced by the emergence of a bi-city primacy (Rio and São Paulo). It is unlikely that the pattern of increasing primacy will continue in the second half of the twentieth century; in Mexico and Brazil, it is the secondary cities that have been growing faster than the primary ones in recent decades. Using Fox's (1975, table 4) projections of urban population in 1980, there is some indication of a decline in primacy. Primacy is likely to decline in the second half of the twentieth century because the scale of immigration required to maintain very high rates of growth in cities of over a million people is increasingly unlikely. Also, as Unikel (1975) points out for Mexico and Faria (1976, 200–19) for Brazil, economies are now sufficiently complex spatially to enable intermediate size centres to grow partly as a result of the diseconomies of scale of the largest cities.

In general, however, there are few underdeveloped countries in which there is, at present, a balanced urban growth based on a thriving regional network of small and medium-sized urban service, commercial and industrial centres. This concentration of population is not simply the product of a desperate rural poverty, but appears to be based, in part, on the attraction of the city and of its economic opportunities for the better-off members of rural society. For such people to move to the large cities and, by and large, to stay in them, suggests that the city economy has some capacity to absorb the increasing numbers of the economically active population. Since the city economy is increasingly dominated by capital-intensive industry, with a low power to absorb labour, we need to look more closely at the structure of the urban economy to understand how employment opportunities continue to expand.

Conclusion

In Latin America, the counterpart to the concentration of economic activities in urban-industrial centres is an increasing diversification of the agrarian structure. The transformation of that structure by the infusion of capitalism remains a partial one, which is likely to be felt most sharply in the rural areas close to the most dynamic cities. Elsewhere, various forms of agricultural production coexist and complement each other: peasant farming expands as a means of colonizing new regions or of exploiting crops which are not commercially viable under other forms of production. The improvement of communications and the generalization of money wages have commercialized the village-level economy, but without transforming it completely into capitalist production. Seasonal labour, often provided by peasant farmers or at times by agricultural workers residing in towns, powers plantations and commercial farms. The result is a situation in which the rural areas retain part of the natural increase in their population and their characteristic economic activities become those of petty trading, petty commodity production and labour intensive farming. The household remains a significant unit in the local economy, but the migration of family members and the fragmentation of economic enterprise undermines its basis as a unit of production.

Centripetal as well as centrifugal forces act upon the rural structure dispersing population, but over a lifetime attracting migrants back. These movements and the commercialization of most rural areas mean that the distinction between rural and urban is not a great one. Economic enterprise spans rural and urban locations. The patterns of consumption of the village may be different in scale from those of the town, but they are not different in kind. Transistor radios, television and refrigerators are found in villages. Canned foodstuffs, bottled drinks, detergents, insecticides are sold in village stores. This is the result of the type of industrialization discussed earlier. It is a sufficiently powerful force to undermine the basis for village craft production and to create wants that cannot easily be satisfied by subsistence farming; but industrialization has not expanded production and employment sufficiently to transform the structure totally. We will find that this uneven development appears in the cities also.

5
The urban economy and social stratification

It is now time to examine more closely the workings or the urban economies of underdeveloped countries. So far the argument has concentrated on the macro-economic and political forces that have shaped contemporary industrialization. It is now necessary to look at the effects of this industrialization on urban employment and on the distribution of income. We can thus tackle the issue of the coexistence of wealth and poverty, modernity and traditionalism in cities of underdeveloped countries. The previous analysis has suggested that such apparent paradoxes can often be explained in terms of the way in which capitalism has expanded in underdeveloped countries. If we are to persist with this claim, it will be necessary to show that the 'traditional' activities of low productivity carried out by the urban poor are linked to, and affected by, contemporary industrialization and by the consumer preferences this industrialization has engendered. Otherwise it would be possible to argue that urban poverty is simply the result of an overurbanization, in which the subsistence activities that have long characterized the rural areas of underdeveloped countries are transferred to the cities.

In pursuing the argument, it will help if we keep in mind two crucial differences in the context of industrialization between contemporary underdeveloped countries and Britain in the nineteenth century. One of these is the presence of a strong, centralized state which, in many underdeveloped countries, has become one of the chief propagators of economic development. The other is that the industrial activities with which contemporary underdeveloped countries begin their industrialization are large-scale and of a high technological level. The channels for transferring technology from advanced to less developed countries are richer than they were in the nineteenth century, leading to rapid transfer and, as we shall see, to a premature displacement of craft production (Felix, 1977).

I shall begin by examining the nature of the linkages between the modern economy and the large numbers of the urban population who are apparently marginal to it. I shall examine the claim that there exists a dual urban economy in which the modern sector is clearly segregated from the subsistence activities of the poor. (See Brookfield, 1975, 54–62, for a discussion of economic development theorizing about dualism.) The existence and growth in numbers of the urban poor suggest, instead, that they fulfil, in a variety of ways, functions as a reserve army of labour for the growth of the modern sector of the urban economy. I shall examine how these functions are fulfilled, seeking also to understand why the poor appear to collaborate in their own exploitation. We need consequently to consider the types of social mobility and class conflict that are produced by this uneven urban economic growth. In the early period of industrialization in Latin America, the existence of extensive opportunities for social mobility was one factor that reduced the class militancy of urban low-income workers. The present economic situation is, in most cities, a very different one: urban incomes are becoming more unevenly distributed and the opportunities for good jobs are expanding less fast than is the urban, economically active population.

Dual economies

An emphasis on the distinctiveness of the two sectors in the urban economy appears in the studies of Clifford Geertz (1963b) in Indonesia. Geertz distinguished between the bazaar economy and the firm economy. The bazaar economy is made up of a large number of small enterprises, which are highly competitive among themselves, which rely on the intensive use of labour, often drawn from the family, and which seek to minimize their risks rather than seek profit maximization. In Geertz's studies, the bazaar economy was mainly found in commercial and personal services—the tertiary sector of the economy. Geertz emphasizes the economic 'irrationality' of the bazaar economy with its large number of *ad hoc* exchanges and its tendency to use labour intensively rather than to raise productivity. The bazaar economy has its counterpart in the rural areas in the tendency to agricultural involution in which increasingly refined techniques of labour utilization absorb extra farm labour, but diminish per capita productivity (Geertz, 1963a, 90–103). Geertz's point is that the bazaar economy prevents capital accumulation and represents a way of life and a means of absorbing surplus labour; it is not conducive to economic development. The firm economy is based on rationalizing production and capital accumulation for further investment and expansion. In Geertz's distinction, the two economies are antithetical to each other. The expansion of the firm economy gradually displaces the bazaar economy by providing a cheaper and more convenient product or service. Likewise, the existence of the bazaar economy limits capital accumulation and can hinder the expansion of the firm economy.

Terrence McGee (1971) extends Geertz's analysis beyond the characteristics of the tertiary sector to examine the systems of production implied in the bazaar and firm economies. He draws on Franklin's (1965) studies of peasant economies to show that the logic of the bazaar economy is that of the household economy. The preoccupation of the household economy is not simply profit but the most effective use of the labour of its members. Thus, jobs which offer little return will be taken on if they allow a household to make use of the labour of one of its members, such as a young child or elderly relative. McGee uses the analysis of the bazaar economy to show that urban–rural distinctions are often misleading as a means of understanding the nature of economic change in underdeveloped countries. The bazaar economy is found in both rural and urban areas and represents a basic strategy of social and economic survival. Its importance in urban areas responds to the shift in the economic dynamic of underdeveloped countries from the agrarian structures to the cities. Populations seeking employment opportunities increasingly turn to the cities and, in order to exploit these opportunities, use similar forms of family-based economic organization which have long prevailed in the countryside. The urban, bazaar economy is thus a dynamic form of economic activity, with a considerable capacity for absorbing labour and representing the transfer of the peasant mode of survival to the cities of underdeveloped countries (McGee, 1971).

The subsistence base of the urban bazaar economy is provided partly by its exchanges with peasant producers and partly by ownership of the tools of the trade and of urban plots of land. The urban bazaar economy is interlinked with the firm economy through a flow of goods and services, just as the peasant economy is linked with capitalist agriculture through labour services. The basis of the bazaar economy is, in this perspective, the internal flow of goods and services, just as in the peasant economy subsistence agriculture remains the basis for economic survival. Some new activities, such as bicycle repairing, are found in the bazaar economy, but the activities are transitional ones which will be displaced eventually by the expansion of the modern economy.

In McGee's (1971, diagram 1) model of these relationships, the flow of goods and services between the urban bazaar economy and the urban firm economy are relatively insignificant compared with the flow of goods and services between the urban bazaar economy and the peasant sector. This dualism in urban economies is thus viewed as an extension of the type of dualism which has long characterized underdeveloped countries, in which an export-orientated commercial sector was juxtaposed to peasant agriculture (McGee, 1971, 165).

This model of the bazaar economy is useful for understanding the early stages of rapid urbanization where the boundaries between city and countryside are often unclear. In his descriptions of southeast

Asian cities, McGee refers to those 'suburbs' in which small-scale agriculture continues as a supplement to urban work. The lots on the periphery of these cities are sufficiently large to allow some animals to be kept, vegetables and fruit to be grown; the shack houses a family in which several members journey to work in the city leaving others (perhaps an elderly relative or a young child) to cultivate the plot. This same kind of mixing of urban and rural occupations has been reported for other underdeveloped regions of the world. In Pons's (1969) description of colonial Stanleyville, in the then Belgian Congo, the housing of low-income urban workers was often located in compounds which permitted animals to be raised and crops to be grown.

When I was working in Guatemala City, I was at first surprised to find the quantity of animals that was kept, even in the densely inhabited squatter settlements; chickens and even pigs were a common sight. Indeed, one of my informants criticized a government project to relocate the squatter settlements on the grounds that it would not work since there would be no place for the families to raise their animals. He himself made a substantial part of his living from butchering pigs which he bought when young, kept in his shack and fed on the refuse of the shanties. These possibilities of the bazaar economy developing a subsistence basis need, however, to be compared cross-culturally. In a comparison of Peru and Guatemala, I pointed out that the interrelationships of the urban bazaar economy and the peasant economy were much stronger in Peru because of the commercial vitality of the Peruvian peasant economy (Roberts, 1974). Likewise, smaller provincial cities, such as Salta in Argentina and Huancayo in Peru, will be more conducive to this development than the large metropolitan cities (Whiteford, 1975; Roberts, 1976b). The smaller places are also more likely to develop interchanges with the peasant economy. Not only will transportation costs be lower between smaller urban places and peasant villages but peasant agriculture and crafts are more likely to flourish close to small provincial cities than to large centres. The size and income distribution of the large urban centre will encourage, as we noted with respect to São Paulo, the development of capitalist agriculture in its vicinity.

With increasing urbanization and larger city sizes, the independent basis of the bazaar economy will be eroded as a larger proportion of the consumption of even the poorest classes become dependent on the market. This change in the consumption patterns is closely related to an increase in the economic and spatial complexity of a city. With increasing complexity, it becomes less likely that work can be obtained close to place of residence. This implies that the costs of the journey to work become a part of most families' budget. Oliveira (1972) and Lopes (1979) both comment on the increasing commercialization of the budgets of low-income families in the large Brazilian cities.

Most food is purchased in local markets and, in the case of São Paulo, this food is increasingly produced on *capitalist* farms close to the city and not in the peasant sector. Canned and other processed 'convenience' foods become an element in the diet of poor families when the wife or other female family members work outside the home and have less time to invest in lengthy food preparation. Other costs, such as educational and health expenses, begin to figure in the budgets of low-income families; amusements such as cinema, sport and gambling become part of family budgets. The budgets of even low-income urban families are thus likely to include an increasingly large expenditure on goods and services which, directly or indirectly, are derived from the firm or modern sector of the economy.

There are several budget studies carried out in urban areas of Latin America which demonstrate the implications of this trend. Webb (1974), for example, reports that in Lima some 75 per cent of the expenditures of families whom he classes as belonging to the traditional sector of the urban economy are spent in the modern sector of the economy. He calculates that a similar proportion of the goods and services of the traditional sector must be 'exported' to the modern sector. As Hart (1973) points out in an account of the 'informal' economy of Accra, in Ghana, some of these transfers may be illicit ones as in the case of robbery or prostitution; but the implication is the same, that the bazaar economy is closely interrelated to the modern economy and, over time, is less likely to have a significant, independent basis for subsistence. John Wells's (1976) survey of consumption patterns in São Paulo and Rio de Janeiro shows that the urban working class is, in fact, an important market for durable consumer goods. In this Brazilian case, the availability of credit facilities enabled even the poorest strata of the two cities to purchase televisions, refrigerators, radios and electric or gas stoves. The poorest 50 per cent of families in São Paulo used almost 11 per cent of their expenditures on debt repayments, mainly for domestic utensils and furniture. Wells suggests that the expenditure on consumer durables by the poor was, to an extent, at the expense of clothing.

These considerations indicate why the type of urban economic dualism which favoured economic growth in Japan does not emerge in Latin America, or possibly in other underdeveloped areas. In Japan, modern, large-scale firms producing mainly for export could keep their workers on low wages since the consumption preferences of these workers remained largely for traditional goods. Felix (1977) remarks on the significance of the Japanese case where, up to the 1950s, about half of urban Japanese household expenditures were on products of Tokugawa origin. The strength of demand for indigenous goods meant that craft industry in Japan was protected from competition from factories based on imported technologies.

In contrast, the integration of Latin America into the world market from the time of the Spanish and Portuguese conquests has created patterns of consumer preference similar to those of the advanced capitalist countries; the control of Latin American markets and of Latin American production by foreign companies reinforced such consumer preferences. The demonstration effect of the high standards of living in the advanced industrial countries had, perhaps, a greater effect in Latin America than in other underdeveloped areas where a local culture has persisted which is sharply distinct from that of the developed world. The small-scale sector in Latin American cities does not, then, cater for the special wants of a segment of the population. There are no truly neighbourhood economies with markets based on goods and principles of organization distinct from those of markets catering to the 'modern' part of the city.

Under these conditions, craft industry and many services in Latin America are adjuncts to the large-scale sector of the economy, producing those goods for which the market is so reduced and so risky that large-scale enterprises are not interested to enter. Consequently, the small-scale sector is left with activities of low profitability that do not permit capital accumulation, making it unlikely that enterprises in this sector will develop into large-scale ones (Eckstein, 1975).

My distinction between the small-scale sector and the large-scale sector is necessarily a crude one, serving to highlight one of the major features of urban economic organization in underdeveloped countries. I define the small-scale sector to include all activities which are not carried out within factories or by those services associated with large-scale production, such as financial and professional services, large retailing and wholesaling establishments or transport and construction enterprises possessing substantial amounts of capital equipment. The small-scale sector includes craft workshops, repair shops, petty traders and the gamut of self-employed artisans or odd-job men and women. We can, for the moment, leave domestic service out of this scheme. The contrasting importance of the two sectors for employment and productivity is brought out in the following table taken from Pinto and Filippo's (1976) analysis of income distribution in Latin America, based on data from ECLA. The modern sector corresponds to what I call the large-scale sector and the intermediate is roughly the small-scale sector. The primitive sector is mainly concentrated in the rural areas (table 5.1).

Table 5.1: Latin America: average productivity per employed person by strata within each sector and population percentages at end of 1960.

	Total		Modern		Intermediate		Primitive		Ratio of productivity in modern stratum to productivity in primitive stratum
	Percentage of employment	Average productivity in dollars at 1960 prices	Percentage of employment	Average productivity in dollars at 1960 prices	Percentage of employment	Average productivity in dollars at 1960 prices	Percentage of employment	Average productivity in dollars at 1960 prices	
Total	100.0	1371	12.4	5909	47.7	1194	34.3	203	29
Agriculture	42.2	694	6.8	4830	27.7	830	65.5	205	24
Mining	1.0	6484	38.0	15606	34.2	1420	27.8	246	63
Manufacturing	13.8	2517	17.5	8938	64.9	1400	17.6	220	41
(a) Industrial	7.7	4168	28.1	9800	71.9	1960	—	—	—
(b) Artisan-type	6.1	419	4.1	1760	55.9	470	40.0	220	8
Construction	4.5	1116	24.8	2322	55.9	800	10.3	203	11
Basic services	5.5	2174	25.0	4276	71.6	1530	3.4	220	19
Trade	10.1	2731	14.0	8990	76.1	1990	9.9	340	26
Other services	17.3	1283	16.2	2713	70.5	940	13.3	160	17

Source: Estimates taken from ECLA, *La mano de obra y el desarrollo económico de América Latina en los últimos años*, E/CN.12/L.1 (Annex).

The economic and spatial significance of the small-scale sector

The small-scale economy is not traditional either in the techniques it uses or in its type of activity. Thus, in our studies of Huancayo and Lima in Peru, we found that the activities that predominated in this sector were complementary to the most productive and tecnhologically sophisticated of the large-scale sector.

In Huancayo, which is an important transport centre, automobile and truck repair workshops proliferated; these were small-scale, informally organized enterprises, but the repairs they undertook and the equipment they used were modern. These enterprises did not have the range of equipment of the repair workshops attached to the large car companies, such as Volkswagen; but between them, they assembled a range of equipment adequate to their tasks. One workshop might undertake general repairs and also have specialized equipment for welding and panel beating; another might specialize in installing mufflers and another in engine jobs.

Traditional activities, such as artisan production of cloth or pottery, are not significant components of the small-scale economies of Latin American countries, though certain types of artisan production, such as jewellery, 'craft' pottery and weaving may find a lucrative market among tourists and high-income families. In the city of Huancayo, set in the 'traditional' highlands of Peru, such activities accounted, at the most, for ten per cent of the employment within the informally organized sector of the city's economy. In Guatemala City, the employment of squatter settlement inhabitants was in the same way anything but traditional; their jobs were in the construction of modern buildings, in transport, in repairing radios and television, in making modern clothes and shoes with the use of a sewing machine and with synthetic material, often imported from the United States. (These points need not be laboured; readers can consult the extensive accounts of economic activity in the informal sector provided by Leeds, 1969, 1971, and Machado de Silva, 1971, for Brazil, by Peattie, 1968 for Venezuela, by Hart, 1973 for Ghana and by Eckstein, 1975, for Mexico.)

The place of the small-scale economy within the urban economy is similar to that of domestic out-work and petty commodity production in the early stages of the Industrial Revolution in England. Thus, in cities of the underdeveloped world, the self-employed worker or small, family enterprise is often dependent on merchants or larger-scale enterprises who provide the capital or the materials. These large-scale operators sell the product in their own shops or use it to complement their own production, as when a shoe factory commissions out-workers to trim shoe leather.

Alison Scott (1978) provides a suggestive account of these relationships between the large-scale economy and independent artisans, small-scale enterprises and casual workers. She points out that the independence of those working outside the large-scale economy is largely illusory. In the situation of Lima, in Peru, very few of the self-employed or of the small enterprises can survive without developing relatively stable relationships of dependence with larger enterprises, to obtain credit or to secure a stable market for their products. Under these conditions, complex networks of production develop in which a modern factory may commission a small, family enterprise to undertake part of its production and, in turn, this enterprise may hire out-workers. Scott provides examples of these networks in the construction sector, in manufacturing and in transport, citing the assembly of refrigerators, the upholstery of microbuses and dressmaking. However, she stresses that, although the independence of these workers and small, family enterprises is largely illusory, they do retain a sense of control of their situation, based at times on ownership of the tools of their trade or of small amounts of factory equipment.

In contrast to the situation in nineteenth-century Britain, these forms of production do not appear to be disappearing in the face of the growth of the factory system (Hobsbawm, 1969b). Indeed, as Scott indicates for Lima, the large-scale sector of the economy fosters the development of other forms of production. One consequence is that in Lima the number of the 'self-employed' continues to increase, so that between 1940 and 1972 this category grew from 79,396 to 264,097 persons. Salaried labour grew much faster, but the proportion of the self-employed in the labour force remained constant.

The basic reason for survival of the small-scale sector of the urban economy is that it is a convenient complement to the large-scale sector. Large-scale enterprises may be unprepared to risk expanding their fixed investments in face of an uncertain market for their product and of fluctuations in demand. It is more profitable to expand production, when necessary, by the out-work systems described earlier, since workers in these can be laid off with little cost when market demand drops. The market for many products in underdeveloped countries is inherently uncertain. Low-income groups mainly spend on inferior quality products which can, at times, be produced competitively by small-scale enterprises; they also have a high demand for repairs, cheap servicing and second-hand goods, leading to the substitution of parts and 'cannibalism' from other products. High income groups demand luxury consumer goods and specialized artisan production of items such as furniture, pottery or clothing. In very few cities of the underdeveloped world is there, in fact, a relatively developed and integrated mass market for factory production. In addition, some industries are faced with seasonal fluctuations in demand, such as in the textile or food and drink industries.

The importance of the small-scale sector of the economy depends on the extent of the middle- and upper-income market. When the size of these markets makes large-scale investment in manufacturing, in commerce and in other services profitable, then the small-scale sector may be gradually displaced. For example, supermarkets, large-scale repair workshops and car-washing machines gradually eliminate the small operator in those cities and in those residential areas where there is a large middle- and high-income market. This development depends, in part, on contemporary urban planning. Single-class residential suburbs, which are emerging on the outskirts of most Latin American cities, encourage car ownership and make profitable large modern garages, shopping centres with supermarkets and department stores.

These variations in the employment structure of cities in underdeveloped countries are part of the international and national social division of labour. We saw, for example, that the high concentration of employment in factories in Britain in the late nineteenth and early twentieth centuries was possible because primary and, to a certain extent, tertiary employment was concentrated in other countries within the British orbit. Also, the 'marginal' employment situation of London in the late nineteenth century, with a heavy concentration of employment in the service sector, was due in part to its function in commercializing, distributing and finishing the factory products of the north of England. Thus, the thousands of seamstresses working under sweat-shop conditions in London complemented factory production in a relationship similar to that between the large- and small-scale sector of underdeveloped economies. Likewise, some countries in the underdeveloped world are taking on what Wallerstein (1974b) describes as a semi-peripheral position, in which they act as intermediate agents for the technological dominance of the core capitalist countries. In countries such as Brazil and Mexico, for Latin America, manufacturing employment in the modern sector has expanded, partly because these countries export manufactures to both developed and underdeveloped countries. These exports are usually basic manufactures, such as textiles or shoes, but they also include cars and electrical goods. Such production is not a sign, as we have seen, of self-sustaining development, but it can create an expansion of employment opportunities in the large-scale sector of the economy.

Within underdeveloped countries, certain cities take on core roles with respect to less developed regions and their cities. This difference is reflected in employment structures. In Brazil, for example, both Rio de Janeiro and São Paulo have higher proportions of their economically active populations employed in the transformative sector than do the less economically prosperous cities of Belo Horizonte, Curitiba and Porto Allegre. These cities, in turn, have a higher proportion of their population employed in the transformative sector than do the less developed cities of the north, Recife, Salvador, Belém and Fortaleza (Faria, 1976, 227; Kowarick, 1975, 149–68). The respective employment ratios of the three groups of cities in terms of tertiary employment to secondary employment are 1.77, 2.26 and 2.83. These differences in employment between the three groups of cities are also reflected in differences in mean family income, industrial productivity and the per capita expenditures on social services (Faria, 1976, 228). On all these variables São Paulo and Rio de Janeiro have significantly higher indices than do the other cities.

Despite these variations, the co-existence and articulation of the large- and small-scale sector is an evident feature of cities in the underdeveloped world. Indeed, this articulation continues to be an important element in the industrial growth of even advanced capitalist countries. In Catalonia in Spain, for example, industry uses outwork systems extensively, not only in textiles but also in engineering and electrical goods. In one case, a modern factory delegated the production of a component of a domestic appliance to a smaller enterprise which in turn sub-contracted to females working in their own homes and to a small workshop. Gordon (1972) has indicated how enterprises often organize their production within the United States to take advantage of cheap labour. Likewise, the analysis of international labour migration suggests that the use of cheap labour continues to be an important element in the expansion of most advanced economies (Castles and Kosack, 1973).

The difference in the underdeveloped situation is one of scale: since markets are more limited and uncertain than in the advanced capitalist world, an extensive small-scale economy is a necessary means of reducing risk and increasing profits for the large-scale sector of the economy. Under these conditions, it is premature to view the small-scale economy as simply an expedient and transitional form. The articulation of small-scale and large-scale economies is likely to limit the expansion of the large-scale sector. This articulation limits the development of a mass market for industrial products and removes incentives towards further rationalization in production and in organization. Industrial managers who base a part of their profitability on dealing informally may not, as a consequence, pay much attention to the latest precepts in economic planning and in plant organization.

The organization of the labour market

The above account of the relationship between the small- and large-scale sectors tells us little about how the labour market is organized in Latin American cities. It might be supposed that the availability of an abundant supply of labour, with experience of jobs that are often similar to those found in the large-scale sector, would be an inducement to adopt more labour-intensive techniques in industry. Also, if this labour supply was fulfilling the classic functions of an industrial reserve army, we might expect wages in the large-scale sector to be under considerable downward pressure; yet, as we shall see later, wages in this sector are many times higher than in the small-scale sector.

The first thing to be noted about labour in the Latin American urban economies is that it is highly mobile geographically. There is little evidence of the type of localized labour markets that Hobsbawm (1964) describes for nineteenth-century London. He notes that a uniform London labour market was emerging in this period even in those industries that were not organized by trade unions, but many trades and their workers were concentrated in certain parts of the city. He stresses the immobility of London labour tied to a walking distance from work to home of three to four miles and dependent for work, in the casual trades, on local contacts.

In contrast, workers in Latin American cities are likely to work far from their place of residence. I calculated that workers from a squatter settlement which I studied in Guatemala City were employed in 15 of the city's 19 zones and that 70 per cent of them worked outside their zone of residence. Similar trends have been reported for other large urban centres in Latin America (Kowarick, 1977). Mobility is facilitated by cheap transport, provided in many cities by small private enterprises which keep costs low by working long hours and using ramshackle buses and taxis. The major factor affecting labour markets is the ease of access to employment. The labour market for the large-scale sector is a highly differentiated one. In part, this is due to the relative scarcity of the skills demanded by this sector. Educational provision in Latin America has been inadequate to the needs of modern industry, both in vocational training and in educating people to secondary school or university standard. Shortages of skilled workers, technicians and professionals are often cited as major bottlenecks to the further industrial development of the continent (Lyons, 1965).

It is also likely that these shortages are artificially created. Balán (1969) noted a tendency to credentialism by which firms demanded qualifications for entry (such as primary or high school certificates) that were not strictly necessary for the performance of the job. Indeed, the recruitment practices of Latin American industries do not encourage a competitive labour market. In many countries, this is the result of the types of agreement reached under populist regimes through which labour unions controlled access to jobs in the large-scale sector. In Mexico, for example, recruitment to a stable job in many large industries depends on the union's prior agreement. However, restrictions on the hiring and firing of certain categories of workers are also present in situations where unions are relatively weak, such as in Monterrey in Mexico. Aside from the question of skills, large-scale enterprises are, in fact, likely to prefer a stable and reliable labour force to a cheap one. The low ratio of labour to capital costs in these enterprises means that industrialists are preoccupied less with high wages than with having production disrupted by industrial strife or with the low level of commitment of the workforce.

The prevalent practice of cheapening labour costs within large-scale enterprises is that of maintaining large wage differentials between a skilled, permanent workforce and a more temporary semi- or unskilled one. Kowarick (1975, 117–23) shows that large-scale enterprises have a high rate of labour turnover and that even the most technologically sophisticated branches of production made extensive use of semi- and unskilled labour. The temporary category is often used as a means to avoid social security obligations and to retain the firm's right to dismiss workers: a 'temporary' worker may, in fact, work many years for the same firm. The temporary workforce is often recruited through the family and friendship networks of the permanent workers, who are at times made responsible for the good behaviour of those whom they sponsor (Roberts, 1978a).

The unskilled workforce of the large-scale sector is often recruited from, and returns to, the small-scale sector. Access to employment in the small-scale sector is unrestricted. The type of craft production that prevails is of a routine nature and often consists in the assembly of ready-made parts. Even the self-employed require little capital since they often receive credit from merchants. Small stores proliferate, for example, in poor areas on the basis of credit, a small amount of savings and a very limited stock. This type of enterprise is the only basis of a neighbourhood economy among the poor, generating, according to one estimate, between 5 and 16 per cent of employment in squatter settlements (Lewis, 1973, 298).

Workers in the small-scale sector look for work wherever they can get it. The contacts they need to obtain work are not based on locality and often consist of relationships with people working in enterprises in the large-scale sector. Thus, in his account of the informal economy in Rio de Janeiro, Luis Machado da Silva (1971) stressed the importance of self-employed or unskilled workers developing an extensive set of relationships with engineers and other professionals or even with janitors of buildings who could give information about the need for domestic help or for repair work. In my account of the two low-income neighbourhoods in Guatemala City, I stressed the extent to which job careers are unstable, involving shifts from one ill-equipped workshop to another or including attempts to peddle merchandise around the city. The rapid growth of Guatemala City entailed considerable competiton among low-income workers for jobs, increasing instability of employment and decreasing the returns to the individual worker. I described the job career of one such worker in the following terms: 'In 1956, he lost his job shortly before the factory closed due to the bankruptcy of the owner. He set up independently as a tailor in the zone. At first, he claimed to do reasonably well and soon bought sewing machines and hired assistants to help with the work. Then his business failed and Luis began to work in small tailor shops. He describes his work in this period from 1956 onwards as moving from shop to shop in search of adequate work. He claims that, due to competition from Salvadoran products, it was becoming increasingly difficult to get enough work to make ends meet. Where before he was given five pairs of trousers to work on in a day, he was now given five pairs to work on in a week' (Roberts, 1973a, 134).

In contrast, conditions in the large-scale sector are not competitive. The limited market and the scale of the enterprise mean that a few large firms dominate. The kind of competition that handloom weavers offered to the power loom in Britain in the early nineteenth century is not possible under contemporary conditions. The new technologies often make a product that cannot be produced by simpler means and, even when this is not the case, the differences in productivity are enormous (see table 5.1).

Wage and salary earners in the large-scale sector thus have greater power than those outside it to negotiate better living conditions. They work under common conditions in large organizations whose economic potential is not only great but is known to those working within it. In contrast, 'at the other end of the scale, we can observe the opposite features. The labour force shows little capacity for organization owing to its fragmentation into a multiplicity of small units, to the low economic solvency of its organizations and its limited access (especially in rural areas) to adequate data and advisory services' (Pinto and Filippo, 1976, 98).

The urban economy is thus organized in such a way that exceptional premiums are obtained by capital, and by technical and skilled labour. This is the basis for urban income inequalities and for the widening of these inequalities in periods of economic growth. For example, in Brazil the inequality of the non-agricultural income distribution increased sharply between 1960 and 1970, so that whereas in 1960 the top 5.8 per cent of the employed received 29.8 per cent of monetary income, in 1970 they received 37.9 per cent (Fishlow, 1973). This increase in inequality was due, in part, to the widening of wage differentials among workers. This wage stretch has been attributed to the demand for skilled workers in an economic growth based mainly on capital-intensive industry (Morley and Williamson, 1977). There was also, as Wood (1977) shows, a drop in real family income in São Paulo.

The result of the type of dualism that has been discussed is that the inequality of income distribution is considerable throughout Latin America. In 1970, the poorest 30 per cent of the population had an average per capita income that was estimated to be 39 times less than that of the top five per cent. Even when the next poorest 50 per cent is considered (the group most likely to include the urban working class), their average income was ten times less than that of the top 5 per cent (Pinto and Filippo, 1976). There is a clear concentration of poverty, as Webb (1974) shows, in the small-scale sector of the urban economy in which the income curve is relatively flat and undifferentiated compared with that of the large-scale sector. However, inequality of income distribution is not simply a question of the difference in earning potential between the small and large-scale sectors.

As we noted above, widely different conditions of work exist even within the large-scale sector. (See Kirsch, 1973, for an overview of the heterogeneity of industrial employment.) Muñoz (1975) has analysed the incomes of workers in Mexico City, showing that all sectors of employment have a proportion of workers earning below the minimum wage of approximately 100 dollars a month (table 5.2). The workers earning below 100 dollars in large-scale enterprises are, in the main, the 'temporary' workers.

Table 5.2: Percentage of workers earning less than 100 dollars a month, Mexico, 1970 (%)

Size of enterprise	Manu- facturing	Con- struction	Distributive services	Producer services	Social services	Personal services
Small	37.7	34.3	33.6	30.6	24.0	50.7
Large	17.5	21.7	16.9	—	5.9	29.5

Source: Muñoz, 1975.

In Muñoz's study, the inequality of income is greater in manufacturing and the services most closely associated with it (producer services) than in other sectors. Thus, the highest income groups in the manufacturing sector (managers and proprietors) obtain, on average, monthly incomes that are seven times greater than unskilled workers and five times greater than skilled workers. Managers and proprietors in finance and business earn, on average, fifteen times more a month than unskilled workers in their sector and six times more than skilled workers. Capital-intensive industrialization thus produces significant income inequalities in the urban sphere, first by the differences in income between the large modern sector firms and small enterprises and then, by the wide income differences found *within* modern sector enterprises.

Social mobility and class relationships

It might be objected that these income inequalities represent too static a picture of urban economies in underdeveloped countries, concealing a social mobility whereby, for example, children improve on their parents' economic position as the economy expands to provide an increasing number of better-paying jobs. The economic trends reviewed in chapter three suggest, however, that the possibilities of a rapid improvement are limited. Capital-intensive industrialization creates relatively few technical or skilled jobs in comparison with the numbers of semi-skilled or unskilled jobs created in the large- and small-scale sector of the urban economy. Kowarick (1975, 116–17) points out that the number of skilled workers continues to be a very small percentage of total workers in Latin America, and that even in São Paulo enterprises, skilled workers are only 23.8 per cent of the total workers. A study of occupational mobility carried out in São Paulo in the 1960s showed that, if anything, members of the working population were downwardly mobile when compared with their parents (Berlinck and Cohen, 1970).

Reliable social mobility studies are hard to come by for Latin America and those that are available are often so different in their methodology that comparisons between them are hazardous. One of the few studies that has tried to provide data comparable to those of studies in developed countries is that by Balán, Browning and Jelin (1973). Monterrey has experienced a rapid industrial expansion powered, in part, by migration from the surrounding and, often, predominantly agricultural regions. Some of Mexico's largest and most modern industrial enterprises are located in Monterrey. It is thus a situation in which fairly high rates of social mobility might be expected, since by Latin American standards the expansion of the large-scale sector has been an exceptionally fast one and part of the workforce has been recruited from people of rural origin.

The study shows that in Monterrey there is less occupational mobility than in developed countries. One of the reasons for the difference is that in Monterrey, as in other Latin American cities, education is closely associated with occupational attainment. Kirsch (1973) provides data from several Latin American countries showing the high degree of association between non-manual work and secondary and higher educational qualifications. In Monterrey, education is more essential for occupational mobility than it is in developed countries, where the generalization of high levels of education has meant, necessarily, that education discriminates less among job seekers.

The near monopoly that the upper and middle classes have of secondary and university education in Monterrey has, it seems, become one of the main means by which their children obtain jobs of similar status to their parents. The authors report a certain amount of mobility and, for example, middle-class men in the older age groups are mainly of working-class origin. They note, however, that credentials such as union membership and education are now becoming more important whereas in the past entry into modern enterprises was relatively unrestricted. For succeeding cohorts, then, there are likely to be fewer possibilities for those with little education or from farm origin to become occupationally mobile. The conditions of poverty such as malnutrition and the need to have children work at an early age also suggest that the educational levels of the poor may not improve sufficiently to offset the growing importance of educational credentials. In fact, education in Latin America seems to be one of the factors that perpetuates inequality. The scarcity value of education and its use as a credential reinforces, I would suggest, the distinction between manual and non-manual work and increases the premium paid to non-manual occupations. The premium paid to the scarcest educational qualifications (professional and technical ones) is, in fact, considerable (table 5.3).

Table 5.3: Mean monthly earnings by occupational group, Mexico City males, 1971 (in US dollars)

	$
Professionals and technicians	417
Managers and proprietors	551
White collar (clerical and sales)	221
Skilled workers	134
Unskilled workers	85

Source: Muñoz, 1975, 226.

The rapid increase in Latin America of private schools catering mainly for the middle classes suggests that in recent years education has become one of the major mechanisms through which these classes appropriate a greater share of the national income (Roberts, 1973b). Equally, there have been considerable middle-class pressures to increase the amount of well paid, non-manual employment. Some of the fastest rates of increase in service employment have been among the predominantly white-collar services in which average incomes are high, such as government services and those provided to industry (Muñoz and Oliveira, 1976).

The size of the non-manual labour force has increased considerably in the most industrialized Latin American countries, reaching an estimated 32.3 per cent in Argentina in 1970, 19.2 per cent in Brazil, 23.2 per cent in Mexico, 26.7 per cent in Chile and 34.5 per cent in Venezuela (Muñoz and Oliveira, 1975). The concentration of non-manual occupations is much greater in the large cities; in Mexico City, for example, 45.6 per cent of the city's male labour was classified as non-manual in 1970 (Muñoz, 1975, 84). Of this percentage, 16.9 per cent were professionals, technicians and managers and the rest white-collar workers.

The income of professionals, technicians and managers means that they are practically the only group that can easily maintain a stable status (see table 5.3). Income provides access to good schools, to segregated housing, and enables the elites to restrict their interactions to their own groups. The degree of income concentration occurring with capital-intensive industrialization means that high income earners are likely *both* to spend on consumer durables and to take advantage of 'cheap' personal services. Thus, in cities of the underdeveloped world there is a considerable demand for domestic servants and for other kinds of personal services. Indeed, the abundance of domestic servants in these cities is directly produced by the demands of the higher income groups. It is in the most developed Brazilian cities (São Paulo and Rio) that domestic service expanded most rapidly as a proportion of all service occupations from 1950 to 1970; in contrast, domestic service declined, in the same period, as a source of service employment in the less developed regions of the northeast (Kowarick, 1975, 167).

This reliance on domestic and personal service is part of the social structure of Latin American cities. Income concentration depends, in part, on the social status of non-manual work; the patterns of social interaction that develop in this situation enforce the tendency for the middle and upper classes to release themselves as far as possible from manual inputs. Women from these classes are 'freed' from the drudgery of work in the house, the carrying of packages and so on. Such freedom allows more time to engage in the social activities—clubs, coffee drinking, sport—that reinforce the economic and social position of these classes (Lomnitz, 1971). Domestic and personal service is thus an important component of the reproduction of the class position and advantages of the privileged groups in underdeveloped countries.

The position of the other classes in the cities of underdeveloped countries is often not clear-cut. Categories such as self-employed, wage earner or proprietor are, as we have seen earlier, more ambiguous in their meaning than is usually the case in developed economies. They imply very little in terms of the independence of the worker or the stability of his job. Indeed, a starting point for the analysis of class relationships is the recognition that, for all but a relatively small number of urban dwellers, occupational position does not entail a relatively fixed and coherent set of status attributes. For the mass of the population the urban milieu is quite heterogeneous. Members of the same family may have completely different job positions, some in the small-scale sector of the economy and others in the large-scale sector. People in the same neighbourhood and even in squatter settlements differ widely in their job position. Geographical mobility continues to be high in Latin American cities, with people moving back and forth from other urban areas or from rural areas.

Also, in place of a division between employers and a mass of industrial workers, employment in the services is more important in Latin America than it was in either Europe or the United States at a comparable moment in their development. Service employment is quite heterogeneous, including government, the professions, domestic service, commerce and entertainment; moreover, the poorest-paid service worker is likely to work in isolation from other members of her or his class, as in domestic service. Cardoso and Reyna (1968) show that around 1880, when the United States, France and Italy had abour half their population in agriculture, they had 26 per cent, 23 per cent and 14 per cent respectively of their employment in the service sector. In contrast, in 1960 when Brazil, Mexico and Peru had about half their employment in agriculture, they had 35 per cent, 30 per cent and 31 per cent respectively of employment in their tertiary sector.

The dynamic of the small-scale sector

To complete this overview of class situations, we need to explore the fragmentation of economic relationships within the small-scale sector. The persistence of forms of labour other than that of wage labour creates a complex social situation within cities of the underdeveloped world. Elizabeth Jelin (1974), basing her analysis on date from Salvador in Brazil, has distinguished four main forms of economic activity outside the large-scale sector of the economy—competitive capitalism present in small and medium-sized firms; family enterprises relying on the intensive exploitation of family members; self-employment in a variety of activities; and domestic service, which can be seen as complementing other forms of economic activity by substituting for the household work of family members whose skills can be devoted to other activities.

Access to the high-income sector of the economy provides the stimulus for entrepreneurial organization in the small-scale sector. Savings from work in the large-scale sector, indemnity payments after leaving work in the mines, the sale of a plot of land, are some of the sources of capital which, in Peru, enabled people to set themselves up in small-scale enterprises. Those who achieved most developed stable relationships with the large-scale sector of the economy. One of the most successful market wholesale traders in Huancayo was a man who had once been a miner and now, on the basis of his previous work contacts, had secured contracts to supply the mines. Another was a family which, until recently, had secured contracts to supply fruit to soft drinks firms in Lima.

To secure and build upon these advantages, the entrepreneurs of the small-scale sector need to cut their cost and provide highly competitive services. This is achieved, in part, by an intensive exploitation of available labour. Family labour is used to its fullest extent; young children run errands, mind the shop, check that loading or unloading is being carried on. Older relatives may sit for long hours minding a shop or selling small quantities of goods that are surplus to the main enterprise. This pattern of organization warns us against assuming too quickly that the individual engaged in what appears to be almost profitless activities is an isolated economic unit. Small-scale market sellers, small shopkeepers, people offering to wash cars and so on, often appear to make little or no income and, in surveys of poverty, are classed among the desperately poor. They are undoubtedly poor, but it is important to examine the houshold and not the individual as a unit of economic enterprise. Many apparently unremunerative occupations are but the tip of an iceberg in which other members of the household earn the major incomes and the person in question simply contributes to his or her upkeep, while minding the children, keeping an eye on the store and disposing of otherwise wasted products. Thus, Robert Lewis (1973) calculated that low-income residents in Lima's *barriadas* offset the risks of unstable employment by increasing the number of people employed per household from the 1950s to the 1960s. This increasing household employment also accounted for part of the rise in the real income of these families.

Entrepreneurship in the small-scale sector is also based on developing organization through personal relationships and trust. The small-scale enterprise cannot afford to take on inflexible commitments; the risks and uncertainties of the competitive market in which it operates makes such commitments hazardous undertakings. For example, a small-scale trader cannot commit himself easily to delivering a fixed quantity of goods at a fixed price over a period of time when he has no control over production or transport. Such a trader prefers to operate with tacit understandings with a variety of purchasers, producers and transporters; he will develop a wide network of contacts among all these categories to ensure that he can maintain a reasonable volume of business without running the risk of over-extending his or her credit or liabilities.

These strategies are important elements in the dynamic of the small-scale sector, since those who operate within it are constrained to seek actively for new contacts to maintain and expand their businesses. This flexibility in operation is a reason for doubting the usefulness of the concept of peasant modes of production in the urban sphere (Franklin, 1965). In the small-scale enterprises I observed in Guatemala and Peru, labour commitment, which is a vital component of the peasant mode, was never a prime consideration of the entrepreneur. The entrepreneur took on the labour of family and friends when he needed it, but equally he laid it off when business was slack. Likewise, there was no evidence that the entrepreneur developed activities simply to occupy household members. It is more useful to focus attention on the *network* of exchanges and obligations which develop in the small-scale sector.

Unskilled workers anticipate the temporary nature of their work by seeking out other job opportunities weeks in advance of the likely end of their job (Machado da Silva, 1971). There are important elements of reciprocity in these work relationships since contacts for a job are repaid by providing information about sources of work in the future, or by giving help on a specific project (Lomnitz, 1977).

Kinship ties, relationships with fellow-villagers or with co-believers are thus important elements in the dynamic of the small-scale economy. These relatively intensive types of relationships provide a basis for trust in economic relationships. Since a great part of the transactions within the small-scale sector depends on tacit understandings and is not directly supervised by the entrepreneur, success depends on working with those one trusts. I am using trust in the sense of being able to anticipate behaviour and having the security of being related to the other by a set of interlocking relationships (Roberts, 1973a). Entrepreneurs, for example, may have to trust individuals with relatively expensive equipment, such as a tricycle vending cart; this trust is less likely to be broken when that individual is someone who interacts with the entrepreneur in other situations than the economic one—as a kinsman, member of the same church, supporter of the same football club. The costs of violating trust are higher in such situations, since the individual would have to forego other important activities of his urban life.

Social relationships provide the basis for quite sophisticated economic organization. Norman Long (1973) has shown how what is in effect a large-scale trucking company in the highlands of Peru was built up through the social relationships of the individual owners. These owners formed a village-based *fiesta* association which included farmers and traders; they were also related to each other by kinship and marriage. The *fiesta* association provided a convenient framework for exchanging information about possible loads, coordinating strategy to fulfil contracts or reward important officials. In these ways, making a living in cities of underdeveloped countries gives vitality to the patterns of social organization.

This degree of organization and enterprise must not obscure the fact that even the most successful small-scale entrepreneurs are not very successful. There are important limitations on accumulation within enterprises of the small-scale sector. Since they are informal they have little access to government or private credit and thus little possibility of capitalizing the enterprise. Credits in underdeveloped countries go to the large enterprises. Thus small-scale enterprises are labour-intensive and highly competitive with each other; and productivity and profits are relatively low. An accident to a truck or machine can effectively wipe out many small-scale sector entre-preneurs.

The expansion of enterprise is limited by the span of control of the entrepreneurs; he will usually prefer to proliferate his enterprises rather than increase any one enterprise in size. Increasing the size of an enterprise makes it liable to government regulation and reduces the possibility of trust developing between employer and employees. In Peru, we found that entrepreneurs in the small-scale sector preferred to invest spare capital in setting up another enterprise whose management they would delegate to a son or other relative; some of these linked enterprises constituted quite impressive investments and in several cases merited listing the entrepreneur in the Peruvian National Biography. However, no single enterprise employed more than four or five people.

These forms of enterprise limit capital accumulation, but they do give the small-scale economy a high degree of flexibility; linked enterprises mean, for example, that the failure of any one enterprise does not necessarily affect the others. Resources and labour can quickly be allocated to exploit new opportunities and shifted out of declining ones.

This discussion warns us of the difficulties of analysing employment and class relationships in cities of the underdeveloped world from the viewpoint of individual members of the labour force. Both poverty and class relationships are determined by the structure of the economy and, in particular, by the relationship between the large-scale sector and the small-scale sector. The small-scale sector is one of unstable employment and low incomes, but it is a highly organized sector which creates opportunities for economic survival for most city dwellers. These opportunities are distributed on the basis of household membership and of other relatively intimate social relationships. It is a small minority of the labour force which is totally isolated from these relationships.

This circumstance does not make poverty a benign condition, but it does help us understand the economic activism of the poor. Declining real standards of life in cities lead families to expand household employment, using all available labour; the networks of the small-scale economy facilitate these strategies. Poverty under the conditions of the small-scale economy means a constant struggle, but it does not imply passivity in the face of overwhelming difficulties, nor does it imply social isolation (Lewis, 1952).

The heterogeneity of low-income groups, their job and geographical mobility prevent the development of strong class consciousness and class organization. The types of economic arrangements which have been described in previous sections individualize the problem of making a living: they obscure, on the one hand, the exploitation that the working class suffers at the hands of the bourgeoisie; on the other hand, they create the sense of economic opportunity for the enterprising individual.

This situation is illustrated by the employment figures for Latin American metropolitan areas in 1970 (Kirsch, 1973, table 9). Some of the rates of unemployment, such as Bogota's 13.1 per cent are very high, but in other metropolitan areas, the rates vary between 4.7 per cent (Greater Buenos Aires) and 8 per cent (Caracas). Open unemployment is not, however, the crux of the problem; the poverty of these cities consists of the very large numbers of people who are underemployed either because of the small amount of work they can get or because of extremely low wages in jobs of very low productivity. In this way, the urban economies of underdeveloped countries create ambiguous job statuses: a worker is not simply employed in the large-scale sector or unemployed, but there are a variety of intermediate statuses (Kritz and Ramos, 1976). The source of the poverty of the working class is obscured; it does not appear as a direct result of the employment practices of the bourgeoisie or of the state.

The situation changes when sectors of the population become more directly dependent on the state or an employer. For example, Perlman (1976) describes the growth of radicalism among low-income populations in Rio after their relocation in a government housing project from a squatter settlement. Difficulties in paying the rent and deficiencies of services led these residents to take on critical attitudes to the government and to begin to organize to defend their interests. In fact, the major force for change in class relationships is likely to be the increase in state intervention in the urban economy. The further development of the large-scale sector of the economy requires substantial investments in economic infrastructure, especially in improved communications and in land-use policies favouring industrial concentration, such as industrial 'parks' (Yujnovsky, 1976). These expenditures not only limit the money available to improve the living conditions of the mass of the population, but they lead to an increasing formalization of land use, restricting the easy access to conveniently located housing or work space that was one element in the dynamic of the small-scale sector. We need, then, to look briefly at the reasons for increasing state intervention in the economy, identifying if possible the sources of variation between countries.

State intervention and the urban economy

State intervention is the underlying factor in the articulation of the large-scale sector of the economy with the small-scale sector. To understand how this takes place, we need first to examine the ways in which the state has become an important participant in the economies of underdeveloped countries. We saw earlier that the origins of this participation lie in the relative weakness of national bourgeoisies in face of technological dependence on the advanced capitalist world and of the large-scale investments needed to acquire such technology.

In underdeveloped countries, the intervention of the state in the economy has been marked in the period of capital-intensive industrialization. Glaucio Dillon Soares (1976) brings together data from Latin America and from Europe and the United States at the period of their industrialization to show that state intervention is greater in the underdeveloped world than it was in the advanced world at the time of its economic development. This intervention is also of a qualitatively different kind in contemporary underdeveloped countries to that of the state in developed countries. The state in underdeveloped countries invests a major part of its funds directly in economic enterprises (Baer *et al.*, 1976). These range from works of economic infrastructure such as roads and other communications to direct investment in basic industries such as mining, oil and steel. This investment may diversify to include shares in petrochemical and even durable consumer goods industries.

As the state has taken on the prime responsibility for sponsoring economic development, so too employment has expanded within the state apparatus. The state's role in economic development requires an extensive bureaucracy for planning and coordinating economic effort. In underdeveloped countries, unlike the advanced capitalist countries in the early stages of industrialization, the state cannot delegate economic development to market forces. The importance of negotiating with foreign countries or with multinational companies, the expense of modern technology and other factors mean that the state in underdeveloped countries develops cadres of trained personnel to supervise the economic process.

Indeed, the structure of the underdeveloped economy necessarily requires the expansion of state employment. Apart from the employment involved with organizing the large-scale sector of the economy, considerable employment is generated in planning ministries to control those sectors of the population outside the large-scale sector of the economy in the urban small-scale sector or in petty agricultural production. The expansion of the police and armed forces in underdeveloped countries is directly related to the economy of underdevelopment. At one level, army personnel may serve as development agents in remote villages, helping to construct roads, build irrigation ditches and so on; all Latin American armies have this developmentalist side to them. More fundamentally, the expansion of police and armed forces has responded to fears of internal subversion and social discontent (Cotler, 1970–71).

This degree of state intervention in the economy has placed significant limits on the development of nationally based private enterprise in underdeveloped countries. These limits already exist, as we have seen, in the nature of capital-intensive industrialization. The state reinforces monopoly tendencies by 'rationalizing' industrial investment to avoid wasteful use of scarce capital. State intervention has limited the development of private enterprise capitalism in another way also: it has meant the restriction of the crudest forms of exploiting labour. Minimum wage legislation and the extension of social security benefits to workers is a common feature of all Latin American economies. Since the state has used its revenues to finance economic expansion, it has also tended to place the costs of social security and welfare on employers. In contrast to the developed world, the underdeveloped state spends only a small proportion of its revenue on social services (Soares, 1976). Indeed, taxing of modern sector enterprises through compulsory social security payments on behalf of workers is one source of state investment funds. Naturally, large-scale sector enterprises derive the compensating advantages of secure markets and high productivity which, in part, is guaranteed by government subsidies or foreign exchange manipulation.

In this situation, state economic intervention creates the basis for the relatively dynamic relationship between the large- and small-scale sector of the urban economy. The small-scale sector of the urban economy survives in the interstices of state regulation. Small-scale sector enterprises make a profit, partly because they lie outside direct state regulation. Small workshops of less than five people, street peddlers or small shops do not incur the overheads of large-scale sector enterprises; they do not pay social security for their workers, they pay below the minimum wage and they pay few, if any, direct taxes. Without these costs, small enterprises can be quite competitive in the production of certain basic goods such as clothing. In Huancayo it was the small workshops producing a range of woollen and cotton goods, not the textile mills with their outdated machinery, that survived the competition from imported textiles (Roberts, 1976a). The transport network that provides low-cost transport for people and goods on the unpaved roads of the highlands of Peru is controlled by informally organized small enterprises. Their profits depend on *not* complying with state regulations governing minimum wages, social security, health and safety. Whereas the small enterprise can more easily avoid such costs, the large-scale enterprise is unlikedly to find it worthwhile to make such savings.

Governments vary, however, both in the scale of their intervention in the economy and in their style of intervention. A way of understanding these variations is the analysis, outlined in chapter three, of the relative strengths and weaknesses of national bourgeoisies, of the industrial working classes and of state institutions. In Brazil, for example, in which there is a strong internal and foreign-linked bourgeoisie, state regulation of the economy has suppressed workers' wages to such an extent that there is relatively little difference between the wages of unskilled and semi-skilled workers in the large-scale sector and those in the small-scale sector. In such a situation, employers may have less incentive to farm out routine work to the small-scale sector. In the 'enclave' countries such as Peru, where the national bourgeoisie was weak, the state under nationalist pressures imposed strict labour regulations on the predominantly foreign-controlled large-scale sector of the economy. This regulation has been so tight that there is a sharp difference in labour costs between these enterprises and the small-scale sector. This has led, in recent years, to the proliferation of arrangements whereby large-scale sector firms farm out work to the small-scale sector.

The greater readiness of the Brazilian state to intervene radically in the urban economy is shown in the policies of eradicating squatter settlements from the centres of cities such as Rio. Squatter settlements that once occupied the hillsides close to Rio's centre have been pulled down and their inhabitants relocated to the periphery of the city. The squatter settlements will be replaced by high-cost residential and commercial developments. In contrast, in Lima the state has sought to regulate and stabilize squatter settlements, granting such settlements legal recognition as 'young towns' (*pueblos jovenes*). Such differences between countries in state intervention remind us that the relative strength of central government and of the classes which compete for its attention continue to be important variables in determining the urban–industrial stage of economic development.

Conclusion

One of the most striking features of the urban economies of underdeveloped countries is the persistence of an apparently traditional sector of small-scale enterprise. In those underdeveloped situations, as in Latin America, in which consumer preferences are similar to those of the developed countries, the small-scale sector is unlikely to have an independent basis on which to develop. The small-scale sector survives as a complement to the large-scale one, taking on those tasks which represent too risky or too limited a market for the large-scale sector. Under these conditions, the possibilities for capital accumulation are negligible. Competition within the small-scale sector and the abundant labour supply drives down wages and profits.

The small-scale sector may benefit from economic expansion since such expansion is likely to reduce unemployment and underemployment; but the position of workers in the small-scale sector may worsen in comparison with those in the large-scale sector whose wages and salaries rise faster in periods of economic expansion. Even within the large-scale sector, however, there are marked differences in income between unskilled workers, skilled workers and white-collar workers. An important feature of class relationships in the cities of underdeveloped countries is the extent to which the distinction between intellectual work and manual work entails substantial differences in income. This distinction is reinforced by the growing importance of credentialism in the labour market. On the one hand, education is a prerequisite for entry into jobs in the large-scale sector and distinguishes manual workers in that sector from those in the small-scale sector. On the other hand, their higher levels of education justify the high salaries paid to technical and professional workers.

Growing income inequalities have not resulted in an increase in overt group and class conflict, partly because of the considerable geographical mobility that is still characteristic of the population of many underdeveloped cities. More important, however, is the fragmentation of much of the working class in small enterprise. Their economic and social relationships are organized around the day-to-day possibilities of making a living, which inhibits the development of broader class organization and action. A force making for change in this situation is the growing role of the state in the urban economy. State intervention is one of the major factors explaining variations in the relationship betwen small- and large-scale sectors of the urban economy. As control of the economy becomes centralized and cities are planned to maximize efficient economic use of space, so too the actions of the state may conflict with the interests of the mass of the urban population. Forced to live far out of the city, with inadequate transport and service facilities, the poor may develop an awareness of their common situation despite the heterogeneity of their occupations.

6
Urban poverty and coping with urban life

So far we have concentrated mainly on the economic aspects of uneven urban development. Even so, political and social relationships have figured prominently in the discussion of the workings of the urban economy and in this chapter these relationships come to the forefront of the analysis. This account will be more ethnographic than previous chapters, attempting to provide some feeling for the quality of life in Latin American cities. The following description of social relationships, religious practices, the problems of housing and of local-level politics may seem far removed from our previous concerns; yet these details enable us to appreciate the extent to which all aspects of life are affected by the pattern of economic expansion that has occurred in underdeveloped countries.

There is also an analytic purpose since we need to explore the ways in which the sheer necessity of coping with urban life sets social and political forces in motion that may affect the path of economic development. This is our chance to bring the individual back into our analysis as someone who is not simply the puppet of forces beyond his or her control, but as a force contributing to shaping the course of events. The individuals will be, in this case, from the low-income populations of the cities and we will explore the extent to which their activities, unplanned and unorganized as they may be, make up undercurrents of change in the political and social structure. We need, then, to see whether the class struggle in the cities of underdeveloped countries, is manifest in other ways than through the actions of political parties and labour unions.

The account to follow will be organized around the theme of social marginality. This has been an important issue in the literature on Latin American urbanization. It is a convenient issue for our purposes since whereas I have chosen to emphasize the integration of the poor into the economic system as the basis for many of the current problems of underdeveloped countries, the marginality perspective has stressed that it is the isolation of the poor that is to blame.

Poverty and social marginality

On most indices of well-being, the situation of the urban poor in underdeveloped countries is appalling. There is widespread malnutrition and mortality rates are many times higher among these groups than among the middle classes, or among low-income populations of the developed world. Even in the more prosperous and economically dynamic cities, such as São Paulo and Belo Horizonte, infant mortality is high among the low-income population and, in recent years, the rate of infant mortality has been rising (Wood, 1977; Kowarick, 1977). The proportion of the urban population that barely subsists is also very high. In Latin America, recent estimates suggest that between 20 and 30 per cent of the urban population have incomes that are insufficient for adequate levels of food and shelter. Kritz and Ramos (1976) show that about 40 per cent of the employed in a sample of Latin American cities have fluctuating incomes that often put them on the fringe of poverty. Although conditions vary from one underdeveloped country to another, it is likely that urban conditions are no better and are probably worse in other underdeveloped areas, such as India and southeast Asia.

Urban poverty is not simply a matter of individual income; it is part of the spatial and physical organization of the cities. These cities are underurbanized in terms of the availability of housing. In Mexico, for example, a group of urban planners estimated that the urban housing deficit would reach 5 million units by 1980 (Araud *et al.*, 1975). Squatter settlements provide housing for between 10 and 20 per cent of the population of many large cities in Latin America. In Asia, figures of 25 per cent of the population of Djakarta and Kuala Lumpur and 26 per cent of Singapore's population are quoted as living in squatter settlements (Laquian, 1971). Squatter settlements are usually rudimentary housing of wood, thatch or even cardboard constructed by the residents on public and private land which they have illegally occupied. Even where land is legally settled with its owners sub-dividing and selling in small lots, the first residences often build the houses with their own labour and materials.

In most large cities of the underdeveloped world, there is also a severe shortage of public services. Many city roads, especially on the outskirts are unpaved; public water supply reaches low-income areas of the city through public hydrants serving a large number of families; and adequate sewage disposal systems serve only a small proportion of the urban population. Health facilities are unevenly concentrated in the richer areas of the city; in low-income areas, a clinic with one doctor may serve over 10,000 people. Educational facilities are also unevenly distributed with the higher-income areas having private schools and better state school facilities; low-income areas such as shanty towns have rudimentary school buildings and overcrowded classes.

The various facets of capitalist development—land speculation, income concentration, capital-intensive industrialization—combine to exclude low-income populations from the benefits of economic growth. This issue has been discussed by Anthony Leeds (1974) in his account of the interlinked processes by which low-income urban populations are unable to obtain adequate housing, incomes and urban services in Brazilian and other Latin American cities. He points out that, despite the diversity of occupational, residential and family situations among the poor, they experience a common set of frustrations in which the 'exclusiveness' of the elites are apparent. These include the practices of public agencies or credit agencies in providing a very limited access for low-income people; these must queue for services and are aware that they receive indifferent treatment (Roberts, 1973a).

Exclusion is also apparent in the uncertainty of tenure of low-income residents; squatter settlements are always liable for demolition and those in rented and government assisted projects can easily be removed for default in payments or nuisances caused by children. Restricted hiring practices in modern enterprises are, as we noted earlier, means by which large segments of the workforce are excluded from stable, high-income work opportunities. These common situations are linked through the activities of work, seeking and defending housing, householding and daily urban activities; no significant group of the low-income population is exempt from them.

The lack of adequate housing and of social services is, some would argue, directly related to the type of urban economic growth that we reviewed in the last chapter. Wells (1976) points out that in Brazil the scarce investment in collective consumption (schools, public services) releases resources for production and for private consumption. Thus, in most Latin American cities, it is common to find radios, televisions and refrigerators even in the poorest squatter settlements. The exclusion of the poor then, is *not* an exclusion from the market for consumer goods.

Since these situations are part of the dynamic of the capitalist system, Leeds argues that it represents the proletarianization of the mass of the urban population. He claims (Leeds, 1974, 84) that this proletarianization 'is even more strongly delineated, less alleviated by "affluence", less ameliorated by great masses of better-paid, highly skilled wage earners, less softened by opportunities for upward mobility, less responsive to political protest and electoral expression, and generally more repressive in the "underdeveloped" dependent societies than in the metropoles like Great Britain and the United States'.

This exclusion of the poor from access to an adequate income and to urban services, has given rise to what Janice Perlman (1976) calls the myth of marginality. In the following sections, I will review the data that show why it is inappropriate to see the poor as socially and politically marginal; but, first, I will outline the concepts of marginality that have perhaps most influenced the way that the 'problem' of urban poverty is viewed generally and acted upon by governments. The first of these concepts is that which sees marginality as consisting in the lack of participation of low-income groups in politics, in their 'traditional' attitudes and in their lack of access to education, health care and adequate standards of consumption. From this perspective, marginality is an unfortunate and avoidable consequence of rapid urban growth in the situation of underdevelopment; marginality is remediable through social welfare and educational programmes and through the creation of job opportunities. In Latin America, this concern with marginality became the basis of an extensive analysis, documenting the exclusion of substantial sectors of the population from the benefits of economic growth in the post-second world war period (Desal-Herder, 1968; Giusti, 1971). It also became the basis for what amounted to a political movement, often associated with Latin American Christian Democrat parties, aimed at remedying the dependence of Latin America vis-à-vis the developed countries.

This dependence was seen as remediable to the extent that the mass of the population could be organized to galvanize traditional structures (Vekemans and Giusti, 1969/70). The economic and political marginality of the mass of the population was seen to hinder this development process in several ways. Illiterate, poverty-stricken families living in urban slums, for example, were viewed as perpetuating from generation to generation feelings of hopelessness. Such populations were also seen as potential supporters of populist or authoritarian politicians and as constituting a barrier to stable democratic development. The remedy to marginality was seen to lie, in part, in the work of popular promotion; various types of cooperatives were to be set up among low-income populations as a means of engendering a spirit of self-help and as a means of promoting the internal integration of the poor. This perspective was one that emphasized the potential benefits to all social classes in ending the marginality of the mass of the population. Vekemans and Giusti (1969/70, 229) expressed this hope as follows: 'The marginal sectors would function as pressure groups to accelerate the process of incorporation, while the ruling elites would provide the guidelines for action and control the general co-ordination for development. Only thus could the nation states provide the basis for hemispheric integrations.'

The second and more complex view of marginality is Oscar Lewis's (1961; 1968) attempts to describe the life styles of the poor by means of the culture of poverty thesis. Lewis developed the concept of the culture of poverty on the basis of intensive observation and interviewing in Mexico City and, subsequently, in San Juan, Puerto Rico and New York. He saw the culture of poverty as most likely to arise in the situation of underdevelopment, in which there is a rapid urban growth without there being jobs in the modern sector of the economy and in which migration from the rural areas was an important component of that growth. He also stressed that his thesis applied to groups that had no strong basis of class or ethnic identity to sustain them in the face of the cumulative difficulties of urban poverty. Lewis argued that low-income casual work, poor living conditions and low levels of education made families and friendships unstable and unreliable. In this context, the culture of poverty develops through the generation of fatalistic orientations, emphasizing living for the moment. The culture of poverty is thus a sub-culture of the national one, enabling the poor to cope psychologically with a different environment.

The culture of poverty, according to Lewis, makes it difficult for people to escape from their impoverished situation even when some (limited) opportunities are provided; children brought up in the culture of poverty experience an unstable and often violent family life, have little chance of being educated and take on at an early age ill-paid and often illegal work. The culture of poverty thus acts to reinforce disadvantages from one generation to the next. Despite the self-perpetuating nature of the culture of poverty, Lewis viewed change as possible when structures were changed from above. At the time of his death, he was working in Cuba and argued that under its communist government, economic and political structures had been changed sufficiently to destroy the basis for a culture of poverty (Lewis, 1968; Butterworth, 1974). In the Cuban research, Lewis and his collaborators showed that incomes were still low in La Habana, but that participation in economic and political life had changed dramatically, creating a sense of optimism about future possibilities among low-income families.

The basic problem with these two views of marginality is that they are elitist in conception; the poor tend to be viewed as being incapable of improving their situation by themselves and change originates from above. Until that time, the poor are relatively ineffectual actors in the urban political and economic scene. Such approaches underestimate the resourcefulness of the poor and the extent to which they participate actively in urban economic and political life. For example, despite the rich texture of his descriptions of the problems facing the poor, Lewis paid little attention to the workings of the urban economy and to the nature of the interconnections, which, as we shall see, exist between the poor and other more powerful members of the city.

The significance of social relationships within the city

In this section, I shall examine the extent to which the urban poor, including rural migrants, are socially isolated and are given to 'traditional' patterns of behaviour. There have been frequent reports of the lack of trust and inter-personal hostility within low-income neighbourhoods (Carolina Maria de Jesus, 1963). Likewise, in some Latin American cities such as Lima and, more markedly, in African and Asian cities, ethnic identities and customs survive in low-income areas, appearing to ruralize the city. In Brazilian cities, magical rites have an extensive following among low-income populations in even the largest and most modern cities.

These and other 'marginal' features must be placed within the context of the patterns of development that characterize cities in the underdeveloped world. We have noted how, in the past, ethnic customs and 'traditionalism' were often the product of capitalist development; this argument can also be applied, with modifications, to the contemporary urban situation. For example, the importance of ethnic identity in urban situations is not simply a survival of rural practices, but is a direct response to the exigencies of survival in a competitive urban economy where economic opportunities are scarce. Ethnic identity permits a certain monopoly of jobs and clients and provides a basis for trust. This type of analysis has been used by Cohen (1969) in describing the significance of religious identification for a particular group of traders in Ibadan in Africa. Such an analysis is in the tradition of those British social anthropologists who showed that it was the urban situation, including its conflicts, anxieties and social interactions, that selectively reinforced rural traits or identities, as for example tribalism in African cities (Mitchell, 1966; 1957).

There is, then, little to be gained in categorizing behaviour as 'traditional', 'rural' or 'fatalistic'. It is more interesting to examine how, in the face of an economically uncertain environment, individuals use the cultural and social resources available to them and adopt a particular pattern of coping with the difficulties of urban life. The uneven development of the urban economy often implies a diversity of means by which people struggle, culturally and socially, not simply to survive but to better their position.

From this perspective, there is no reason to assume that rural migrants will have inherent problems in adjusting to urban life and to urban occupations. In fact, studies in Latin America have often shown that there is little difference between migrants and city-born in their occupational attainments, their education and their place of residence within the city (Gilbert, 1974, 111–20). A more interesting approach is to look at the resources, such as capital, social relationships, educational and other skills, that different groups of migrants and city-born are able to marshall to cope with urban life. The relative significance of the different types of resources will vary depending on the size of the city and its stage of economic development.

Balán (1969) used the concept of credentialism to stress that the disadvantages of migrants were not due to cultural inadaptation or to differences in capacity between migrants and city-born: 'This variable [credentialism] is of strategic importance in the present context, since migrants more often than natives lack the proper credentials. They may know how to read and write, but they lack the primary school certificate. They may be hard workers, but they lack a letter testifying to this fact. They may be skilled in their jobs, but they find it difficult to become members of the union that controls the jobs. Therefore, the more important credentials become, the more handicapped migrants tend to be.' Balán thus extends the discussion of education in the last chapter by emphasizing the way in which such attributes are used as means of selecting and excluding population in terms of the benefits of economic growth. Migrant marginality is a product of a type of economic development rather than of any innate incapacities in the migrant himself.

Among low-income families, the strength of kinship will vary with the urban situation of the individual and of the family. Thus, among small-scale entrepreneurs operating extended domestic enterprises, kinship relationships are important. Family events will be celebrated and there is intensive interaction between kin members both within the city and outside it. In contrast, those with jobs that do not require collaboration with trusted others are perhaps less likely, as Smith (1975a) reports for Lima, to maintain kinship ties. In the extreme case, a high degree of poverty and job instability in a city may undermine the stability of the nuclear household. Eames and Goode (1973) review a series of studies in the Caribbean and Central America that indicate that single-parent families and unstable households are the result of economic uncertainty. They suggest that under conditions of poverty and job instability, men may be unwilling to commit themselves to relatively permanent obligations; likewise, women may be unwilling to take on the liability of a permanent attachment when the man might prove a drunkard, unable to earn a living or prone to violence.

This explanation for marital instability in cities of underdeveloped countries emphasizes the elements of rational calculation entering into arrangments that, to the casual observer, may seem to be the result of individual and social disorganization. In my study in Guatemala, I found that 58 per cent of couples living together in the shanty town and 46 per cent in the legally settled neighbourhood were not married by either church or state. Guatemala is a Catholic country and many of these couples living in consensual unions were active church members. These unions were, on the average, very stable and, when I questioned families about marriage, I was often told quite explicitly that it was not worth being legally married since, apart from the expense, it meant that it would be more difficult to separate. The women, in particular, emphasized the risk of attachment to a man who drank too much, brought in no money and consumed her earnings. While these women were satisfied with their present union, they stressed that in a place like Guatemala the future was always uncertain.

Likewise, the number of social relationships which an individual or family maintains with non-kin, both inside and outside their neighbourhood of residence, depends on factors such as the level of income of a family, the location of their neighbourhood, age and the type of work of family members. Other factors are recency of arrival in the city and number of prior contacts in the city. For example, in my Guatemala study I found that older people travelled less frequently outside the neighbourhood, relied on neighbours or were dependent on others visiting them; likewise, poverty inhibited external visits because of the expenses of travel, but increased reliance on neighbours (Roberts, 1973a, 150–92). Those living in more centrally located neighbourhoods found it easier to visit outside the neighbourhood than did those in peripheral locations; from peripheral locations, travel to the centre involved considerable time and expense. More recent migrants and those without prior contacts in the city had less opportunity to develop extended relationships.

Despite these qualifications, both neighbourhood-based and city-wide networks are maintained by low-income families and it is rare for families not to have people on whom they can rely for help and information. Similar conclusions have been reached by, among others, Perlman (1976, 132–41) for Rio de Janeiro and by Peattie (1968) for Ciudad Guayana in Venezuela. Among the Guatemalan sample, the large majority of informants were able to cite people who would help in illness, with small loans, with advice or with help with a job (Roberts, 1973a, 167). In my observations of these families and in my trips with them around the city, I found that they had a relatively detailed knowledge of where kin, fellow-villagers and friends were living (Lomnitz, 1976; 1977).

The networks of low-income families provide a basis for inter-neighbourhood linkages whereby, for example, carnival or betterment committees in one low-income neighbourhood collaborate with those in quite distant parts of the city. There are examples of such linkages for Guatemala and Brazil (Roberts, 1973a; Leeds, 1974). Low-income families put much effort into maintaining and creating these social networks. Someone who happens to be in another part of the city on a job or errand, for example, will take the opportunity to call on an old friend and kinsman and exchange information about jobs, housing and the like (Roberts, 1973a, 150–92).

Kin living in different parts of the city will visit each other on holidays or meet in some public park or at a sporting event. Commentators on urban life in Latin America have frequently observed the vitality of social relationships and the extent to which kinsmen, friends, or fellow-villagers living in different parts of a city will maintain contact with each other (Kemper, 1974; 1977; Smith, 1975b). The social relationships of urban low-income families often include friends and kin in the provinces and, also, in foreign countries. Cornelius (1976) reports the extensive network of relationships maintained by Mexican urban and rural families with friends and kin who have migrated to the United States.

Indeed, the few studies of the behaviour of the middle and upper classes in Latin America indicate considerable particularism in their use of social relationships. The existing reports emphasize the significance of both kinship and friendship relationships for these classes, arguing that it is through the maintenance and manipulation of their social networks that the class advantages of upper- and middle-class families are maintained (Caplow, 1964; Leeds, 1964; Lomnitz, 1971). Lomnitz describes the importance of reciprocal exchange among the urban middle class of Chile; these exchanges included an extensive use of non-kin friendships. The exchanges were mainly of favours such as information and services, often connected with bureaucratic regulations. These exchanges often brought considerable economic benefit to the participants (Lomnitz, 1971).

Many upper-income urban families in underdeveloped countries depend on maintaining kinship solidarity for the success of new businesses. In Mexico City, recent immigrant groups such as the peninsular Spaniards have built up important economic enterprises partly on the basis of kinship ties. Spaniards migrating to Mexico in the early years of the century, found it difficult to conduct business because of the political and economic uncertainties of the country and could not rely on local businessmen and politicians to fulfil agreements.

It is also the wealthy in cities of the underdeveloped world who are most likely to develop 'provincial' attitudes to urban space. Most middle- and upper-income families confine their activities either to the centre of the city or to the relatively isolated residential suburbs in which many of them now live. Special recreational clubs provide additional enclaves for these families. The increasing use of the motor car in cities of Latin America reinforces this tendency for the middle and upper classes to avoid any use of public facilities or public urban space; thus, such classes rarely use public transportation, rarely walk streets outside the fashionable business areas and rarely shop in places used by low-income residents.

Even those families without many social relationships may find ways of obtaining social support. I attributed the development of Pentecostal and other sects in predominantly Catholic Guatemala to the attempts of those without extensive social relationships to develop the basis for such relationships (Roberts, 1968b). In the two low-income neighbourhoods I studied, members of the sects were often those without kin in the city and included women separated from their husbands or whose husbands were alcoholic. The self-employed were frequently found in these sects. The relationships established in the sects were reinforced through frequent meetings and travel, on church business, throughout the city, and were often the basis of business partnerships or of the exchange of economically useful information. I also found that the Catholic *hermandades* (voluntary religious groups) performed similar functions for other low-income residents. They provided the opportunity for single women with children, for example, to have a stable basis of interaction with others who could help them find work or obtain some benefits from social welfare agencies (Roberts, 1973a, 188–9).

Peter Fry's (1978) analysis of Pentecostalism and Umbanda (a spirit cult of Afro-Brazilian origin) in urban Brazil and of Methodism in nineteenth-century Manchester takes this kind of argument further. He stresses that urban religious movements are not simply means of obtaining social support or of integrating people into urban life. Such movements also provide a framework for interpreting daily events in ways that are broadly congruent with an individual's social and economic position and prospects. Fry suggests that movements like Umbanda challenge the dominant ethos of economic development while others, like Pentecostalism and Methodism, support that dominant ethos.

Pentecostalism in urban Brazil has certain similarities with Methodism, providing a stable congregation, hierarchically organized into federations, and a unified cosmology in which clear-cut notions of good and evil lead to a rigorous moral ethic emphasizing the values of hard work, thrift and abstinence. For many of the middle class, and for the skilled working class of both Manchester and of urban Brazil, such values are congruent with the possibilities of material improvement. These values served besides to provide a standard of behaviour by which to judge the less fortunate classes.

Fry contrasts this religious affiliation with that of Umbanda, which has a large and growing following among low-income groups, often drawn from the small-scale sector of the urban economy. Umbanda is organized around cult centres which are controlled autocratically by cult leaders; it has an eclectic and variable cosmology in which both good and evil are necessary parts of ritual efficacy and by which individuals develop particularistic relations with their spirits. The devotees demand help against malevolent forces that have been inflicted on them undeservedly, such as ill-health, unemployment, frustrations in love or other basic problems of urban living. Umbanda, then, is organized by clientage and specializes in short-term ritual solutions to the difficulties and insecurities of life in the cities and rural areas.

Umbanda represents one, and in under-developed countries, often the predominant face of capitalist development: thus, alongside the large-scale sector of the economy, based on 'rational' principles of organization and allocation of resources, there exists a cruder form of economic exploitation based on a combination of authoritarianism and particularism. Fry shows how the organization of Umbanda, such as the entrepreneurial nature of individual cult centres, its rivalries and schisms, fits the Brazilian urban environment in which people seek individual solutions to their problems: 'Umbanda thrives . . . as magic thrives in social relations and magic thrives in such relations where formal power is wielded autocratically and apparently illogically over those who suffer its consequences and, who having no formalized channels of influencing the exercise of these powers . . . continue to "make out" in urban Brazil by a cunning conjunction of the obtaining of professional qualifications and . . . by the manipulation of personal relationships.'

Despite initial repression, the São Paulo state government had begun to sponsor Umbanda festivals. However, the newspaper and business journal, which reflects the views of the São Paulo bourgeosie, continued to denounce Umbanda as a source of perversion and corruption and criticized government sponsorship of the cult. As Fry points out, the government could not afford to ignore this mass movement which, in any event, was playing the same kind of game as the politicians. It was left to the bourgeoisie to imply that the movement was contrary to the moral and political behaviour needed by a modern capitalist state.

Living conditions and neighbourhood

To obtain a fuller understanding of the significance of social relationships for low-income groups, we need to look more closely at the living conditions generated by urban growth and especially at housing. The first point to be made is that finding shelter is a problem that requires considerable energy and the helping hand of kin or friends.

There is no single integrated housing market catering for low-income families in which allocation is determined by need and ability to pay; instead, there are a large number of fragmented and localized markets. The original establishment of squatter settlements is often based on prior social relationships among the invaders; subsequent settlement also depends on having some relationships with the existing squatters. In Guatemala City, squatters would send to tell friends or relatives of a vacant space or shack. The characteristics of squatter settlements, such as their illegality, their densities and the predominance of owner-occupation, make it unlikely that people settle in them simply as a result of an individual search for rented or purchasable accommodation. This argument applies to other low-income settlements also; in cities of the underdeveloped world there are few public, 'impersonal' agencies to which those in search of housing can go to obtain information or to be placed on a waiting list.

Also, the search for housing is complementary to the other attempts of low-income families to secure a living in the city; individuals and families often prefer to locate near friends or kin who can help them find work or assist in times of emergency. This is especially apparent among recent migrants to Latin American cities. Most studies report that newly arrived migrants have prior contacts in the city before their arrival and that they settle with or near to kin or fellow villagers (Roberts, 1973a; Kemper, 1974; Lomnitz, 1974; Gianella, 1969; Perlman, 1976, 74–6). This practice can range from that of villagers in Guatemala and Peru who come and reside for a period of weeks with relatives before seeking their own accommodation, to that of migrants whose contacts in the city are less strong but who still feel happier about settling close to some prior contact. Consider, for example, this comment from one low-income informant in Guatemala City who did not have strong contacts prior to his arrival: 'We rented a house in . . . Zone 12. There was a relative living near that area, I felt a little protected by him, although he was very poor, but I felt protected.'

As Pahl (1974) points out, social relationships have an important utilitarian function in surviving amidst the complexities of the job and housing market produced by rapid urban growth. A similar use of friendship and kinship ties has been reported by Anderson (1971) in his account of the urban growth of Preston, an English industrial town, in the nineteenth century. Anderson examined housing registers to show the concentration of kin and fellow villagers in the same streets of the town; he also argued that migrants from the villages tended to come and first lodge with kin or villagers who had previously arrived in the city.

In contrast, however, with the situation that had developed in the northern English industrial cities by the second half of the nineteenth century, housing in cities of the underdeveloped world is more heterogeneous in construction and in patterns of tenure. Given the low incomes and job insecurity of the mass of the urban population, low-income housing is not an attractive investment for the large-scale sector of the economy. Even the state is loath to commit funds to what is seen as non-productive investment. Housing provision is thus left, in the main, to different types of private initiative. Small-scale entrepreneurs sub-divide older housing or build rudimentary apartments. Individuals construct their own housing and the state provides only the most basic assistance which, in many countries, is simply the indirect assistance of permitting the illegal occupation of land.

Under these conditions, finding housing is a bewildering and complex operation which often constitutes the basic problem of city residents. Consider this report (Roberts, 1973a, 80–1) by one of my Guatemalan informants who is now a relatively prosperous small businessman but continues to live in a squatter settlement: 'I went searching in all of Zone 12 and there would be a sign saying this room is for rent. When I asked, "how much is the apartment, ma'am?", she says to me, "Its only seventy-five *quetzales* a month". I was astonished, then I went back and not to shame myself I said to the lady that I would come back. We continued looking for humbler little houses . . . we asked how much is the rent of this room. "This is worth twenty-five *quetzales*", she says to me. I did not think that this one was the one for me either, since I was going to earn forty-five *quetzales* and to pay twenty-five *quetzales* did not suit me. Eventually we came to a little house, a shack like the one we are living in now [in a squatter settlement] and I asked the lady, "how much is the little room?". "Eight *quetzales*," she says, "do you have children?" "Yes", says I, "I have four." "Ah, we don't want anyone with children." '

In any urban economy in which there is a considerable amount of casual and low-paid work, housing provision is unlikely to be adequate for the needs of the population, mainly because there is no profit incentive to private builders to build working-class housing. Thus, in late nineteenth-century London where casual employment and sweat shops abounded, the working-class housing market was also highly restricted and complex. Compare, for example, this comment of a silver plater trying to find accommodation in the 1870s and 1880s with that of the Guatemalan informant: 'I know cases where people cannot get room; I experienced the difficulty myself sometimes. The first question I asked was, "What is the rent?", and I was told 10*s* for two rooms; I could not afford to pay 10*s* a week because my wages are very uncertain. I am upon a piece of work . . . so that I have nothing I can regularly depend upon as a regular stipend. Then they asked me the question "How many children?" When I told them, they said, "We cannot have you at all" ' (Stedman Jones, 1971, 218).

Leeds (1971) provides an account of the diversity of low-income settlement types in Latin American cities and stresses this diversity and the social heterogeneity with which it is associated, as part of his critique of the culture of poverty thesis. He distinguishes several very different types of low-income living environment. These include the central city tenements which are often formed from the sub-division of former elite residences. This type of housing is made up of a large number of rooms, many of which accommodate transients or single people. Other housing, in contrast, may have more of a communal organization, such as the *callejones* of Lima and the *vecindades* of Mexico (the type described by Oscar Lewis) which are smaller units, organized around an interior courtyard and sharing facilities. Other types of housing are usually found on the periphery of the city, often at one or two hours commuting distance from the centres of work. The most frequent type of government sponsored housing for low-income groups is in such locations. Residents are selected according to their ability to pay and are provided with adequate, but rudimentary, housing and services. Another peripheral type is the sub-division of land by government or private developers for privately owned houses; these houses are often built by the first purchasers of the land in a variety of shapes and sizes and will often have space for a garden and animals. Finally, there are the squatter settlements, where land is occupied illegally and the squatters erect their own housing, though subsequently this housing may be sold or rented. Squatter settlements appear at whatever point of the urban landscape there is empty space, that for one reason or another is not in great demand. Usually these spaces are also on the periphery of the city and in undesirable locations such as swampy land; but they also exist close to the centre when topography discourages other uses, such as in ravines of Guatemala City or on the steep hillsides of Rio de Janeiro.

The one type of housing that has been relatively rare in underdeveloped countries is mass public housing built close to the centres of work. The exceptions to this are government financed housing designed for occupations which are well organized in labour unions or which have a special relation to the government. Thus, in Mexico, government subsidizes housing for workers in the major unions; housing colonies are constructed for workers belonging to the same enterprise or branch of industry (Araud *et al.*, 1975). In Rio, there are high-rise housing blocks for bank clerks, sailors, industrial workers and public functionaries.

Despite these last examples, the diversity of low-income housing types has not contributed to any marked social segregation within the low-income population. There are tendencies in this direction and several studies have reported that changes in income, in size of family or in the stage of life-cycle lead families to seek housing to meet their new needs (Leeds, 1969; Roberts, 1973a; Mangin, 1967). However, the housing market for low income families is highly imperfect since, as we have noted, people tend to seek housing close to kin or friends and have not the time or resources to hunt for accommodation over a long period. Consequently, low-income settlements are internally heterogeneous in terms of the occupations of residents, stages in their life-cycle and length of residence in the city. For example in Perlman's (1976, 73–84) study of three low-income settlements (two shanty towns and a peripheral legally settled community), residents had a range of occupations, including skilled and white-collar occupations; educational levels varied from illiterate to secondary school and alongside recently arrived migrants from the countryside, there lived people born in the city and those who had lived many years in the city.

Similar results have been reported by most studies of Latin American low-income communities. There is little evidence that the socially marginal, such as the unemployed or underemployed, the most recent migrants or broken families, are the majority of residents of even the most marginal settlements (such as squatter settlements). In these ways, low-income housing reflects and facilitates the type of dualistic urban economy that was examined in the last chapter. We can appreciate this by considering the social forces involved in squatting and the contributions that squatters make to urban development.

Squatter settlements are physically very diverse types. In some of the oldest settlements of Rio de Janeiro, the process of housing improvement has reached a point where the settlements are hardly distinguishable from legal housing areas with a reasonably good standard of housing. Neighbours in squatter settlements will often over time install basic urban services through both cooperative and individual enterprise (Turner, 1967; Mangin, 1967; Leeds, 1969; Perlman, 1976). In cooperative ventures, neighbours combine to install sewage and water supplies, petitioning government and international agencies for aid.

I provided a case study of such attempts in a Guatemala squatter settlement in which, over a period of eight years, neighbours, through their own initiative, succeeded in building a church, a community centre, a small school, and in installing sewage disposal and piped water (Roberts, 1973a). They were helped by the municipal and national governments of Guatemala and also by the North American Agency for International Development; this assistance was granted after considerable and sophisticated lobbying from squatters. Neighbours often arrange individually to install electricity, where necessary bribing a company employee to let them install a light meter; then the person with the meter runs a large number of independent lines to other houses in the settlement, charging for this service and making a profit on the whole undertaking (Roberts, 1973a; Leeds, 1971). By these processes, squatter settlements acquire a distinct character; the major variables that contribute to this character are the age of the settlement, the average income of the residents and the size of the settlement.

Leeds (1969) has provided a detailed study of the importance of such variables in analysing the range of squatter settlement in Rio de Janeiro. He points out that large squatter settlements are likely to generate their own economic activity, providing clients for small storekeepers, craftsmen and so on; other smaller settlements are more likely to be dormitories, dependent on surrounding legal neighbourhoods for needed services.

Leeds is careful to emphasize that such factors in squatter settlement organization do not account for all the variation that is found. The major point about squatter settlements is that they cater for diverse housing and settlement needs (Turner, 1967; Frankenhoff, 1967). Squatting is attractive to people whose families are growing in size and who find themselves increasingly inconvenienced by the cramped quarters of the inner-city tenements. For such people, squatting may provide the only cheap alternative that is also near to their work. Other squatter types are people with unstable jobs who wish to avoid the difficulties of constantly having to pay rent, but who cannot afford to put the money down for a house or a legal plot of land. In the Guatemala squatter settlements, I found a disproportionate number of single women with children; these women worked outside the settlement in domestic or other low-paying services, often leaving the children to look after themselves in the shanty town. They valued the security that their shack gave them.

Even people with stable, relatively well-paying jobs, may prefer to settle in squatter settlements, because such housing allows them to save income for alternative investments. Thus, in Guatemala, small businessmen might locate temporarily in a squatter settlement while building up capital; likewise, school teachers and policemen are often found in squatter settlements as a means of saving for other kinds of housing or to meet the expenses of educating, feeding and clothing their families adequately. Also, as several studies have shown, residents of squatter settlements value the help they get from neighbours; the material deprivation and the external threats to the settlement foster at least as high a community spirit as is found elsewhere in the city (Mangin, 1965).

In the studies of squatter settlements in different parts of the world, there has been a similar emphasis on the diversity of these settlements. Laquian (1971), for example, emphasizes the range of squatter settlements in Asia and also argues strongly against the idea that these settlements are the refuges of the most poor or the most recent migrants. Instead, he surveys the range of economic activity found within squatter settlements and stresses the many forms of social, political and economic participation found in such settlements.

Local-level politics

The final type of marginality to consider in this chapter is political marginality, or the extent to which low-income families are ignorant of urban or national political issues and are unable to organize to influence decision-making. Most recent studies have agreed that it is incorrect to view low-income urban populations in underdeveloped countries as politically passive and unaware of issues (Handleman, 1975). Thus, Perlman (1976, 165–73) documents the complex political organization of *favelas* in Rio de Janeiro and points out that the levels of political awareness among *favelados* are higher than those found in rural areas of Brazil. Their level of direct participation in politics, through demonstrations or political meetings, is comparable with that of poor people in United States cities, as is their level of contact with local and national administrative agencies. Likewise, in my own research in Guatemala City (1968) I found high levels of political involvement and awareness among the poor; indeed, two thirds of the families in one squatter settlement owned and listened to a radio and the large majority of them claimed that they occasionally heard both Radio Havana from Cuba and the Voice of America from the United States.

The poor are not politically marginal in the sense of not participating in or affecting urban politics in Latin American cities (Leeds, 1971; Cornelius, 1974; Uzzell, 1972; Dietz, 1977). When the political structure permits, the poor enter readily in the electoral game, organizing on behalf of middle-class candidates and extracting what benefits they can for themselves or for their neighbourhoods. Even where authoritarian regimes severely restrict party politics or abolish them altogether, the poor are still active in bureaucratic politics, seeking to lobby the various branches of urban and national government and to develop patronage relationships with influential military and civilian leaders. The political opportunities created by organizing the urban poor leads Collier (1975) to observe that the creation of squatter settlements in Lima was based to a large extent on the desire of politicians to obtain political support.

For the mass of the urban population, the neighbourhood has become the main basis on which their grievances and deprivations are articulated (Portes and Walton, 1976; Cornelius, 1975, 9; Roberts, 1970). As Cornelius points out, there are few other agencies for developing political organization and consciousness in Latin American cities. Labour unions organize only a minority of low-income workers and there are few large-scale economic enterprises. Political parties, even under populist regimes, rarely attempted to organize low-income families on a permanent basis. Instead, the 'mass' parties of Latin America relied on local organizers to use various kinds of patronage to bring out crowds for demonstrations or on election day. Other city-wide bases for organization do not include significant proportions of low-income families. Voluntary associations or movements based on ethnic, regional or other issues have, on the whole, been relatively weak. One major exception to this has been the importance of regional associations in city life of Lima in Peru and, in this case, such associations have been a vehicle for political organization at the local and national levels (Mangin, 1965; Doughty, 1972; Roberts, 1974).

Furthermore, among low-income families, the neighbourhood is a highly salient basis for political organization. Most low-income neighbourhoods are deficient in many basic services such as water, electricity and transport services. In squatter settlements, land tenure is also uncertain, requiring residents to organize to press government to legalize their settlement or, at least, to take no action against it. There have, consequently, been a large number of urban social movements in Latin American cities, based on neighbourhood issues, and often expanding to become city-wide movements. These movements have frequently been linked to, and formed the popular base of, political parties. The Christian Democrat party in Chile, Venezuela and Central America gained a great deal of its electoral strength in urban areas from linked movements based on low-income neighbourhoods. In Chile, the communist and other left-wing parties also organized on a neighbourhood basis and over neighbourhood issues (Portes, 1971). Castells (1976, 413–69) cites a figure of 800,000 people as being involved in the Chilean *movimiento de pobladores*, which by 1972 was a large-scale network of neighbourhood-based organizations, some with almost total responsibility for administering law and order, services and urban planning in their local area.

Castells viewed this urban popular movement as a potential means of class organization among the mass of the urban population in Latin America, radicalizing workers threatened or 'displaced' by the increasing dominance of capital-intensive industrialization. The urban contradictions of dependent capitalism thus make its political contradictions more acute. For example, the very success of the Christian Democrats in organizing low-income neighbourhoods in Santiago led, under Christian Democrat government, to a situation in which escalating demands for improved housing and urban services brought repressive measures by government and made clearer the class basis of Christian Democracy. These conflicts paved the way for the victory of Allende in 1970. From this perspective, then, the neighbourhood and neighbourhood issues are essential elements in the class struggle. Urban protest makes populist alliances more difficult to maintain while at the same time bringing into the class struggle those groups that have been politically marginalized by the uneven development of the urban economy. Most workers are employed in small- or medium-sized enterprises and are rarely unionized. Also, the close supervision and paternalistic control maintained by the boss in this type of enterprise impedes class organization in the work place.

Why, then, have the contemporary authoritarian regimes in Latin America been so successful in excluding working-class participation and suppressing the demands of urban popular movements? Observers agree, for example, that neighbourhood-based political movements have been less effective under the Brazilian military regime than under the previous populist regimes, despite a worsening of the living standards of urban low-income groups (Leeds, 1974; Perlman, 1976). Likewise, the ruling party, the PRI, in Mexico, has successfully co-opted most urban social movements and used them as a means of consolidating its own authority (Cornelius, 1975).

Indeed, the political activity of the urban poor is not necessarily in support of left-wing parties or governments. Perlman (1976, 187) cites the support given by many inhabitants of the *favelas* to the military coup in Brazil in 1964 and characterizes the attitudes of her sample of poor families in Rio de Janeiro as basically conservative, loyal to the regime and patriotic. Collier (1975) emphasizes the support that the Peruvian military dictator, Odria, received from squatter settlements. Portes summarizes the literature dealing with collective action among the poor of Latin American cities and also finds a relative absence of political radicalism. He attributes this lack of radicalism to a rational adaptation to what structural circumstances permit and encourage and to the perceived impracticality of challenging the existing order (Portes and Walton, 1976, 108).

Political mobilization over specifically urban demands is difficult to sustain, partly because it is relatively easy for government to buy off or placate these demands. Although no government could afford to accede to *all* demands for improved services from low-income families, it can provide some of the services demanded to some of the neighbourhoods demanding them. Unlike labour union demands for improved wages, government agreement to a demand for urban services does not entail an across-the-board settlement. In practice, Latin American urban authorities have tended to alternate repression and concession over demands for improved urban services and the legalization of squatter settlements. When a neighbourhood obtains a needed service after a degree of struggle, its own militancy declines and it does not contribute to the struggles of those neighbourhoods still in need of urban services.

Mobilization over urban services tends to encourage vertical structures of dependence between local community and central authorities. Since it is possible for certain communities to be advantaged when others are not, it is to the advantage of local communities and to their leaders to develop client relationships with important politicians or government agencies. In this way, demand-making on urban government often becomes a means of extending government control over localities at relatively little cost. Collier (1975), for example, describes how the Peruvian military government's organization of squatter settlements, renamed 'new towns' (*pueblo jóven*), became a means of ensuring the loyalty of the poor and of excluding rival political parties. The reorganization involved very little capital outlay and consisted, mainly, in setting up a bureaucratic structure of control, in legalizing the settlement and in promoting self-help projects. Government is provided with information about conditions and grievances at the local level, is directly in contact with local leadership and is able to reward, selectively, communities and individuals.

Several commentators have pointed out that while local community leadership tends to be more politically aware and more politically sophisticated than the majority of residents, it also lends itself more easily to co-option by government (Cornelius, 1975, 130–1; Machado, 1967; Roberts, 1973a, 283–330). Perlman (1976, 186) cites a conclusion of Fernando Cardoso and Carlos Martins that 'the socio-economic determinants tend to focus the anti-conservative or opposition attitudes in those sectors in which there is the greatest concentration of apathy and political inactivity; and, conversely, tend to accumulate in the most mobile, informed and active sectors exactly the attitudes and values which predispose the most conformist forms of intervention in the political process'.

Since leadership over neighbourhood issues requires time and also a certain amount of cash, it tends to be taken up by those whose work, or lack of it, makes them easily available for community business. I found that the self-employed, or those with irregular timetables, were disproportionately active in local community politics in Guatemala. They were able to make afternoon visits to the town hall, to government offices or could spend time making the rounds of the neighbourhood. In contrast, those residents with steady jobs in factories left early and arrived home relatively late and tired from their work. Factory workers found it difficult to devote time to local politics. Those most ready to become politically active over local neighbourhood issues tended to be those who were committed to the neighbourhood as a place of business and who, to a certain extent, gained from the existing neighbourhood structure. Thus, owners of electricity meters in both Guatemala and Brazil figure prominently in local community politics, as do local storekeepers and the like. The economic position of many leaders thus makes them particularly susceptible to co-option. Contacts with government officials, politicians or businessmen can bring them individual economic favours as well as possible benefits for the neighbourhood. These processes are the bases for the clientelism that has often been seen to characterize the political systems of Latin America and other underdeveloped areas (Kaufman, 1974). Although patron-client relationships exist under most political systems, they flourish under the conditions of an unevenly developed economy, in which neighbourhoods are occupationally heterogeneous and access to resources is not determined by standard administrative procedures. In the Latin American urban economies, unemployment neither means access to welfare nor does it preclude access to a multitude of 'informal' economic opportunities. Likewise, there are a variety of ways in which access to housing or to other urban services can be obtained. To a much greater extent than in developed economies, individuals neither gain access as of right to these services nor are they debarred from access by standardized qualifications. Under these conditions, vertical relationships of the patron-client type are convenient means to increase state control over local areas. This is the dilemma of most urban social movements in Latin America; although they contribute to the political experience and organization of the disadvantaged, they have also become an instrument in the vertical control of poor populations.

This pattern of co-option does not occur in those situations where there is a basis for local community organization other than the neighbourhood and its issues. Those cases of a strong and militant local community organization, which Castells (1976, 457–69) reports for Santiago in Chile, are those in which communist and other left-wing political parties have organized the neighbourhoods *and* where workers with labour union experience link the urban conflict with industrial conflict. Also, the experience of defending rights to land or battling for basic services has enduring effects. Thus, several studies show that those who participated in the actual land invasion that established a squatter settlement remain, years afterwards, significantly more politically aware than their fellows and more ready to recognize the value of solidary local organization (Cornelius, 1975, 103–4; Portes, 1971; Roberts, 1973a, chapter 3). One factor in the high levels of community cohesion is that invasions and defending rights against outsiders emphasize a sense of community identity and reinforce the sense of territorial boundaries. Residents recognize more sharply their dependence on each other and are more likely to develop the trust necessary for effective organization.

The situation of urban poverty in cities of the underdeveloped world is thus a volatile one, giving rise to a variety of individual and group attempts to master the urban environment. In these attempts, there is neither a sense of progress, of, for example, cumulatively improving access to services and to decision-making, nor of failure. This fluid situation is truer of some cities than of others and any analysis of a specific city would need to take systematic account of the sources of diversity outlined above—the size and spatial organization of the city, the presence or relative absence of an organized industrial working class, the amount of 'informal' housing and the amount of resources that urban governments have for distribution. Differences in the development of state institutions also affect local-level activity, as between authoritarian governments which have little need of grass-roots support and those governments which are less well consolidated and use administrative favours to seek support.

Conclusion

The poor in cities of Latin America are not socially or politically isolated. The activities in which they must engage to make a living mean that they develop complex patterns of social interaction that are not confined to neighbourhood. The urban poor also find ways of interpreting the uncertainties of their economic and social position which are compatible with an active attempt to cope with the day-to-day problems of urban living. Thus, the religious practices of the urban poor can be viewed in this way and also demonstrate the cultural heterogeneity that accompanies uneven economic development.

Social relationships are crucial to survival in these cities. Obtaining housing as well as jobs is a question of developing an effective social network. Indeed, the striking feature about the urban poor is their activism in the face of seemingly appalling conditions. The study of squatter settlements show what can be achieved by people who have few material resources. Although squatter settlements are not social problems, neither are they a solution to resource-scarcity in cities of the underdeveloped world. Indeed, squatter settlements are often used by governments as a means of patronizing low-income populations at little cost. Expenditures on housing or social services are thus avoided which need to be made if existing income inequalities are to be remedied.

Exclusion on many fronts from the benefits of urban economic growth places the bulk of the population in a similar situation. Although they are skilful participants in local-level politics, the poor have been unable to sustain protests or political organization enough to constitute a serious threat to government. Their protests against the inadequacy of urban services are rendered ineffective because urban issues offer a fragile basis for political organization. Protests can be bought off cheaply and one neighbourhood set against another by government provision of partial services. The activism of the poor is, however, a factor in urban politics since their behaviour constitutes an unknown element which is alternatively feared and sought after, depending on the strength and political complexion of the government of the day.

The urban poor receive few benefits from the dominant form of economic organization and have little reason to accept as a norm any one standard of family life, of social and political behaviour or of moral worth. This means that in Latin American cities there is no well developed civil society in the sense of an implicit consensus over values and behaviour among the mass of the population. In the absence of such consensus, government and the dominant classes are deprived of one of the most valuable bases of potential support, that of legitimacy.

7
Urbanization and marginality in underdevelopment

In this concluding chapter, I shall reconsider the patterns of economic and social organization discussed earlier. My aim is to use this material to understand current trends in urban development and political change. In some respects, then, this chapter is not intended to be conclusive and much of what will be said is open-ended and speculative. My perspective, however, will be similar to that of the rest of the book, seeing economic growth as the main force shaping the course of events.

One of the themes of this book has been that growth influences political change by bringing new class forces into play and altering the balance of power within a country. Also, growth may weaken class organization, marginalizing sectors of the population so that they cease to be important factors in influencing events. I will now take this argument further by contrasting two views of social and economic marginality. The first regards marginality as a permanent and irreversible phenomenon while the second focuses on how marginality enables the dominant classes to resolve temporary bottle-necks in economic growth. Both views seek to understand the nature of the urban working class in underdeveloped countries. The potential for organization of this class and its collective aspirations are likely to be crucial factors in influencing the future development of cities in underdeveloped countries.

We will also need to examine, once more, the role of the state in shaping urban development. The intervention of the state in the urban economy has widened in range as the economy expands and becomes more complex. We must examine how this intervention alters the relationship of the state to the urban population and, in particular, to the working class. We have noted, for example, that in many urban situations, economic growth has widened income inequalities and done little to remedy the inadequacy of the housing and social services provided for the bulk of the population. We need now to consider the political implications of this situation: whether, for example, it leads to authoritarian government.

Marginality as a permanent phenomenon

We saw earlier that marginality is defined as the exclusion of part of the urban population from better-paying jobs, a say in politics, adequate housing and so on. In the first perspective on marginality that we review in this section, marginality is seen as a permanent and irreversible result of capitalist development. It is this irreversibility that, it is claimed, distinguishes contemporary marginality from previous patterns of urban poverty. For example, in nineteenth-century British cities, marginality was ultimately reversed by the expansion of employment opportunities in the urban economy (Hobsbawm, 1969a).

To those who see contemporary marginality as irreversible, such as Quijano, the issue is not simply one of extreme poverty. He points out that the situation of the poor in nineteenth-century cities beginning their industrial development was probably worse than that of the marginalized populations of Latin America: the nineteenth-century poor had few political rights and obtained little protection or help from the state (Quijano, 1973, 202).

In this section I will outline Quijano's interpretation of marginality, reserving my criticisms for the subsequent section. Quijano bases his analysis on the capital-intensive nature of the contemporary industrialization process. He claims that this industrialization cannot absorb the increase in the population of underdeveloped countries who are seeking work. Moreover, this industrialization actually displaces workers from productive activity. This can happen directly as when new technology reduces the labour needs of an industry. Also, the increased productivity of new industries displaces workers in traditional sectors. Artisan production is increasingly destroyed as machine-made cloth replaces the products of domestic looms and as plastic and aluminium utensils replace earthenware. Traditional food and drink industries give way to modern bottling plants. The new industries are capital-intensive and cannot replace the employment opportunities lost by the destruction of older, more labour-intensive forms of production. These processes create, according to his argument, a substantial surplus labouring population.

In Quijano's argument, this surplus population does *not* have the functions of an industrial reserve army. Jose Nun (1969) develops this point by distinguishing that marginality which is functional for the capitalist system (the industrial reserve army) and that which is not, the *masa marginal* (marginal mass). Nun claims that Marx's concept of the relative surplus population of workers produced by capitalist production should not be exclusively identified with the concept of the industrial reserve army (Marx, 1867, I, 628–38). A surplus labouring population forms a disposable reserve army only under the conditions where it acts as a downward pressure on wages or as an indirect means whereby capitalists control their labour power. From Nun's perspective, the unemployed and under-employed populations of Latin American cities are not a reserve army because they are not directly functional for capitalist expansion in underdeveloped countries. He claims that marginalized workers do not help to keep salaries generally low in modern industry since they are not competing for the key jobs which require relatively high levels of skill and education. Also, the high productivity and profita-bility of capital-intensive industry means that firms are able to accept restrictions on their ability to dismiss workers and are willing to pay high wages. It follows from this argument that since Latin American countries and other third-world countries cannot pass through a stage of more labour-intensive industrialization in their present situation of economic dependency, the limitation on employment is irreversible.

Quijano's emphasis on irreversibility is based, in part, on his assessment of the contemporary international division of labour in industry. He points out that those working in capital-intensive industry in underdeveloped countries often constitute an industrial reserve army for the industrial production of the advanced capitalist countries. They are already, in this sense, providing the basic cheap production of the capitalist world economy. Quijano (1973, 237–40) hypothesizes that the possibilities of industrial expansion at the periphery are limited by external control of technological innovation and by the direct control by multi-national companies of the most dynamic sectors of local industry. In contrast, industrialization in nineteenth- and early twentieth-century Europe and the United States could expand employment opportunities by seeking new and more differentiated markets, both internally and externally.

Those who are marginalized by the dynamic of capital-intensive industrialization find work in those sectors of the economy in which there is little or no possibility for capital accumulation. These sectors are primarily the urban-based tertiary sector of the economy, such as petty trade, personal services, small repair shops and so on. Accord-ing to Quijano (1973, 262) this marginal employment is likely to concentrate in the large cities of each underdeveloped country. Earn-ing opportunities are greater in these centres given the concentration of high-income earners. Also, access to educational and to welfare facilities and proximity to the centres of government make possible a greater range of strategies for survival. In contrast, demographic pressure on inadequate land resources, diminishing opportunities for craft work and relative isolation make rural areas less attractive places for survival.

Quijano's hypotheses fit reasonably well with our earlier account of the urban economy; in fact he explicitly recognizes that there is a transitional period in which capital-intensive industrialization may actually create employment opportunities in other sectors. However, he points out that these opportunities are purely transitional. Modern capitalism will eventually expand to provide capital-intensive services such as supermarkets, car-washing machines, modern automobile repair services and so on. These modern sector services use little labour relative to the smaller enterprises, which are relegated to servicing the needs of the poorest segment of the urban population. Marginalization is thus the increasing concentration of workers in activities that are risky, do not provide full-time employment and generate low incomes or very low profits.

From this perspective, the development of class organization among the working class is weakened because many urban workers cease to have a significant role in capital accumulation. In contrast, the urban poor of nineteenth-century Europe were, as an industrial reserve army, necessary to capital accumulation and, consequently, it was important for the dominant classes to develop the organization to maintain and control the poor as an industrial reserve. Likewise, it was in the interests of nineteenth-century industrial workers to extend labour unions to include members of the industrial reserve in order to avert the possibility that the reserve might be used to lower wages or break strikes.

In the underdeveloped situation, the dominant classes are mainly concerned with the poor as potential threats to political order; the economic relationships between the dominant classes and the marginalized groups are, according to Quijano (1973, 220), inconsistent, precarious, unstable and fragmentary. Instead, the marginals are more likely to relate *as a group* to the state. Indeed, the state becomes one of the major sources of survival for these groups, providing social and economic assistance and creating a network of patron-client relationships between agencies of the state and groups and individuals among the marginals.

Jose Nun (1969) provides an analysis of the political and economic fragmentation of the poor in city and countryside and argues that their lack of integration takes a form which poses little threat to the dominant system: the poor are afunctional and not dysfunctional for monopoly capitalism under the conditions of uneven development. The types of activity to which the poor must resort are of a kind which, as we have seen, force them to exploit each other; small shopkeepers charging high prices for unit purchases so that squatters pay more for produce than do middle-class shoppers using supermarkets. The involvement of the poor in neighbourhood issues, as in squatter settlement community betterment projects, can also divert attention from class exploitation and focus it on local quarrels and marginal possibilities of improvement.

In the situation described by Quijano and Nun the relationships of the industrial working class and the marginal poor are ambiguous. It is not the case that there is a conflict of interest between the two groups (Quijano, 1973, 267–9). Their identity of interest, however, is not sufficiently strong to permit effective organization against the dominant classes. This type of analysis suggests, then, that current economic trends in underdeveloped countries produce relatively low levels of overt class conflict. This argument can be extended to claim that the increasing spatial concentration of economic activities lessens class conflict outside the dominant metropolitan centres.

In provincial urban centres, the possibilities of capital accumulation are likely to have been diminished by the concentration of capital-intensive industry in the large cities; factory production in these centres will be displaced and survival will depend on the proliferation of small-scale labour-intensive activities. In this way, the whole economy of the secondary centres will become marginal; indeed, in these centres, the state may become an important source of income through the extension of educational services or administration.

In this provincial situation, the contradictions of current economic developments are less sharp because of the absence of the capital-intensive sector and its component classes—the bourgeoisie dependent on capital-intensive industrialization and the industrial working classes. Outmigration from these smaller centres to the larger centres channels out the energies and the frustrations of those attempting to progress in a marginal situation.

A similar analysis can be applied to the agrarian situation. Poverty persists in the agrarian situation and, with increasing pressure on land, the relative prosperity of peasants and rural workers may decrease. As we have seen earlier, more members of the household seek work externally, intensify labour inputs into agriculture and work longer hours. Yet, the contradictions of current economic developments may be less apparent in the rural area and be less likely to give rise to class struggle than was the case in previous stages of dependency. The *latifundia* are a less crucial form of economic exploitation in the stage of capital-intensive industrialization and, in many underdeveloped countries, may decline absolutely. Agrarian reform, for example, as in Peru and Chile, may remove the most overt forms of exploitation of the peasant population. Increasingly, the exploitation of the rural population during capital-intensive industrialization can take on the characteristics of the self-exploitation of peasant groups. Thus in Lopes's (1976) study of agrarian change in Brazil, we noted that the peasant sector of the population was both absolutely and relatively growing in Brazil. Though this peasant sector is exploited through marketing monopolies held by merchants and landowners, the form of exploitation is less sharp than that of the direct relationships between the large landowners and the dependent peasantry.

This perspective on marginalization enables us to extend the discussion of core-periphery relationships in interdependent development (chapter 1; Brookfield, 1975; Friedmann, 1972a, b). Peripheral groups or regions find difficulty in reversing their subordinate status because their economic and social fragmentation is not conducive to class organization and thus to a coherent struggle against exploitation from the centre. This hypothesis suggests a fruitful line of research which can include core-periphery relationships within cities of underdeveloped countries.

David Harvey (1973, 139–40) made this point with reference to the capitalist market system when he remarked that the wealth of the centre of the urban system is based on creating scarcity at the periphery (Pahl, 1971). Kowarick (1977) documents the apalling consequences of this process in an analysis of the pattern of land settlement in São Paulo and the creation of peripheral low-income housing. Land scarcity is artificially created by market mechanisms, concentrates low-income populations far from centres of work, produces overcrowding, unhealthy living conditions and a rising rate of infant mortality. In the analysis of both Quijano and Nun, urban marginality is an example of the creation of scarcity to permit capitalist expansion. The expressions of marginality—squatter settlements, labour-intensive occupations with low productivity, subsistence standards of living, low levels of demand for educational and other services—are produced by the necessities of capital accumulation in the dominant economic sector. Marginality provides an effective means of reducing demands on scarce capital, while contributing transitionally to its accumulation.

Alternative perspectives to marginalization

In discussing the alternatives to the above analysis, we will be examining a different approach to the contemporary class struggle in underdeveloped countries. The major difference is that the alternative approaches emphasize the variety of situations of underdevelopment and the various forms that the class struggle can take in contemporary underdevelopment. To a greater extent than in the anlysis of Quijano and Nun, capitalism is viewed as an internally expanding force which, even when unevenly developed, has a capacity to transform local social and economic structures. Capitalist development, not dependency and external forces, produces the contradictions of contemporary underdeveloped countries (Kowarick, 1975, 137–54). This internal dynamic of capitalism is, however, conditioned by the nature of a country's resources and prior history of underdevelopment. This dynamic is heavily dependent on the state and, consequently, varies with the strength and nature of the state apparatus in different underdeveloped countries.

This focus on the internal transformations generated by capitalism is that of the group of sociologists and economists who, in the main, have been associated with the Brazilian research institute, the Centro Brasileiro de Analise e Planejamento (CEBRAP). These include names we have already cited previously, such as F. H. Cardoso, P. Singer, F. de Oliveira, J. B. Lopes, V. Faria and L. Kowarick. The reason for singling out this group is not only because of the amount of analysis they have produced, but because, working closely together, their interpretations have evolved in similar directions and with a relatively high degree of internal consistency. Thus, a fuller understanding of the position of any one member can often be obtained by placing his arguments within the context of the work of his colleagues. Fernando Enrique Cardoso's (1971) attack on Jose Nun's (1969) distinction between a relative surplus population and an industrial reserve army is best understood in the context of the work of Oliveira and Singer which I shall consider shortly.

Another reason for emphasizing the national and institutional affiliation of these analysts is that, in their case, as in that of Quijano, their interpretations are necessarily and explicitly influenced by the historical experience of their own country. Likewise, the development model to which Quijano's analysis is most applicable is that of Peru. As we have seen, Peru and Brazil have had a very different experience of capitalist penetration; Peru, for example, has a much lower level of 'independent' industrialization and has a weakly developed middle class. Marginal populations are more evident in Lima than they are in the highly industrialized city of São Paulo. These comments are not intended to question the theoretical usefulness of the interpretations we are considering, but to warn the reader of the importance of national experiences in their formulation.

Both Faria (1976) and Kowarick (1975) have recently provided an extensive critique of marginality theories, using a range of quantitative data on the performance of the Brazilian economy and on urban occupational trends. I shall rely heavily on both works in these next pages, supplementing their observations with data from other countries.

A major criticism of Quijano's and Nun's marginality position is that it underestimates the extent to which even capital-intensive industrialization generates employment opportunities and contributes to the capitalist transformation of an underdeveloped country. The first part of this criticism concerns the rate of increase in industrial jobs in the years since 1950. Faria provides data to show that from 1950 to 1970, the transformative sector (manufacturing and construction) added some 1,633,553 new jobs to the Brazilian economy. In fact, all sectors of the economy added jobs in this period to absorb the increasing number of new entrants into the labour force. Though the agricultural sector increasingly reduced its share of total employment, this sector also added some 2,836,000 new jobs. In the same period, the tertiary sector (distribution, personal and industrial services, social services) showed the fastest rate of growth, adding some 6,782,000 jobs and expanding at a rate of 4.78 per cent a year; in comparison, the secondary sector (transformation and construction) grew at a rate of 3.98 per cent a year and the primary sector grew at a rate of 1.23 per cent a year.

At first sight, these figures might appear to support the arguments of those stressing the 'excessive' concentration of employment in the service sector of the economy in which employment is concealed by underemployment in non-productive occupations such as street vendors, car-minding and so on. Faria (1976, 167–81) shows, however, that from 1950 to 1972 the geometric rate of growth of the real product was high in all sectors of the economy, including commerce, transport and communication; the geometric rate of growth of the real product in industry, in the period 1966–72, was, for example 10.3 per cent and that of commerce was 9.3 per cent. Moreover, the trend of employment has not been consistently in favour of the tertiary sector; from 1960 to 1970 it was the secondary sector that showed the fastest rate of growth in employment and not the tertiary sector. Also, when the tertiary sector is disaggregated into its component parts, it is the social services that show the fastest growth in employment, expanding at an annual rate of growth from 1950 to 1970 of 5.75 per cent compared with the 4.08 per cent of the distributive sector (commerce and transport). From 1950 to 1970, nearly 2 million new jobs were created in the social service sector. This sector, which includes all those services provided by government, is an integral part of the apparatus of capital-intensive industrialization in Brazil.

These figures question the generality of Quijano's marginality hypotheses since those sectors most closely linked to capital-intensive industrialization appear to be among the most dynamic in creating job opportunities; there is little sign of capital-intensive industrialization displacing workers. A similar conclusion was reached for the Peruvian economy by Richard Webb (1974) in his analysis of the economic performance of the different sectors. Webb introduced into his analysis a sectoral distinction between what he called the modern sector and the traditional sector. In practice, the distinction was based on the size of the economic unit, so that transformative activities or commercial activities employing less than five people were classified as traditional. Webb claimed that this cut-off point provided a rough approximation to the division between modern, capital-intensive enterprises and those more likely to be based on household labour. Webb's traditional sector approximates to the marginal sector in urban and rural areas.

The calculations indicate that the modern sector continued to create employment opportunities in the period 1950–70, though its relative share in employment scarcely increased from 19 per cent to 21.6 per cent. However, there was evidence that the per capita incomes of *both* modern and traditional sectors rose in this period; this rise was substantially greater in the modern sector, but it was appreciable in the urban traditional sector also. Webb shows that it is the urban traditional sector that absorbs most of the increase in urban labour power: between 1950 and 1970, the urban traditional sector grew from 24.1 per cent to 33.1 per cent of the total labour force in Peru and migrants into this sector obtained higher and more rapidly growing incomes than those in the rural areas.

This evidence from both Peru and Brazil on employment creation and on the productivity of the large-scale and small-scale sectors of the economy does not suggest an increasing marginalization of the urban population with capital-intensive industrialization. Quijano was, in part, basing his argument on a United Nations table of the distribution of the economically active population in Latin America between 1925 and 1960 (ECLA, 1965, tables 2 and 16; ILPES–CELADE, 1968). This table shows that the manufacturing sector decreased its share of total employment after 1955, but this decrease (from 14.5 per cent of the economically active in 1950 to 13.4 per cent in 1960) occurred because of the decline in artisan employment; the factory sector increased its share in total employment and the decline was mainly in rural artisan activities; as ECLA (1965, 170) indicates, the urban artisan sector grew in these years through the establishment of small workshops and repair establishments.

These comments do not mean, however, that the real wage of the urban worker has been improving in recent years. We have seen that, in fact, there may have been a reduction in that wage, forcing greater female participation in the labour force. The critique of marginalization consists instead of a different interpretation of the linkage between the urban poor and the capital-intensive industrialization process. From the CEBRAP perspective, the poor are a necessary, rather than an afunctional, part of the capitalist industrialization process in underdeveloped countries. Also, the sectoral concentration of labour in the services is not marginality but is required for the expansion of capitalist production under the conditions of underdevelopment.

This perspective is expressed in detail in Oliveira's (1972) analysis of the importance of cheap labour for the industrialization of São Paulo. Oliveira claims that in a situation of relative capital scarcity it is necessary for the industrial sector to make use of the services of a labour-intensive tertiary sector. The existence of small-scale, commercial and transport activities and of repair and maintenance activities organized in labour-intensive ways, facilitates the distribution of the industrial product and saves capital. Consequently, industrialization develops on the basis of labour-intensive services which are not well remunerated and which add to capitalist accumulation (Oliveira, 1972, 31). Concentration of employment in the tertiary sector is consequently not due to the 'inflation' of such a sector, but results from the expansion of industrial production in a situation in which capital is reserved for production activities. The existence of marginal occupations subsidizes capitalist production in other ways also; they reduce the labour costs of large-scale industry by reducing the reproduction costs of that labour power. Thus, cheap food produced in the peasant sector of the economy is an important element in the survival of the urban worker on low wages. Likewise, the fact that industrial workers can obtain services cheaply reduces pressure on wages; Oliveira (1972, 32) points out that the self-construction of housing by the working class (*favelas* or shanty towns) constitutes an effective subsidy to the capitalist class by lowering the urban subsistence costs of the workers.

State intervention in the economy is the crucial factor in distinguishing the contemporary forms of an industrial reserve army from those which Marx (1867, I, 628–48) described for nineteenth-century England. For Marx, the labouring population made surplus by the increases in machine productivity served to provide a reserve which could be easily incorporated into the active workforce at times of sudden expansion or of the rise of new branches of production. At other times, this surplus labouring population created a downward pressure on wages by their competition for jobs. As a result of state regulation, employers in many underdeveloped countries face indemnity payments and other costs in taking on or laying off workers, making direct competition for jobs less of a function for an industrial reserve army. (But see Kowarick, 1975, 115–23.) Consequently, out-work and the small-scale economy are, it can be argued, the modern equivalent of the industrial reserve army, fulfilling the necessary function of reducing the labour costs of production for industrial capital. Under these conditions, an underdeveloped country can undertake its own internal capitalist transformation. Capital is initially provided by the export sector (mainly coffee in the case of Brazil) but, increasingly, expansion is based on accumulation within the industrial sector. This process is affected by external factors, such as the terms of foreign trade and the structure of foreign investments; but it is not determined by external factors.

From this viewpoint, there is no reason to suppose any immediate end to the process of capital accumulation. There may be economic crises and rates of growth may fluctuate, but the internal market for industrial production is likely to continue to increase and to attract new investment, either from abroad or domestically. Though income concentration may encourage the production of technologically sophisticated consumer durables, the market for these goods has spread to include, as we have seen, even the poorest strata of the population (Wells, 1976). Finding the political solutions to the problems created by the bottlenecks of scarce capital is, it is argued, essential for the dominant classes. As long as the mass of the urban population can be denied an adequate social infrastructure (education, sanitation, housing and social security), while encouraged to participate fully in the economy as consumers and workers, then the state is able to reserve its funds to encourage economic expansion.

Thus, capitalist expansion in Brazil after 1930 is interpreted by Oliveira and others in terms of the internal class struggle. Industrialization proceeds by exploiting labour power in the ways described above. This pattern of capitalist industrializaiton also involves the state in an increasing regulation and support of economy activity. The state regulates the relations of workers and employers and creates the conditions for a stable industrialization; the state is also pressed to provide the infrastructural investment in communications that make the expansion of industrial production possible.

The alliances among the dominant classes reflect the uneven nature of internal capitalist transformation. Alongside relatively stagnant traditional industries such as textiles are others with greater economic dynamic, such as the technologically sophisticated consumer durable industries. These latter are, however, dependent on foreign technology and are often restricted in their freedom to innovate in product and to expand into new markets. Thus, even in those sectors most dependent on foreign technology or finance, conflicts as well as complementaries of interest exist between local firms and new 'parent' companies. In the agrarian sector, a similar diversity of economic interests is found. No one group within the dominant classes, it can be argued, is strong enough to ignore the others, especially in face of their common interest in controlling the demands of labour. Consequently, state economic policy is determined in often ambiguous ways: some industrial branches are protected from foreign competition, while the inflow of foreign capital into other sectors is subsidized and infrastructural investments are made in still other sectors (Faria, 1976, 163). Marginality has been displaced, it is argued, to poorer regions of the country such as the northeast. As we have seen, it is in the poorer regions that small-scale enterprises develop to transport, market and provide the services needed to expand the market for the industrial production of the developed region. Likewise, it is in these poorer regions that subsistence farming continues to provide the bulk of foodstuffs for the local urban populations.

From this perspective, marginality is thus the direct product of capitalist expansion, facilitating its early industrial stages and, subsequently, the expansion of its internal market. The implications of this version of marginality are different from those considered in the previous section. In the first place, the increasing ratio of tertiary sector employment to secondary sector employment is seen as temporary fluctuation which resolves the bottle-necks to capitalist expansion in an unevenly developed economy. Also, marginality, representing the horizontal extension of non-productive occupations, is seen to be more likely to occur in the less dynamic urban centres. Faria (1976) provides documentation on these points, showing that marginal occupations are more likely to predominate in the more peripheral cities of Brazil such as Salvador or Recife and less likely to occur in the larger and most dynamic cities such as São Paulo or Rio de Janeiro. Faria also makes the point that there may have been a greater urban 'surplus' population in the early twentieth century than later in the capital-intensive stages of industrialization (Faria, 1976, 109–12). Cowell's (1975) examination of migration to nineteenth-century Recife supports this argument by showing that, as a consequence of fluctuations in the sugar economy, there was a considerable surplus population in the city by the end of the century.

Faria argues that rapid urbanization, and the consequent increases in the economically active population, is not the product of capital-intensive industrialization in the sense that this industrialization displaces previous activities. Instead, rapid urbanization results from an uneven capitalist development in which cheap labour and services are the basis for expansion in both rural and urban areas. The significance of labour to this form of capitalist expansion has, he argues, the demographic consequence of high birth-rates. High birth-rates suit both capitalist interests and family strategies in which domestic labour can be used from an early age in a variety of poorly remunerated ways.

The line of reasoning of the CEBRAP group also leads them to a somewhat different view of the class struggle from that of Quijano. From their angle, the expansion of the large-scale sector sharpens class conflict by placing all urban workers in an increasingly similar position. Those in the small-scale sector become 'proletarianized' by their increasing dependence on contract work from the large-scale sector. Most workers, whether in the small- or large-scale sectors are forced to seek housing in peripheral areas of the city and family budgets become more inflexible as a result of commitments to pay for transport, rent and a range of consumer goods.

The political structure of marginality

This analysis of marginality suggests a way of understanding the political developments of the capital-intensive stage of urban industrialization. In this stage, the dominant capitalist classes in underdeveloped countries are faced not so much with the problem of controlling the demands of their labour power, but of excluding the mass of the urban population from a significant share of the national income (O'Donnell, 1975). Under these conditions, populist regimes and political parties (see chapter three) may appear socially and economically dangerous to the dominant classes because they both raise the aspirations of the masses and give the masses some organized means to struggle for higher incomes. At the same time, the dominant classes do not have a sufficiently wide social and economic appeal to develop class alliances that would enable conservative political parties to gain and retain power electorally. As those who report on the progress of the so-called emergent middle classes of Latin America indicate, intermediate classes remain numerically and politically weak (Ratinoff, 1967). It is this situation which many recent commentators have linked to the increasing preominance of authoritarian military regimes in Latin America (Horowitz, 1967; Cotler, 1970; Quijano, 1971; Cardoso, 1975b; Stepan, 1971).

Quijano described the situation as that of a crisis in hegemony. By hegemony he means the institutional apparatus and practices (for example, political parties, ideologies) by which the dominant capitalist classes obtain sufficient legitimacy to maintain their control of power. In Peru he identifies this crisis with the failure of civilian political parties to develop ideological appeal and, when in power, to develop effective means of satisfying the economic and social demands of the population during rapid urbanization. Bourricaud (1970) refers to the same phenomen under the concept of social mobilization and documents the increasing appearance in Peru of groups that could not be controlled by traditional political means. These groups, such as urban slum dwellers and small peasant farmers, were deeply affected by the changes brought about by urbanization; but they did not share significantly in the benefits of economic growth. The 1968 military coup in Peru is thus interpreted as, in part, an attempt to establish the degree of control over the aspirations of the mass of the population necessary for capital-intensive industrialization. The military coup in Brazil in 1964 and the various Argentinian coups in recent years have similarly been interpreted as responses to the inability of civilian elites to restrict access to social and economic benefits, when depending on mass political support (O'Donnell, 1977).

O'Donnell (1975, 1977) sees these military regimes as a new form of corporate state, one which he characterizes as bureaucratic-authoritarian. Unlike previous forms of corporate state in Latin America, the bureaucratic-authoritarian regime develops the state apparatus so that it is technically capable of managing the economy and of organizing and controlling, vertically, the different sections of the population. This state plays an important direct role in the economy through state-controlled enterprises; the state also extends its vertical control through, for example, government agencies responsible for squatter settlements or labour organization.

The bureaucratic-authoritarian state develops, then, as a consequence of the most recent stage in urban and industrial development; this stage is one in which, as we have seen in chapter three, economic expansion depends on deepening the urban productive structure through more complex activities such as petrochemicals, the motor industry and other consumer durables, machines and other relatively simple capital goods. The deepening is most easily achieved in cooperation with multi-national corporations and foreign capital. This economic expansion benefits those sectors of national capital linked to the multi-nationals, but, increasingly, marginalizes other sectors of national capital whose product or service cannot compete with those of technologically advanced enterprises. (But see Ferner, 1977, for a full discussion of this process which generates new forms of complementarity as well as conflict.) The situation of these 'marginalized' middle sectors is made more difficult since the alliance with international capital often requires the state, as a condition of loans, to adopt an austere budgetary policy; this policy threatens the traditional sources of middle-class employment in the services and raises taxes.

Consequently, bureaucratic-authoritarian regimes seek to control middle-class access to decision-making by severely reducing, or eliminating, the role of civilian political parties and by restricting the operation of such middle-class interest groups as businessmen's associations. The low-income population is excluded entirely from political participation, thus removing a potential support for middle-class political organization and reducing pressure to adopt welfare policies that redistribute income. Thus capital can be 'saved' for technological expansion.

The contradiction implicit in the development of the bureaucratic-authoritarian state is that those sectors of national capital and of the middle class who are disadvantaged by the influx of foreign capital and by budgetary control may seek alliances with the popular classes to resist foreign encroachment. The extent to which the middle sectors see themselves as more threatened by popular pressures for redistribution of income than by foreign control is thus a variable in differentiating the responses to the bureaucratic-authoritarian state in Latin America. Where, as in the case of Chile, this 'threat' was seen by the middle classes to be a great one, then the military have a relatively free hand in opening the doors to foreign capital and in pursuing policies that restrict middle-class, as well as popular, consumption. In contrast, in the 1966 military coup in Argentina, the relative absence of a perceived popular threat meant that the middle classes were not unqualified in their support for the coup and the military regime encountered considerable resistance to its attempts to encourage foreign capital (O'Donnell, 1975).

Thus, variations in the nature of the bureaucratic-authoritarian regime must be understood in terms of the particular historical experiences of each country and in terms of the forms that the class struggle has taken. For example, the Peruvian military inherited a situation in which their freedom of action, in terms of rival class interests, was greater than in either Brazil or Argentina. The reformism of the Peruvian regime contrasts with the economically conservative authoritarianism of the Brazilian regime. In Mexico, the 1910 revolution early secured the organized participation of the working class in government; there, the dislocations produced by rapid urbanization have been handled through the development of a sophisticated and complex one-party apparatus through which segments of organized labour and of the middle classes have a regulated access to decision-making.

But, as O'Donnell remarks, the similarities in the economic problems of underdeveloped countries are a powerful force for convergence. Despite institutional differences, the recent actions of the Mexican state to encourage foreign capital and to control labour have been similar to those of the Brazilian and Argentinian regimes.

Eventually, all bureaucratic-authoritarian regimes must seek to reincorporate the middle sectors and ensure their cooperation in expanding the national market. Thus, in Brazil the military regime has increasingly sponsored the development of national enterprise through subsidy and through excluding foreign capital from certain sectors of the economy. Likewise, a limited political participation favouring middle-class interest groups has been permitted and serves to provide jobs and patronage for the middle-class civilian population (Banck, 1974).

This analysis of the bureaucratic-authoritarian regime is that of an ideal type, ignoring many of the complexities of current political practice in Latin America. It serves to highlight the similarities in the political context, not only of Latin America, but of other underdeveloped countries as well. O'Donnell (1975) remarks, in discussing the bureaucratic-authoritarian state, 'our theme is "Latinamerican" only in a trivial sense. The relevent historical context is that of the political economy of nations which, initially, were exporters of primary materials and then were extensively industrialized at a later stage, in dependence on the major centres of world capitalism.'

The dynamic of local-level transformation

Throughout the volume, I have argued that development constitutes a two-way process of political and economic interaction between governed and government. If the analysis of class struggle is to be deepened, then we need to examine the ways this struggle expressed itself even among the apparently powerless and un-organized.

The concentration in cities and other urban places of large numbers of highly mobile people who are not incorporated into the career and reward structures of modern economic organizations creates a series of risks and uncertainties for government and elite groups. Many of these risks and uncertainties arise from the lack of information on the responses of such populations to political and economic changes initiated from above. The characteristics of squatter settlement populations and their likely responses to problems such as food shortages are constant preoccupations of government and elites in underdeveloped countries. In such situations the apparatus of the state often becomes orientated to information-gathering about the underprivileged and to the development of organizations suited to monitor any potential disturbances. Low-income populations are equally adept at this game and seek to bargain with government agencies and elite groups. Also, the planning function which is so essential to the continuing dynamic of modern capitalism becomes, at best, a set of intelligent guesses when so little can be predicted for so much of the population. The sources of political change are thus to be found in the shifting alliances that have developed during the period up to and including the dominance of authoritarian regimes. The support for the authoritarian regime is a conditional one—conditional on that regime providing the economic expansion that will offset the growing dominance of foreign capital in the economy.

It is in this fluctuating situation that the analysis of local-level urban politics and economic activity contributes to the understanding of political change. We have seen the conditions that make the mass of the urban population a weak, but unpredictable, political force. Though it is unlikely that the low-income urban population will spontaneously organize against authoritarian rule, they represent a force which is potentially mobilizable. The pressures on authoritarian regimes to guarantee the stability of capital accumulation forces them, as we have seen, into measures designed to organize and rationalize the urban milieu and in ways that are likely to provoke increasingly popular discontent. Since the urban poor are also necessary to the dynamic of modern urban capitalism, they cannot easily be physically isolated or totally removed. In this situation, despite the apparent political stability of authoritarian regimes, undercurrents of political change prepare the way for different types of political regime.

Conclusion

In this chapter, I have tried to identify the directions of change in urbanization in underdeveloped countries through looking at urban class organization and at the relationship of the state to the different classes. I have emphasized that changes in the patterns of economic organization are not simply produced by technological develop-ments, but by the choices people make, or force others to make, about the ways resources are allocated and consumed. This does not mean that the study of technological change is irrelevant to under-standing underdevelopment. Changes in technology create the basis for new relationships of dependency between developed and under-developed countries and between dominant and peripheral regions with the same country. Class relationships have likewise been pro-foundly affected in the contemporary period by the technological dualism of urban economies. Eventually, we may find that there are technological constraints on growth as energy supplies and energy crises constrain future technological developments and make it increasingly difficult to maintain vast urban agglomerations. Rather than deal with the imponderables of such technological develop-ments, I have chosen to concentrate on the political and social context of future developments in underdeveloped countries.

Despite the arguments advanced by Quijano and Nun, it does not seem that economic growth in underdeveloped countries is in-herently limited by its capital-intensive nature. Even when capitalist expansion is limited by the peripheral role of underdeveloped coun-tries in the capitalist world economy, economic growth continues to transform local social and economic structure, though at a slower and more uneven pace than was the case in the developed world. The unevenness of development is shown in the ways in which factors of production are combined to secure growth: capital is reserved for the most profitable economic activities with little of it 'wasted' on purely social investments or on those services not closely connected with the large-scale sector of production. Labour is used intensively and cheaply in the less profitable areas, such as craft production and many of the repair, commercial and personal services, helping to reduce, directly and indirectly, the labour costs of production in the large-scale sector of the economy. This form of capitalist develop-ment is convenient to the dominant classes since it permits economic growth while maintaining high standards of consumption among the wealthy. Such a pattern of growth depends, however, on a political context in which the mass of the population has no effective means of influencing the allocation of resources and thus securing improvements in living standards. This political context is partly produced by authoritarian government and partly by the weak development of political and labour organization among the urban working class, under social and economic conditions that tend to divide and isolate members of this class from each other.

This form of capitalist expansion will reinforce the present pattern of urban and industrial concentration. Diseconomies of scale may lead to a certain degree of decentralization, as industries seek cheaper and less congested sites; but decentralization will be countered by the attractive force of the large cities which contain the biggest consumer markets and the greatest concentration of skilled labour, financial and technical resources. Under these conditions, as we saw in chapter three, decentralization may mean little more than the suburbanization of industry or the creation of outlying industrial parks which are more closely linked to the metropolitan centre than to their provincial hinterland. The political forces counteracting the continuing concentration of economic activities are weak. In few countries is there an economic or social basis for strong regional elites or for a strongly organized provincial working class. These provincial classes rarely have common interests to further by combining to force government into a policy of redistributing resources among the regions. We have seen earlier how current economic developments fragment economic activity in provincial areas and inhibit class organization. Unless such political pressure is brought, the 'natural' tendency is for capital and the most qualified people to concentrate in the centres where the most profitable opportunities are to be found.

The situation is not, however, as straightforward as the above description suggests. Economic expansion is likely, over time, to increase the pressure on government from the urban working classes. To further economic growth by making most efficient and profitable use of capital, those in charge of policies in underdeveloped countries are likely to permit and at times encourage a spatial reorganization of the large cities which will make it more difficult to survive on low incomes. This reorganization will entail an increasing inflexibility in choice of housing, a long journey to work and the rising cost of foodstuffs produced on capitalist rather than peasant farms. At present, the largest Latin American cities are becoming increasingly difficult places to govern in face of popular protest. Despite the fragmentation of the urban working class, there are thus powerful forces acting to homogenize their situation. This process may not result in political or labour union organization, but it makes the working class an evidently volatile element in urban politics. The situation will become more fluid because continued economic expansion will probably increase the potential conflicts of interest among the dominant classes, due, in part, to the different rates of growth of different sectors of the economy.

In this context, authoritarian government provides an increasingly ineffective 'solution' to the problems of uneven economic growth. Lacking secure internal bases of support, authoritarian governments are likely to become over-dependent on external support, intensifying technological and financial dependence which, in turn, creates further sources of internal dissatisfaction. The point to be made here is not, however, that the solution to current urbanization problems is to be found in the return of representative government. Such governments would be as unstable as their predecessors under the present balance of economic forces in underdeveloped countries. Rather, the point is that pressures are building up which make it easier for governments to seek radical solutions to present dilemmas.

The problem of the crisis of rapid urban growth in under-developed countries is not, basically, one of the appropriate solution to apply. Most commentators are agreed that what is required is a more balanced regional development, based on smaller-size cities and towns and on a mix of capital- and labour-intensive tech-nologies. To make such a development possible, however, requires among other things radical changes in income distribution and in patterns of consumption. The crucial question thus becomes one of identifying the conditions that stimulate governments to initiate measures which go against the present interests and consumer habits of much of the population and which induce the different classes to tolerate these changes. Although conditions in most countries of Latin America are reaching a point where radical changes in policy are now more feasible than before, there will still be considerable variation in the timing and character of these policies. This quali-fication is a necessary one if we are to continue with the analysis of this volume, since class organization and the state itself differ in the strength of their development from country to country. The initia-tion of policies is always, in any event, a somewhat fortuitous event responding to particular moments in a country's history; but the successful implementation of policies depends on the underlying forces making for change.

This conclusion is, in some respects, special to the situation of Latin America. More than any other underdeveloped area, it has become over the centuries an integral part of the capitalist world economy not simply in terms of international trade and division of labour, but also in becoming permeated by ways of life and of consumption that are basically similar to those of the developed world. This is why radical change is perhaps more difficult in Latin America than in Africa and in Asia. Latin American cities and the general pattern of the continent's urbanization are, as we have seen, similar to the developed world in spatial and economic organization. The consumer aspirations of the developed world are also less alien to Latin America than to other underdeveloped areas. Thus, though the forces making for change in Latin America are perhaps greater than elsewhere, it is also true that the forces resisting a departure from present patterns of concentrated urban development are also greater. The freedom of action of those who seek change is reduced in Latin America, though equally the urgency of the problem is likely to encourage heroic efforts.

Bibliography

ADAMS, Richard N., 1965: *A community in the Andes: problems and progress in Muquiyauyo*. Seattle and London: University of Washington Press.

ADAMS, Richard N., and HEATH, Dwight, B. (eds.), 1965: *Contemporary cultures and societies of Latin America*. New York: Random House.

ALAVI, Hamza, 1972: The state in post-colonial societies: Pakistan and Bangladesh. *New Left Review* **74** (July-August).

ANDERSON, M., 1971: *Family structure in nineteenth-century Lancashire*. Cambridge: Cambridge University Press.

ARAUD, Ch., BOON, G. K., GARCIA, Rocha A., RINCON, S., STRASSMAN, W. P. and URQUIDI, V. L., 1975: *La construcción de vivienda y el empleo en México*. Mexico City: Colegio de México.

ARIAS, Evanisto Piñon, 1971: *Las empresas multinacionales y sus efectos sobre la economia*. Buenos Aires.

AMIN, Samir, 1973: *Neo-colonialism in West Africa*. Harmondsworth: Penguin.

1974: *Accumulation on a world scale I*. New York and London, Monthly Review Press.

ASSADOURIAN, Carlos S., 1973: Sobre un elemento de la economia colonial: producción y circulación de mercancias al interior de un conjunto regional. *Revista Latinomericana de Estudios Urbanos Regionales* (EURE) **3** (December), 135–81.

1977: *La producción de la mercancia dinero en la formación del mercado interno colonial*. Documentos CEED, Colegio de México.

BAER, Werner, TREBAT, Thomas and NEWFARMER, Richard, 1976: State capitalism and economic development: the case of Brazil. Paper presented at conference on Implementation in Latin America's Public Sector: Translating Policy into Reality. University of Texas at Austin, April/May.

BALÁN, Jorge, 1969: Migrant-native socio-economic differences in Latin American cities: a structural analysis. *Latin American Research Review* **4**, (1), 3–29.

1973: Migrações a desenvolvimento capitalista no Brazil: ensaio de interpretação histórico-comparativa. *Estudos CEBRAP* **5** (July –September), 5–80. São Paulo.

1976: Regional urbanization under primary sector expansion in neo-colonial societies. In Portes and Browning, 1976.

BALÁN, J., BROWNING, H. and JELIN, E., 1973: *Man in a developing society*. Austin and London: University of Texas Press.

BANCK, Geert A., 1974: The war of reputations: the dynamics of the local political system in the state of Espirito Santo, Brazil. *Boletín de Estudios Latinomericanos y del Caribe* **17**, 69–77.

BANTON, Michael (ed.), 1966: *The social anthropology of complex societies*. London: Tavistock.

BARKIN, David, 1975: Regional development and inter-regional equity: a Mexican case study. In Cornelius and Trueblood, 1975, 277–99.

BARRATT BROWN, Michael, 1974: *The economics of imperialism*. Harmondsworth: Penguin.

BARTRA, Roger, 1974: *Estructura agraria y clases sociales en México*. México, D. F. Serie Popular, Editorial Era.

BERLINCK, Manoel T. and COHEN, Youssef, 1970: Desenvolvimento econômico, crescimento econômico e modernização na cidade de São Paulo. *Revista de Administração de Empresas* **10**, 1 (Jan/Mar), 45–64. Rio de Janeiro.

BERRY, Brian J. L., 1967: *Geography of market centers and retail distribution*. Englewood Cliffs, N. J.: Prentice-Hall.

1973: *The human consequences of urbanization*. London: Macmillan.

BOURRICAUD, François, 1970: *Power and society in contemporary Peru*. New York: Praeger.

BOYER, RICHARD E., 1972: Las ciudades Mexicanas: perspectivas de estudio en el siglo XIX. *Historia Mexicana* **22**, 2 (October/December), 142–59.

BOYSON, Rhodes, 1970: *The Ashworth cotton enterprise*. Oxford: Clarendon Press.

BRADING, David A., 1971: *Miners and merchants in Bourbon Mexico, 1763–1810*. Cambridge: Cambridge University Press.

1976: The city in Bourbon America: elite and masses. Paper presented at 42nd International Congress of Americanists, Paris.

BRIGGS, Asa, 1971: *Victorian cities*. Harmondsworth: Penguin.

BROMLEY, J. S. and KOSSMANN, E. H. (eds), 1971: *Britain and the Netherlands* **4**, The Hague: Nijhoff.

BROOKFIELD, Harold, 1975: *Interdependent development*. London: Methuen.

BROWN, Richard (ed.), 1973: *Knowledge, education and cultural change*. London: Tavistock.

BROWNING, Harley L., 1958: Recent trends in Latin American urbanization. *Annals of the American Academy of Political and Social Science* **316** (March), 111–20.

1968: Urbanization and internal migration in Latin America. Paper delivered at the Undergraduate Conference on the Population of Latin America, Cornell University, January 24–7.

1972a: Primacy variation in Latin America during the twentieth century. *Acta y Memorias del XXXIX Congreso Internacional de Americanistas, Lima 1970* **2**, 55–77.

1972b: Some problematics of the tertiarization process in Latin America. Paper presented to the 40th Congress of Americanists, Rome, September.

1971: Migrant selectivity and the growth of large cities in developing societies. In National Academy of Sciences, 1971, 273–314.

BROWNING, Harley L. and FEINDT, W., 1971: The social and economic context of migration to Monterrey, Mexico. In Rabinovitz and Trueblood, 1971, 45–70.

BROWNING, Harley L. and SINGELMANN, J., 1975: The development of the service sector in Latin America: an international historical perspective. Mimeo, Population Research Center, Austin.

Bureau of the Census, 1975: *Historical statistics of the United States*. Washington, D.C.: Government Printing Office.

BUTTERWORTH, Douglas, 1974: Grass roots political organization in Cuba: a case of the committees for the defense of the revolution. In Cornelius and Trueblood, 1974, 183–206.

CALDWELL, John C., 1969: *African rural-urban migration: the Movement to Ghana's towns*. Canberra: Australian National University Press.

1976: Towards a restatement of demographic transition theory. *Population and Development Review* **2**, 3–4 (September/December).

CAPLOW, Theodore, 1964: *The urban ambiance: a study of San Juan, Puerto Rico*. Ottowa, New Jersey: Bedminster Press.

CARDOSO, Fernando H., 1971: Comentários sobre os conceitos de superpopulação relativa e marginalidade. *Estudos CEBRAP* **1**, 99–130.

1977: The consumption of dependency theory in the United States. *Latin American Research Review* **12**, 3, 7–24.

1973: Dependency revisited. Hachett Memorial Lecture, Institute of Latin American Studies, University of Texas at Austin.

1975a: The city and politics. In Hardoy, 1975, 157–90.

1975b: *Autoritarismo a democratização*. Paz e Terra: Rio de Janeiro.

CARDOSO, Fernando H. (ed.), 1968: *Cuestiones de sociologia del desarrollo de América Latina*. Santiago de Chile: Editorial Universitaria.

CARDOSO, Fernando H. and FALETTO, Enzo, 1969: *Dependencia y desarrollo en América Latina*. México: Siglo Veintiuno.

CARDOSO, Fernando H. and REYNA, J. L., 1968: Industrialización, estructura ocupacional y estratificación social en América Latina. In Cardoso, 1968.

CASTELLS, Manuel, 1972: La urbanización dependiente en América Latina. In M. Castells (ed.), *Imperialismo v urbanización en América Latina*. Barcelona: Editorial Agusto Gilli.

1976: *La cuestion urbana*. Mexico, Madrid and Buenos Aires: Siglo Vientiuno.

1977: *The urban question: a marxist approach*. London: Edward Arnold.

CASTLES, Stephen and KOSACK, Godula, 1973: *Immigrant workers and class structures in Western Europe*. London: Oxford University Press for Institute of Race Relations.

Censo Nacional de Población y Ocupación (Peru), 1940: Vol. 1. Lima: Ministerio de Hacienda y Comercio, Dirección Nacional de Estadística, 1944.

Censos Nacionales (Peru) VII de Población, II de Vivienda, 1972: Vol. 1. Lima: Officina Nacional de Estadística y Censos, 1974.

Census of England and Wales, 1901: Census Office, 1902–3. London: HMSO.

CIDA, 1970: *Estructura Agrária v Desarrollo Agrícola en México*. Vols 1–3, Mexico: Centro de Investigaciones Agrárias, Comité Interamericano de Desarrollo Agrícola.

CHAPMAN, Sidney, 1904: *The Lancashire cotton industry*. Manchester: Manchester University Press.

CHEETHAM, Rosemond, 1973: El sector privado de la construcción: patrón de dominación. *Revista Latino Americana de Estudios Urbano Regionales* **1**, 3 (October).

CHI, Peter S. K. and BOGAN, Mark W., 1975: Estúdio sobre migrantes y migrantes de retorno en el Peru. Notas de Población.

Revista Latinoamericaná de Demografía **3**, 9 (December), 95–114.

CLIFFE, Lionel, 1977: Rural class formation in East Africa. *Journal of Peasant Studies* **4**, 2, 195–224.

COHEN, Abner, 1969: *Custom and politics in urban Africa*. London: Routledge and Kegan Paul.

COLLIER, David, 1975: Squatter settlements and policy innovation in Peru. In Lowenthal, 1975, 128–78.

CONNIFF, Michael H., NOHLGREN, Stephen and HENDRIX, Melvin, 1971: Brasil. In Morse, 1971c.

CONNING, Arthur, 1972: Rural-urban destinations of migrants and community differentiation in a rural region of Chile. *International Migration Review* **6**, 2 (summer), 148–57.

COPELAND, M. T., 1912: *The cotton manufacturing industry of the United States*. Cambridge, Massachussetts.

CORNELIUS, Wayne, A., 1971: The political sociology of city-ward migration in Latin America: towards empirical theory. In Rabinowitz and Trueblood, 1971.

1974: Urbanization and political demand-making: political participation among the migrant poor in Latin American cities. *American Political Science Review* **68**, 3, 1125–46.

1975: *Politics and the migrant poor in Mexico City*. Stanford, Calif.: Stanford University Press.

1976: Mexican migration to the United States: the view from rural sending communities. Paper presented at conference on Mexico and the United States, The Next Ten Years. School of International Service, The American University, Washington, D.C., 18–19 (March).

CORNELIUS, Wayne and TRUEBLOOD, Felicity (eds), 1974: *Latin American urban research* **4**. Beverly Hills and London: Sage.

1975: *Latin American urban research* **5**. Beverly Hills and London: Sage.

CORTÉS CONDE, Roberto and GALLO, Ezequiel, 1967: *La formación de la Argentina moderna*. Buenos Aires: Paidos.

COTLER, Julio, 1970/71: Political crisis and military populism in Peru. *Studies in Comparative International Development* **6**, 5.

COWELL, Bainbridge Jr, 1975: Cityward migration in the nineteenth century: the case of Recife, Brazil. *Journal of InterAmerican Studies and World Affairs* **17**, 1 (February).

DALTON, G. (ed.), 1971: *Studies of economic anthropology*. Washington, D.C.: American Anthropological Association Studies **7**.

DANDLER, Jorge, HAVENS, Eugene, SAMANIEGO, Carlos and SORJ, Bernardo, 1976: La estructura agraria en America Latina. *Revista Mexicana de Sociologia* **38**, 1 (January–March), 29–50.

DAVIS, Kingsley, 1965: The urbanization of the human population. *Scientific American* **214** (September), 40–53.

1972: *World urbanization, 1950–70* **1** and **2**. *Population Monograph Series* **9**. University of California, Berkeley.

DEAN, Warren, 1969: *The industrialization of São Paulo, 1880–1945*. Latin American Monographs **17**. Institute of Latin American Studies, Austin and London: University of Texas Press.

DESAL–HERDER, 1968: *La Marginalidàd en América Latina: Un Esayo de Diagnóstico*. Barcelona.

DIETZ, Henry A., 1977: The office and the *poblador*: perceptions and manipulations of housing authorities by the Lima urban poor. Malloy, 1977.

D'INCAO e Mello, M. C., 1976: O 'Bóia-Fria': acumulação e miséria. Petropolis, Brazil: Editora Vozes.

DI TELLA, Torcuato, 1965: Populism and reform in Latin America. In Veliz, 1965, 47–74.

1967: *Sindicalismo y comunidád*. Buenos Aires: Editoria del Instituto Torcuato di Tella.

DOUGHTY, Paul, 1972: Peruvian migrant identity in the urban milieu. In Weaver and White, 1972.

DOWD, Douglas F., 1956: A comparative analysis of economic development in the American West and South. *Journal of Economic History* **16**, 4, 556–74.

DRAKE, Michael (ed.), 1973: *The process of urbanization*. Bletchley: Open University Press.

DYOS, H. J. (ed.), 1968: *The study of urban history*. London: Edward Arnold.

1971: Greater and greater London: notes on metropolis and provinces in the nineteenth and twentieth centuries. In Bromley and Kossmann, 1971, 89–112.

DYOS, H. J. and ALDCROFT, Dennis, 1969: *British transport*. Leicester: Leicester University Press.

DYOS, H. J. and REEDER, D. A., 1973: Slums and suburbs. In Dyos and Wolf, 1973.

DYOS, H. J. and WOLFF, M. (eds), 1973: *The Victorian City*. London and Boston: Routledge.

EAMES, Edwin and GOODE, Judith Granich, 1973: *Urban poverty in a cross-cultural context*. New York: Free Press; London: Collier-Macmillan.

ECLA, 1957: Change in employment structure in Latin America. *Economic Bulletin for Latin America* **2**, 1 (February), 15–42.

1965: Structural changes in employment within the context of Latin America's economic development. *Economic Bulletin for Latin America* **10**, 2 (October) 163–87.

1970: *Development problems in Latin America*. Austin: University of Texas Press.

ECKSTEIN, Susan, 1975: The political economy of lower-class areas in Mexico City: societal constraints on local business opportunities. In Cornelius and Trueblood, 1975, 125–45.

EDMONSON, Munro S., CARRASCO, O., FISHER, G. and WOLF, E. 1957: *Synoptic studies of Mexican culture*. Tulane University: Middle American Research Institute, publication **17**.

EFFRAT, Marcio P. (ed.), 1974: *The community: approaches and applications*. New York: Free Press.

ELIZAGA, Juan C., 1972: Internal migration: an overview. *International Migration Review* **6** (summer), 121–46.

FARIA, Vilmar E., 1976: Occupational marginality, employment and poverty in urban Brazil. PhD dissertation, Harvard University.

FARIS, R. E. L. (ed.), 1964: *Handbook of modern sociology*. Chicago: Rand McNally.

FAUSTO, Boris (ed.), 1975: *O Brasil Republicano* 3. São Paulo: Difel.

1976: *Trabalho urbano e conflito social, 1890–1920*. São Paulo and Rio de Janeiro: Difel.

FELDMAN, A. and MOORE, W., 1962: Industrialization and Industrialism: convergence and differentiation. *Transactions of the Fifth World Congress of Sociology* 2, International Sociological Society.

FELIX, David, 1977: The technological factor in socio-economic dualism: toward an economy-of-scale paradigm for development theory. In Nash, 1977, 180–211.

FERNANDES, Florestan, 1969: *The negro in Brazilian society*. New York: Columbia University Press.

FERNER, Anthony, 1977. The industrial bourgeoisie in the Peruvian development model. PhD thesis, University of Sussex.

FISHLOW, Albert, 1973: Some reflections on post-1964 Brazilian economic policy. In Stepan, 1973, 69–118.

FITZGERALD, E. V. K., 1976: Peru: the political economy of an intermediate regime. *Journal of Latin American Studies* 8, 1 (May).

FLINN, William L., 1971: Rural and intra-urban migration in Colombia: two case studies in Bogota. In Rabinovitz and Trueblood, 1971.

FONG, H. D., 1930: *Triumph of factory system in England*. Tientsin, China: Chihli Press.

FOSTER, John, 1974: *Class struggle and the Industrial Revolution*. London: Weidenfeld and Nicolson.

FOX, Robert W., 1975: *Urban population growth trends in Latin America*. Washington, D.C.: Inter-American Development Bank.

FOXLEY, Alejandro (ed.), 1976: *Income distribution in Latin America*. London: Cambridge University Press.

FRANK, André Gunder, 1971: *Capitalism and underdevelopment in Latin America*. Harmondsworth: Penguin.

FRANKENHOFF, C. A., 1967: Elements of an economic model for slums in a developing economy. *Economic Development and Cultural Change* 16, 1, 27–35.

FRANKFURTER, Felix, 1962: *The case of Sacco and Vanzetti*. New York: Grosset and Dunlap (A. Little, Brown and Company edition).

FRANKLIN, S. H., 1965: Systems of production, systems of appropriation. *Pacific Viewpoint* 6, 2, 145–66.

FRIEDEL, Edward and JIMENEZ, Michael F., 1971: Columbia. In Morse, 1971c.

FRIEDEN, B. J. and NASH, W. W. (eds), 1969: *Shaping an urban future*. Cambridge, Mass.

FRIEDMANN, John, 1969: The role of cities in national development. *American Behavioral Scientist* 12, 5, 13–21.

1969/70: The future of urbanization in Latin America. *Studies in Comparative International Development* 5, 9.

1972a: The spatial organization of power in the development of urban systems. *Comparative Urban Research* **1** (spring), 5–42. New York.

1972b: A general theory of polarized development. In N. M. Hansen (ed.), *Growth Centers in Regional Economic Development*. New York: Free Press.

FRIEDMANN, John and SULLIVAN, F., 1974: The absorption of labor in the urban economy: the case of developing countries. *Economic Development and Cultural Change* **22** (April) 385–413.

FRISBIE, W. Parker, 1976: *The scale and growth of world urbanization*. Population Research Center, University of Texas at Austin.

FRY, Peter, 1978: Two religious movements: Protestantism and Umbanda. In Wirth, 1978.

FURTADO, Celso, 1976: *Economic development of Latin America*. Cambridge: Cambridge University Press.

GALEY, John, 1971: Venezuela. In Morse, 1971c.

GALLO, Ezequiel, 1974: *El 'boom' cerealero y cambios en la estructura socio-política de Santa Fé (1870–1895)*. Documento de trabajo **88**, Centro de Investigaciones Sociales, Instituto Torcuato Di Tella.

GANS, Herbert J., 1965: *The urban villagers*. New York: Free Press.

GEERTZ, Clifford, 1963a: *Agricultural involution: the process of ecological change in Indonesia*. Berkeley and Los Angeles: University of California Press.

1963b: *Peddlers and princes: social development and economic change in two Indonesian towns*. Chicago: University of Chicago Press.

GERMANI, Gino, 1962: *Política y sociedád en una epoca de transición*. Buenos Aires: Paidos.

1966: Social and political consequences of mobility. In Smelser and Lipset, 1966, 364–94.

1969/70: Stages in modernization in Latin America. *Studies in Comparative International Development* **5**, 8.

GERSHRENKRON, Alexander, 1962: *Economic backwardness in historical perspective*. Cambridge, Mass.: Belknap Press.

GIANELLA, J., 1969: *Marginalidád en Lima Metropolitana*. Lima: Cuadernos, DESCO.

GIBBS, Jack P. and BROWNING, Harley L., 1966: The division of labor, technology and the organization of production in twelve countries. *American Sociological Review* **31**, 1 (February).

GILBERT, Alan, 1974: *Latin American development: a geographcial perspective*. Harmondsworth: Penguin.

1975: Urban and regional development programs in Colombia since 1951. In Cornelius and Trueblood, 1975, 241–75.

GIUSTI, Jorge, 1971: Organizational characteristics of the Latin American urban marginal settler. *International Journal of Politics* **1**, 1, 54–89.

GLADE, William, 1969: *The Latin American economies: a study of their institutional evolution*. New York: American Books, Van Nostrand, Reinhold.

GOLDTHORPE, John, 1978: The current inflation: towards a sociological account. In Hirsch and Goldthorpe, 1978.

GONZÁLEZ CASANOVA, Pablo, 1965: Internal colonialism and national development. *Studies in Comparative International Development* 1, 4, 27–37.

GOODMAN, David and REDCLIFT, Michael, 1977: The 'Bóias-Frias': rural proletarization and urban marginality in Brazil. *International Journal of Urban and Regional Research* 1, 2, 348–64.

GORDON, David M., 1972: *Theories of Poverty and Unemployment*. Lexington Mass.: D. C. Heath.

GRAHAM, Douglas, 1970: Divergent and convergent regional economic growth and internal migration in Brazil. *Economic Development and Cultural Change* 18 (April), 362–82.

1972: Foreign migration and the question of labor supply in the early economic growth of Brazil. Mimeo, Economic History Workshop, Instituto de Pesquisas Economicas, Universidade de São Paulo.

GRAHAM, Richard, 1973: *Britain and the onset of modernization in Brazil*. Cambridge: Cambridge University Press.

GRAHAM, Richard and SMITH, Peter (eds.), 1974: *New approaches to Latin American history*. Austin and London. University of Texas Press.

GREAVES, Thomas C., 1972: The Andean rural proletarians. In *Anthropological Quarterly* 45, 2, 65–83.

GRIFFIN, Keith, 1969: *Underdevelopment in Spanish America: an interpretation*. London: Methuen.

GRONDIN, Marcelo, 1975: Un caso de explotación calculada: la comunidád campesina, de Muquiyauyo, Peru. PhD dissertation, Universidad Iberoameiicana, Mexico.

HABAKKUK, H. J., 1967: *American and British technology in the nineteenth century*. Cambridge: Cambridge University Press.

HALL, Michael, 1974: Approaches to immigration history. In Graham and Smith, 1974.

HALL, P. G., 1962: *The industries of London since 1861*. London: Hutchinson.

HALPERIN, Donghi, Tulio, 1963: La expansión ganadera en la compania de Buenos Aires (1810–52). *Desarrollo Economico* 111, 1–2 (April–September). Buenos Aires.

1970: *Historia contemporánea de América Latina*. Madrid: Alianza Editorial.

HANDELMAN, Howard, 1975: The political mobilization of urban squatter settlements. *Latin American Research Review* 10, 35–72.

HANKE, Lewis, 1956: *The imperial city of Potosí: an unwritten chapter in the history of Spanish America*. The Hague: Nijhoff.

HANSEN, Niles M. (ed.), 1972: *Growth centers in regional economic development*. New York: Free Press.

HARDOY, Jorge (ed.), 1975: *Urbanization in Latin America: approaches and issues*. Garden City, N.Y.: Anchor.

HART, Keith, 1973: Informal income opportunities and urban employment in Ghana. *Journal of Modern African Studies* 11, 61–89.

HARVEY, D., 1973: *Social justice and the city*. London: Edward Arnold.

HAUSER, Phillip M. and SCHNORE, Leo F. (eds), 1965: The study of urbanization. New York: Wiley.

HAWLEY, Amos, 1950: *Human ecology*. New York: Ronald Press.
1971: *Urban society: an ecological approach*. New York: Ronald Press.

HAYTER, Teresa, 1971: *Aid as imperialism*. Harmondsworth: Penguin.

HERMANSEN, T., 1972: Development poles and related theories: a synoptic review. In Hansen, 1972.

HERRICK, Bruce H., 1965: *Urban migration and economic development in Chile*. Cambridge, Mass. and London: MIT Press.

HILL, Richard C., 1977: Two divergent theories of the state. *International Journal of Urban and Regional Research* 1, 1, 76–99.

HIRSCH, Fred and GOLDTHORPE, John H. (eds), 1978: *The political economy of inflation*. London: Martin Robertson.

HIRSCHMAN, Albert O., 1977: A generalized linkage approach to development with special reference to staples. In Nash, 1977, 67–98.

HOBSBAWM, Eric, 1964: The nineteenth-century London labour market. In Centre for Urban Studies (ed.), *London: aspects of change*. London: Macgibbon and Kee, 3–28.
1969a: *Industry and empire*. Harmondsworth: Penguin.
1969b: La marginalidád social en la historia de la industrialización europea. *Revista Latinoamericana de Sociologia* 5, 2 (July), 237–48.

HOROWITZ, Irving Luis, 1967: The military elites. In Lipset and Solari, 1967, 146–89.

ILPES-CELADE, 1968: Elementos para la elaboración de una política de Desarrollo con integración para América Latina. Sintesis y Conclusiones. Mimeo.

JANVRY, Alain de and GARRAMON, Carlos, 1977: The dynamics of rural poverty in Latin America. *Journal of Peasant Studies* 4, 3.

JACOBSON, L. and PRAKASH, V. (eds), 1970: *Urbanization and National development*. Beverly Hills, Calif.: Sage.

JELIN, Elizabeth, 1974: Formas de organización de la actividad económica y estructura ocupacionál: el caso de Salvador, Brazil. *Desarrollo Económico* 53, 14 (April–June), 181–203.

JESUS, Carolina Maria de, 1963: *Child of the dark*. New York: Signet/E. P. Dutton.

JOHNSON, E. A., 1970: *The organization of space in developing countries*. Cambridge, Mass.: Harvard University Press.

KATZ, Friedrich, 1974: Labor conditions on *haciendas* in Porfirian Mexico: some trends and tendencies. *Hispanic American Historical Review* **54**, 1 (February), 1–47.

KATZMAN, Martin T., 1977: *Cities and frontiers in Brazil: regional dimensions of economic development*. Cambridge: Harvard University Press.

1978: São Paulo and its hinterland: evolving relationships and the rise of an industrial power. In Wirth, 1978.

KAUFMAN, Robert R., 1974: The patron-client concept and macropolitics: prospects and problems. *Comparative Studies in Society and History* **16**, 284–308.

KEMPER, Robert V., 1974: Family and household organization among Tzintzuntzan migrants in Mexico City. In Cornelius and Trueblood, 1974, 23–46.

1977: *Migration and adaptation: Tzintzuntzan peasants in Mexico City*. Beverly Hills and London: Sage.

KEMPER, Robert V. and FOSTER, George M., 1975: Urbanization in Mexico: the view from Tzintzuntzan. In Cornelius and Trueblood, 1975, 53–75.

KIRSCH, Henry, 1973: Employment and the utilization of human resources in Latin America. *Economic Bulletin for Latin America* **18**, (2), 46–94.

KLAREN, Peter F., 1973: *Modernization, dislocation and aprismo*. Austin and London: Institute of Latin American Studies/University of Texas Press.

KOWARICK, Lúcio, 1975: *Capitalismo e marginalidade na América Latina*. Rio de Janeiro: Paz e Terra.

1977: The logic of disorder: Capitalist expansion in the metropolitan area of greater São Paulo. Discussion Paper, Institute of Development Studies at the University of Sussex.

KRITZ, Ernesto and RAMOS, Joseph, 1976: The measurement of urban underemployment: a report on three experimental surveys. *International Labour Review* **113**, 1 (January/February), 115–127.

LACLAU, Ernesto, 1971: Feudalism and capitalism in Latin America. *New Left Review* **67** (May–June), 19–38.

LAITE, Andrew J., 1977: The migrant worker: a case study of industrialization and social stratification in highland Peru. PhD thesis, University of Manchester.

LAKE, Nathan, 1971: Argentina. In Morse, 1971c.

LAMPARD, Eric E., 1965: Historical aspects of urbanization. In Hauser and Schnore, 1965, 519–54.

1968: The evolving system of cities in the US: urbanization and economic development. In Perloff and Wingo, 1968.

LANDES, David, 1970: *The unbound prometheus*. Cambridge: Cambridge University Press.

LAQUIAN, Aprodicio A., 1971: Slums and squatters in South and Southeast Asia. Jakobson and Prakash, 1971.

LASUEN, J. R., 1969: On growth poles. *Urban Studies* **6**, 2 (June).

LAWTON, R., 1962: Population trends in Lancashire and Cheshire from 1801. *Transactions of the Historical Society of Lancashire and Cheshire* **114**, 189–213.

LEACOCK, E. (ed.), 1971: *The culture of poverty: a critique*. New York: Simon and Schuster.

LEEDS, Anthony, 1964: Brazilian careers and social structure: an evolutionary model and case history. *American Anthropologist* **66**, 6, 1321–47.

1969: The significant variables determining the character of squatter settlements. *Améric Latina* **12**, 3, 44–86.

1971: The culture of poverty concept: conceptual, logical and empirical problems, with perspectives from Brazil and Peru. In Leacock, 1971, 226–84.

1974: Housing-settlement types, arrangements for living, proletarianization and the social structure of the city. In Cornelius and Trueblood, 1974.

LEES, Lyn, 1973: Metropolitan types: London and Paris compared. In Dyos and Wolf, 1973, 413–28.

LEFF, Nathaniel, 1972: Economic development and regional inequality: origins of the Brazilian case. *Quarterly Journal of Economics* **86** (March), 243–62.

LEHMAN, David (ed.), 1974: *Agrarian reform and agrarian reformism: studies of Peru, Chile, China and India*. London: Faber.

LERNER, Daniel, 1958: *The passing of traditional society*. New York: Free Press.

LEWIS, Oscar, 1952: Urbanization without breakdown: a case study. *Scientific Monthly* **75**, 1, (July).

1961: *The children of Sanchez*. New York: Random House.

1968: *La vida: a Puerto Rican family in the culture of poverty—San Juan and New York*. New York: Vintage Books, Random House.

LEWIS, Robert Alden, 1973: Employment, income and the growth of the *barriadas* in Lima, Peru. PhD thesis, Cornell University.

LIPSET, Seymour Martin and SOLARI, Aldo (eds), 1967: *Elites in Latin America*. New York: Oxford University Press.

LOMNITZ, Larissa, 1971: Reciprocity of favors among the urban middle class of Chile. In Dalton, 1971.

1974: The social and economic organization of a Mexican shanty town. In Cornelius and Trueblood, 1974, 135–56.

1976: Migration and network in Latin America. In Portes and Browning, 1976.

1977: *Networks and marginality: life in a Mexican shanty town.* New York and London: Academic Press.

LONG, Norman, 1973: The role of regional associations in Peru. In Drake, 1973, 173–91.

1977: *An introduction to the sociology of rural development.* London: Tavistock.

LONG, Norman and ROBERTS, Bryan (eds), 1978: *Peasant cooperation and capitalist expansion in the central highlands of Peru.* Austin and London: University of Texas Press for Institute of Latin American Studies.

LOPES, Juarez Brandão, 1961: Relations industrielles dans deux communautés brasiliennes. *Sociologie du Travail* **4**, 61, 18–32.

1976: Do latifúndio à empresa: unidade e diversidade no campo. *Caderno,* CEBRAP **26**, Editors Brasiliense, São Paulo.

1977a: Developpement capitaliste et structure agraire au Bresil. *Sociologie du Travail* **19**, 1, 59–71.

1979: Capitalism in the periphery: notes on the development of the proletariat in São Paulo. *International Journal of Urban and Regional Research,* forthcoming.

LOVE, Joseph, 1975: Autonomia e interdependencia: São Paulo: e a Federação Brasileira, 1889–1937. In Fausto, 1975.

LOWDER, Stella, 1973: Aspects of internal migration in Peru. PhD dissertation, University of Liverpool.

LOWENTHAL, Abraham (ed.), 1975: *The Peruvian experiment.* Princeton and London: Princeton University Press.

LYONS, Raymond F. (ed.), 1965: *Problems and strategies of educational planning.* UNESCO.

McGEE, T. G., 1967: *The South East Asian city.* London: G. Bell.

1971: Catalysts or cancers? the role of cities in Asian society. In Jakobson and Prakesh, 1971, 157–82.

McGREEVEY, W. P., 1971a: *An economic history of Colombia, 1845–1930.* New York: Cambridge University Press.

1971b: A statistical analysis of primacy and lognormality in the size distribution of Latin American cities, 1750–1960. In Morse, 1971c.

MACHADO DA SILVA Luiz Antonio, 1967: A politica nas favelas. *Cuadernos Brasileiros* **9**, 3.

1971: *Mercados metropolitanos de trabalho manual e marginalidade.* MA dissertation presented to the postgraduate programme of social anthropology of the National Museum, Rio de Janeiro.

MALLOY, James M. (ed.), 1977: *Authoritarianism and corporatism in Latin America.* Pittsburgh: University of Pittsburgh Press.

Manchester University Economics Research Section, 1936: *Readjustment in Lancashire*. Manchester: Manchester University Press.

MANGIN, William P., 1965: The role of regional associations in the adaptation of rural migrants to cities in Peru. In Adams and Heath, 1965, 311–23.

1967: Latin American squatter settlements: a problem and a solution. *Latin American Research Review* **2**, 3, 75.

MARSHALL, J. D., 1961: The Lancashire rural labourer in the early nineteenth century. *Transactions of the Lancashire and Cheshire Antiquarian Society* **71**, 90–128.

1968: Colinization as a factor in the planning of towns in northwest England. In Dyos, 1968, 215–30.

MARTINE, George, 1972: Migration, natural increase and city growth: the case of Rio de Janeiro. *International Migration Review* **6**, 2 (summer), 200–15.

MARX, Karl, 1867: *Capital*. Edited by Frederick Engels, vols 1–111, New York: International Publishers Co. Inc.

MEILLASSOUX, Claude, 1977: *Mujeres, graneros y capitales*. Mexico: Siglo Veintiuno.

MELLOR, Rosemary, 1977: *Urban sociology in an urbanized society*. London: Routledge.

MERRINGTON, J., 1975: Town and country in the transition to capitalism. *New Left Review* **73**, 71–92.

MILLER, Rory, 1976: Railways and economic development in central Peru, 1880–1930. In Miller *et al*., 1976, 27–52.

MILLER, Rory, SMITH, Clifford T. and FISHER, John (eds), 1976: *Social and economic change in modern Peru*. University of Liverpool, Centre for Latin American Studies, monograph series **6**, 27–52.

MINGIONE, Enzo, 1977: Pahl and Lojkine on the state: a comment. *International Journal of Urban and Regional Research* **1**, 1, 24–36.

MITCHELL, J. Clyde, 1957: *The Kalela dance: aspects of social relationships among urban Africans in Northern Rhodesia*. Rhodes Livingstone Paper **27**, Manchester: Manchester University Press for Rhodes Livingstone Institute.

1966: Theoretical orientations in African urban studies. In Banton, 1966.

MOORE, Wilbert, 1964: Social aspects of economic development. In Faris, 1964.

1977: Modernization as rationalization: process and restraints. In Nash, 1977, 29–42.

MORENO TOSCANO, Alejandra, 1972: Cambios en los patrones de urbanización en México, 1810–1910. *Historia Mexicana* **22**, 2, 160–87.

MORENO TOSCANO, Alejandra and AGUIRRE, Carlos A., 1975: Migrations to Mexico City in the nineteenth century. *Journal of Interamerican Studies and World Affairs* **17**, 1, (February), 27–42.

MORENO TOSCANO, Alejandra and FLORESCANO, Enrique, 1974: El sector externo y la organización espacial y regional de México, 1521–1910. *Cuadernos de Trabajo del Departamento de Investigaciones Historicas*, Instituto Nacionál de Antropologia y História, Mexico.

MORLEY, Samuel A. and WILLIAMSON, Jeffrey G., 1977: Class pay differentials, wage stretching, and early capitalist development. In Nash, 1977, 407–27.

MORSE, Richard M., 1962: Latin American cities: aspects of function and structure. *Comparative Studies in Society and History* **4** (July).

1971a: Trends and issues in Latin American urban research, 1965–1970. *Latin American Research Review* **6**, 1 (spring), 3052.

1971b: Trends and issues in Latin American urban research, 1965–1970 (Part II). *Latin American Research Review* **6**, 2 (summer), 19–75.

1971c: The urban development of Latin America, 1750–1920. Stanford University: Center for Latin American Studies.

1974: Trends and patterns of Latin American urbanization, 1750–1920. *Comparative Studies in Society and History* **16**, 4 (September), 416–47.

1975: The development of urban systems in the Americas in the nineteenth century. *Journal of Interamerican Studies and World Affairs* **17**, 1 (February), 4–26.

MOYNIHAM, D. P. (ed.), 1970: *Towards a national urban policy*. New York: Basic Books.

MUÑOZ, Humberto Garcia, 1975: Occupational and earnings inequalities in Mexico City: a sectoral analysis of the labour force. *PhD dissertation*, University of Texas at Austin.

MUÑOZ, Humberto and OLIVEIRA, Orlandina de, 1975: La mano de obra en América Latina. In CLACSO, *Fuerza de trabajo y movimientos laborales en América Latina*. Social Science Research Council and Grupo de Movimientos laborales del Consejo Latino-americano de Ciencias Sociales.

NASH, Manning (ed.), 1977: *Essays on economic development and cultural change in honor of Bert F. Hoselitz. Economic Development and Cultural Change* **25**, supplement, Chicago: University of Chicago Press.

National Academy of Sciences, 1971: *Rapid population growth: consequences and policy implications*. Baltimore and London: Johns Hopkins Press.

NELSON, R., SCHULTZ, T. P. and SLIGHTON, R., 1971: *Structural change in a developing economy*. Princeton: Princeton University Press.

NUN, José, 1969: Sobrepoblación relativa, ejército industrial de reserva y masa marginal, *Revista Latinoamericana de Sociología* **4**, 2 (July), 178–237.

O'DONNELL, Guillermo, 1975: Reflexiones sobre les tendencias generales de cambio en al estado burocrático-autoritario. Documento CEDES–CLACSO **1**. Buenos Aires.
  1977: Corporativism and the question of the state. In Malloy, 1977.

OLIVEIRA, Francisco de, 1972: A economia brasileira: crítica á razão dualista. *Estudos CEBRAP* **2** (October), 5–82.

OLIVEIRA, Orlandina de Muñoz, 1975: Industrialization, migration and entry labor force changes in Mexico City: 1930–1970. Based on 1971 sample survey of Mexico City (1,104 males), PhD dissertation, University of Texas at Austin, 15–64.

OLSEN, Donald J., 1973: House upon house. In Dyos and Wolff, 1973, 333–86.

PAHL, R. E., 1971: Poverty and the urban system. In Chisholm and Manners, 1971.
  1974: Instrumentality and community in the process of urbanization. In Effrat, 1974.

PEATTIE, Lisa R., 1968: *The view from the barrio*. Ann Arbor: The University of Michigan Press.
  1975: Tertiarization and urban poverty in Latin America. In Cornelius and Trueblood, 1975, 109–24.

PERLMAN, Janice E., 1976: *The myth of marginality*. Berkeley, Los Angeles, London: University of California Press.

PERLOFF, Harvey S. and WINGO, Lowdon. Jr, 1968: *Issues in urban economics*. Baltimore and London: Johns Hopkins Press.

PETIAS, James and ZEITLIN, Maurice (eds), 1968: *Latin America: reform or revolution*. New York: Fawcett.

PICKVANCE, Christopher G., 1976: On the study of urban social movements. In Pickvance (ed.) 1976, 198–218.
  (ed.), 1976: *Urban sociology: critical essays*. London: Tavistock/Methuen.

PINTO, Anibal and Di FILIPPO, Armando, 1976: Notes on income distribution and redistribution strategy in Latin America. In Foxley, 1976, 91–106.

PONS, Valdo, 1969: *Stanleyville*. London: Oxford University Press for International African Institute.

PORTES, Alejandro, 1971: Political primitivism, differential socialization and lower-class leftist radicalism. *American Sociological Review* **36** (October), 820–35.

PORTES, Alejandro and BROWNING, Harley (eds), 1976: *Current perspectives in Latin American urban research*. Austin and London: University of Texas Press.

PORTES, Alejandro and WALTON, John, 1976: *Urban Latin America: the political conditions from above and below*. Austin and London: University of Texas Press.

PREOBRAZHENSKY, Ergenii, 1965: *The new economics*. Oxford: Clarendon Press.

PRESSNELL, L. S., 1956: *Country banking in the industrial revolution*. Oxford: Clarendon Press.

QUIJANO, Aníbal, 1968: Dependencia, cambio social y urbanización en América Latina. *Revista Mexicana de Sociologia*, July–September, 525–70.

  1971: *Nationalism and capitalism in Peru*. New York: Monthly Review Press.

  1973: Redefinición de la dependencia y proceso de marginalización en América Latina. In Weffort and Quijano, 1973, 171–329.

  1974: The marginal pole of the economy and the marginalized labor force. *Economy and Society* **3**, 4 (November), 393–428.

  1975: The urbanization of Latin American society. In Hardoy, 1975.

RABINOVITZ, Francine F. and TRUEBLOOD, Felicity (eds), 1971: *Latin American urban research* **1**. Beverly Hills and London: Sage.

RATINOFF, Luis, 1967: The new urban groups: the middle classes. In Lipset and Solari, 1967, 61–93.

RAVENSTEIN, E. G., 1885: The laws of migration. *Journal of the Royal Statistical Society* **48**, 2, (June), 167–227.

REDFORD, Arthur, 1926: *Labour migration in England, 1800–1850*. Manchester: Manchester University Press.

REDFORD, Arthur and RUSSELL, Ina S. 1940: *The history of local government in Manchester* **2**. London: Longmans, Green.

REISSMAN, Leonard, 1964: *The urban process: cities in industrial societies*. London: Collier-Macmillan, Glencoe: Free Press.

RIIA, 1937: *The problem of international investment*. Royal Institute of International Affairs, London: Oxford University Press.

ROBERTS, Bryan R., 1968a: Politics in a neighbourhood of Guatemala City. *Sociology* **2**, 2, 185–204.

  1968b: Protestant groups and coping with urban life in Guatemala City. *American Journal of Sociology* **73**, 6, 753–67.

  1970: Urban poverty and political behaviour in Guatemala. *Human Organization* **29**, 1 (spring), 20–28.

  1973a: *Organizing strangers*. Austin and London: University of Texas Press.

  1973b: Education, urbanization and social change. In Brown, 1973, 141–62.

  1974: The interrelationships of city and provinces in Peru and Guatemala. In Cornelius and Trueblood, 1974, 207–36.

  1975: Center and periphery in the development process: the case of Peru. In Cornelius and Trueblood, 1975.

1976a: The social history of a provincial town: Huancayo, 1890–1972. In Miller *et al.*, 1976, 130–97.

1976b: The provincial urban system and the process of dependancy. In Portes and Browning, 1976.

1978a: The bases of industrial cooperation in Huancayo. In Long and Roberts, 1978.

1978b: Agrarian organization and urban development. In Wirth, 1978.

ROBSON, Brian T., 1973: *Urban growth: an approach*. London: Methuen.

ROSENSTEIN-RODAN, P., 1943: Problems of industrialization in Eastern and Southeastern Europe. *Economic Journal* **53** (June–September), 202–11.

ROTHSTEIN, Morton, 1966: Antenellum wheat and cotton exports: a contrast in marketing organization and economic development. *Agricultural History* **41**, 4, 91–100.

1967: The antebellum South as a dual economy: a tentative hypothesis. *Agricultural History* **42**, 4, 373–82.

SAMANIEGO, Carlos, 1974: Location, social differentiation and peasant movements in the central sierra of Peru. PhD dissertation. University of Manchester.

SAVILLE, John, 1957: *Rural depopulation in England and Wales, 1851–1951*. London: Routledge.

SCHNORE, Leo F., 1961: The statistical measurements of urbanization and economic development. *Land Economics* **37**, 229–45.

1965: On the spatial structure of cities in the two Americas. In Hauser and Schnore, 1965, 347–98.

1975: *The new urban history*. Princeton: Princeton University Press.

SCOBIE, James R., 1964: *Revolution on the pampas: a social history of Argentine wheat, 1860–1910*. Austin: University of Texas Press.

1975: Patterns of urbanization in Argentina, 1869–1914. *Latin American Research Review* **10**, 2, 132–4.

SCOTT, Alison M., 1976: Who are the self-employed? In C. Gerry and R. Bromley (eds): *The casual poor in third world cities*. London and New York: John Wiley.

SCOTT, Christopher, 1976: Peasants, proletarianization and the articulation of modes of production; the case of sugar-cane cutters in northern Peru, 1940–1969. *Journal of Peasant Studies* **3**, 3, 321–42.

SHIRLEY, Robert W., 1978: Legal Institutions and early industrial growth. In Wirth, 1978.

SIMMONS, A. B. and CARDONA, G., 1972: Rural–urban migration: who comes, who stays, who returns?—the case of Bogota, Columbia. *International Migration Review* **6**, 2, 166–81.

SINGELMAN, J., 1974: The sectoral distribution of the labour force in selected European countries. PhD dissertation, University of Texas at Austin.

SINGER, Paul, 1973: *Economía política da urbanização*. São Paulo: Editora Brasiliense (Edições CEBRAP).

  1975a: O Brasil, no contexto do capitalismo internacional, 1889–1930. In Fausto, 1975, 347–90.

  1975b: Urbanization and development: the case of São Paulo. In Hardoy, 1975, 435–56.

SJOBERG, Gideon, 1965: Cities in developing and in industrial societies: a cross-cultural analysis. In Hauser and Schnore, 1965, 213–63.

SMELSER, Neil J. and LIPSET, Seymour Martin (eds), 1966: *Social structure and mobility in economic development*. London: Routledge.

SMITH, Gavin A., 1975a: The social basis of peasant political activity: the case of the *huasicanchinos* of central Peru. PhD thesis, University of Sussex.

  1975b: Internal migration and economic activity: some cases from Peru, *working paper* **17**, Centre for Developing Area Studies, McGill University, Montreal, Canada.

SOARES, Gláucio Ary Dillon, 1976a: The web of exploitation: state and peasants in Latin America. Mimeo, University of Florida, Gainesville.

  1976b: The state in Latin America. Mimeo, University of Florida, Gainesville.

SORJ, Bernando, 1976: *The state in peripheral capitalism*. PhD dissertation, University of Manchester.

SOUZA, Herbert and AFFONSO, Carlos A., 1975: The role of the state in the capitalist development in Brazil. *Brazilian Studies* **7**, York University, Toronto, Canada.

STAVENHAGEN, Rodolfo, 1965: Classes, colonialism and acculturation. *Studies in Comparative International Development* **1**, 6, 53–77.

STEDMAN JONES, G. 1971: *Outcast London*. London: Oxford University Press.

STEPAN, Alfred, 1971: *The military in politics: changing patterns in Brazil*. Princeton: Princeton University Press.

  (ed.) 1973: *Authoritarian Brazil*. New Haven and London: Yale.

TAEBUR, Karl E., CHIAZZE, Leonard Jr, and HAENZEL, William, 1968: Migration in the United States: an analysis of residence histories. *Public Health Monograph* **77**, US Department of Health, Education and Welfare.

THERNSTROM, Stephen, 1964: *Poverty and progress: social mobility in a nineteenth-century city*. Cambridge, Mass.: Harvard University Press.

THERNSTROM, Stephen and KNIGHTS, Peter B., 1970: Men in motion: some data and speculations about urban population mobility in nineteenth-century America. *Journal of Interdisciplinary History* **1** (autumn), 7–35.

THOMAS, Brinley, 1973: *Migration and economic growth: a study of Great Britain and the Atlantic economy.* Cambridge: Cambridge University Press.

THOMPSON, Edward P., 1970: *The making of the English working class.* Harmondsworth: Penguin.

THORP, Rosemary and BERTRAM, Geoff., 1976: Industrialization in an open economy: a case study of Peru, 1890–1940. In Miller *et al.*, 1976.

1978: *Peru, 1890–1977: growth and policy in an open economy.* London and New York: Macmillan and Columbia University Press.

TURNER, John F. C., 1967: Barriers and channels for housing development in modernizing countries. *Journal of the American Institute of Planners* **32**, 3 (May), 167–81.

1970: Squatter settlements in developing countries. In Moynihan, 1970.

UNIKEL, Luis, 1975: Urbanism and urbanization in Mexico: situation and prospects. In Hardoy, 1975, 391–434.

UN, 1948: *National income statistics of various countries: 1938–1947.* New York: Statistical Office of the United Nations.

1964: *Statistical yearbook.* New York: Statistical Office of the United Nations.

1967: *Statistical yearbook.* United Nations.

1975: *Statistical yearbook.* United Nations.

UZZELL, Douglas, 1972: Bound for places I'm not known to: adaptation of migrants and residence in four irregular settlements in Lima, Peru. PhD dissertation, University of Texas at Austin.

1974: The interaction of population and locality in the development of squatter settlements in Lima. In Cornelius and Trueblood, 1974, 113–34.

VAPÑARSKY, César A., 1975: The Argentine system of cities: primacy and rank-size rule. In Hardoy, 1975, 369–90.

VEKEMANS, Roger and GIUSTI, Jorge: 1969/70: Marginality and ideology in Latin American development. *Studies in Comparative International Development* **5**, 11.

VELIZ, Claudio (ed.), 1965: *Obstacles to change in Latin America.* London: Oxford University Press for Royal Institute of International Affairs.

WADE, Richard C., 1959: *The urban frontier: the rise of western cities, 1790–1830.* Cambridge, Mass.: Harvard University Press.

WALLERSTEIN, Immanuel, 1974a: *The modern world system.* New York and London: Academic Press.

1974b: The rise and future demise of the world capitalist system. *Comparative Studies in Society and History* **16**, 387–415.

WALTON, John, 1977: *Elites and economic development: comparative studies on the political economy of Latin American cities.* Austin and London: University of Texas Press for Institute of Latin American Studies.

WARD, D., 1968: The emergence of central immigrant ghettoes in American cities: 1840–1920. *Annals of the Association of American Geographers* **58** (June), 343–59.

WARNER, William Lloyd and LUNT, Paul S., 1941: *The social life of a modern community.* New Haven.

WATKINS, Melville H., 1963: A staple theory of economic growth. *Canadian Journal of Economics and Political Science* **29** (May), 141–58.

WEBB, Richard, 1974: Government policy and the distribution of income in Peru, 1963–73. PhD dissertation, Harvard University.
    1975: Public policy and regional incomes in Peru. In Cornelius and Trueblood, 1975.

WEBER, Adna Ferrin, 1899: *The growth of cities in the nineteenth century.* Ithaca, N.W.: Cornell University Press.

WEFFORT, Francisco C., 1973: Classes populares y desarrollo social. In Weffort and Quijano, 1973, 17–169.

WEFFORT, Francisco C. and QUIJANO, Aníbal (eds), 1973: *Populismo, marginalización y dependencia,* San José, Costa Rica: Editorial Universitaria Centroamericana.

WELLS, John, 1976: Subconsumo, tamanho de mercado e padrões de gastos familiares no Brasil. *Estudos CEBRAP* **17** (July–September), 5–60.

WHITEFORD, John H., 1975: *Urbanization of rural proletarians and Bolivian migrant workers in northwest Argentina.* PhD thesis University of Texas at Austin.

WIBEL, John and DE LA CRUZ, Jesse, 1971: Mexico. In Morse, 1971c.

WILHEIM, Jorge, 1977: São Pualo 77: housing within the context of underdevelopment. Paper presented to conference on Manchester and São Paulo, The Crisis of Rapid Urban Growth, Stanford University, April.

WILLIAMS, Eric, 1944: *Capitalism and slavery.* Chapel Hill: University of North Carolina Press.

WILS, Fritz, 1975: *Industrialists, industrialization and the nation-state in Peru.* The Hague: Institute of Social Research.

WINGO, Lowdon Jr, 1967: Recent patterns of urbanization among Latin American countries. *Urban Affairs Quarterly* **2**, 1 (March), 81–109.
    1969: Latin American urbanization: plan or process? In Frieden and Nash, 1969, 115–46.

WIRTH, John, 1975: Minas e a Nação: un estudo de poder e dependencia regional, 1889–1937. In Fausto, 1975.

(ed.) 1978: *Manchester and São Paulo: problems of urban growth.* Stanford, Calif.: Stanford University Press.

WIRTH, Louis, 1938: Urbanism as a way of life. *American Journal of Sociology* **44** (July).

WOLF, Eric, 1957: The Mexican Bajio in the eighteenth century. In Edmonson *et al.*, 1957, 180–98.

WOOD, Charles H., 1977: Infant mortality trends and capitalist development in Brazil: the case of São Paulo and Belo Horizonte. *Latin American Perspectives* **4**, 56–65.

YEPES, Ernesto, 1972: *Peru: 1820–1920: un siglo de desarrollo capitalista.* Lima: Instituto de Estudios Peruanos.

1974: Some aspects of Peruvian socio-economic history. PhD thesis, University of Manchester.

YUJNOVSKY, Oscar, 1975: Urban spatial structure in Latin America. In Hardoy, 1975, 191–220.

1976: Urban spatial configuration and land use policies in Latin America. In Portes and Browning, 1976, 17–42.

Subject Index

Author Index

307.76
RC43

112019